Harold Pinter Collected Screenplays Three

Harold Pinter was born in London in 1930. He is married to Antonia Fraser. In 1995 he won the David Cohen British Literature Prize, awarded for a lifetime's achievement in literature. In 1995 he was given the Laurence Olivier Award for a lifetime's achievement in theatre.

HAROLD PINTER

Collected Screenplays Three

The French Lieutenant's Woman

The Heat of the Day

The Comfort of Strangers

The Trial

The Dreaming Child

Introduced by the author

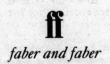

faber and faber

First published in this collection in 2000
by Faber and Faber Limited
3 Queen Square London WC1N 3AU

Photoset by Parker Typesetting Service, Leicester
Printed in England by Mackays of Chatham plc

A CIP record for this book
is available from the British Library

ISBN 0–571–20733–2

2 4 6 8 10 9 7 5 3 1

CONTENTS

INTRODUCTION

The problem with adapting John Fowles' *The French Lieutenant's Woman* was that of the active role the author plays in the book. To have the author on screen, talking to us, as it were, seemed to Karel Reisz and me to be impossible. Karel solved this dilemma brilliantly, I thought, by proposing that the actors playing Sarah Woodruff and Charles Smithson in 1860 also play the actors themselves in the present, so that the two narratives run concurrently and the perspectives constantly shift. The two narratives, in other words, complement and illuminate each other. The screenplay took a long time to write but was very rewarding.

Elizabeth Bowen's shadowy, dense wartime novel *The Heat of the Day*, a spider's web of dubious loyalties and betrayals, I found compelling. It was shot by Christopher Morahan for television and the framework of blacked-out London was most persuasive. Patricia Hodge gave a very intelligent and touching performance, Michael Gambon one of his very best and Michael York his best. The film was shown at 10pm on a Saturday night the day after Boxing Day and about three people saw it. It was not reviewed in the press and was never shown again.

Ian McEwan's *The Comfort of Strangers* is a truly frightening book. It slid onto the screen. Paul Schrader moved about a dark Venice almost on tiptoe and the deepening magnetism of evil (with a smiling face) is, I think truly disconcerting. I found in it an echo of silent movies where the audience would cry, 'Don't go through that door!' But the two victims did go through that door and the fearsome Christopher Walken ate them up.

I had wanted to have a crack at *The Trial* for many years and the BBC finally gave me the opportunity. David Jones and I decided to set it in pre-First World War Prague, where and when the world appeared to be solid and stable. The growing shadow of another world, seeping into K's consciousness I thought was very well conveyed in the film, which seemed to me a rich piece of work altogether.

I adapted Karen Blixen's *The Dreaming Child* a couple of years ago and the film has not yet been made. The short story is wonderfully elusive and mysterious and I believe it will make a very arresting and affecting film. I hope it comes about.

I have never written an original film. But I've enjoyed adapting other people's books very much. Altogether, I have written twenty-four screenplays. Two were never shot. Three were rewritten by others. Two have not yet been filmed. Seventeen (including four adaptations of my own plays) were filmed as written. I think that's unusual. I certainly understand adapting novels for the screen to be a serious and fascinating craft.

Harold Pinter
13 September, 2000

The French Lieutenant's Woman

Note. The writing of this screenplay took over a year. This is the final version with which we began shooting. Inevitably a number of scenes were cut and some structural changes were made during the course of production.

HAROLD PINTER

The French Lieutenant's Woman was first presented in Britain by United Artists in 1981 with the following cast:

SARAH WOODRUFF/ANNA Meryl Streep
CHARLES SMITHSON/MIKE Jeremy Irons
SAM Hilton McRae
MARY Emily Morgan
MRS TRANTER Charlotte Mitchell
ERNESTINA FREEMAN Lynsey Baxter
MR FREEMAN Peter Vaughan
VICAR Colin Jeavons
MRS FAIRLEY Liz Smith
MRS POULTENEY Patience Collier
DAIRYMAN John Barrett
DR GROGAN Leo McKern
NATHANIEL DYSON Edward Duke
SIR THOM BURGH Richard Griffiths
MONTAGUE Michael Elwyn
MRS ENDICOTT Toni Palmer
SERJEANT MURPHY David Warner
GRIMES Alun Armstrong
DAVIDE Gerard Falconetti
SONIA Penelope Wilton
TOM ELLIOTT Orlando Fraser
GIRL Fredrika Morton
SECOND GIRL Alice Maschler
BOY Matthew Morton
MRS TRANTER'S MAID Vicky Ireland
MRS POULTENEY'S MAID Claire Travers-Deacon

Produced by Leon Clore
Directed by Karel Reisz

EXT. THE COBB. LYME REGIS. DAWN. 1867.

A clapperboard. On it is written: The French Lieutenant's Woman. Scene 1. Take 3.

It shuts and withdraws, leaving a close shot of Anna, the actress who plays Sarah. She is holding her hair in place against the wind.

VOICE
(off screen)

All right. Let's go.

The actress nods, releases her hair. The wind catches it.

Action.

Sarah starts to walk along the Cobb, a stone pier in the Harbour of Lyme. It is dawn. Windy. Deserted. She is dressed in black. She reaches the end of the Cobb and stands still, staring out to sea.

INT. HOTEL ROOM. THE CUPS. HOTEL. LYME. DAY.

Charles sitting at a table, examining a fossil through a microscope. He is wearing a dressing gown and is whistling to himself.

Fossils lie on various shelves. A variety of scientific instruments and books are about the room.

Charles stops, looks up, considers, and suddenly calls:

CHARLES

Sam!

(He turns.)

3

Sam!

> (*He mutters.*)

Where the devil is he?

He stands and goes to the window.

EXT. LYME HIGH ST. CHARLES'S P.O.V.

The High Street at early morning. Men on horse-back. A shepherd with a flock of sheep. A street market. In background Lyme Bay.

INT. HOTEL ROOM.

Charles picks up a telescope and looks through it out of the window.

THE STREET MARKET. CHARLES'S P.O.V.

The telescope moves through sheep and people to focus finally on Sam, who is standing by a flower stall. He holds a bunch of flowers. He is talking to a young girl. He gives her a flower. She giggles, and turns away.

CLOSE-UP. CHARLES WATCHING.

EXT. THE STREET.

Sam walking between horses, and treading with distaste over horse dung, the bunch of flowers in his hand.

Charles's voice-over.

CHARLES

Sam!

> (*Sam looks up.*)

EXT. THE CUPS HOTEL.

Charles at his window.

> CHARLES

Come up here!

> SAM

At the double, sir.

INT. HOTEL ROOM. DAY.

Charles dips his shaving brush in a bowl and begins to lather his face.

Sam enters.

> SAM

Sir?

> CHARLES

Where the devil have you been?

> SAM

I was just taking the flowers up to the house, sir, as you —

> CHARLES

Change of plan. I'll want my grey suit.

> SAM

Your grey suit? But I thought you were going fossilling this morning, sir.

> CHARLES

No fossils today, Sam. Today is a day for action.

> SAM

Yes, sir.

> CHARLES

I shall do it this morning, immediately after breakfast!

SAM

Do what, sir?

CHARLES

I should have done it weeks ago.

SAM

Ah. Well better late than never, sir.

Sam picks up the razor.

Charles takes it from him.

CHARLES

I'll shave myself this morning. Breakfast! A double dose of muffins. And kidneys and liver and bacon.

Sam goes to the door.

And Sam!

SAM

Mr Charles?

CHARLES

When we get there be sure you don't dally with Miss Ernestina's maid.

SAM

Me, sir? Dally, sir?

CHARLES

This is my day, not yours.

Sam goes out. Charles looks at himself in the mirror, shaves.

EXT. STREET. LYME. DAY.

Carriage, with Charles and Sam in it, going up hill along the High Street.

EXT. COUNTRY LANE. DAY.

The carriage out of Lyme and into open landscape.

EXT. MRS TRANTER'S HOUSE. DAY.

The carriage arrives. Charles jumps out, strides to the front door. It is opened at once by Mary.

MARY

Good morning, sir.

CHARLES

Good morning. Please tell your mistress I would like to see her. Ah! Mrs Tranter!

He takes off his hat and walks in.

Mary remains at the door for a moment, looking for Sam.

SAM WINKING AT MARY.

INT. MRS TRANTER'S HOUSE. HALL.

Mrs Tranter walks towards Charles.

MRS TRANTER

Charles! My goodness, you are up early!

CHARLES

Good morning Mrs Tranter. A beautiful morning.

MRS TRANTER

It is indeed.

CHARLES

Is Ernestina ... awake?

MRS TRANTER

Mary, is my niece awake?

                        MARY

She is, mu'm.

                    MRS TRANTER

Tell her Mr Charles is here.

                        MARY

Yes, mu'm.

Mary bobs and goes up the stairs.

                      CHARLES

Might it be possible for me to see Ernestina ... alone?

INT. STAIRCASE.

Mary stops and looks down into the hall.

                    MRS TRANTER

But of course. Of course.

She leads Charles towards the garden room.

Mary turns quickly and hurries up the stairs.

INT. ERNESTINA'S BEDROOM.

Ernestina half-dressed. Mary knocks and enters.

                        MARY

Mr Charles is here, Miss, to see you.

                    ERNESTINA

Mr Charles?

                        MARY

He's downstairs waiting for you Miss. He wants to
speak to you.

                    ERNESTINA

Oh, dear! What shall I ... What dress shall I wear?

MARY

Oh your green is so lovely Miss. You look as pretty as a picture in your green.

ERNESTINA

Yes, yes. My green. I'll wear that.

INT. LIVING ROOM.

MRS TRANTER

The conservatory ... is a private place. Will that suit?

CHARLES

It will suit. Thank you. I shall wait for her ... in the conservatory.

INT. KITCHEN.

The Cook at the sink.

Sam at the window, looking across the garden into the conservatory. Charles's figure can be discerned, walking about.

COOK

I always thought you from London spent half the day in bed.

SAM

No ma'm. Up and about, we're always up and about, early birds ready to catch the early worm, ma'm. Us Londoners.

Ernestina can be seen going into the conservatory.

Mary comes into the kitchen.

She's gone in to him.

MARY

Doesn't she look a princess?

COOK

What's going on in this house this morning?

INT. LIVING ROOM.

Mrs Tranter looking at Ernestina and Charles through the conservatory window. Charles is talking.

INT. CONSERVATORY. DAY.

CHARLES

Ernestina, it cannot have escaped your notice that it is fully six weeks since I came down here to Lyme from London.

ERNESTINA

No. It has not escaped my notice.

Charles clears his throat.

CHARLES

I came to Lyme to explore the flint beds of the Undercliff, to look for fossils – but I have stayed for you.

ERNESTINA

Ah!

CHARLES

For your sweet company.

ERNESTINA

Thank you.

INT. ERNESTINA'S BEDROOM. DAY.

Mrs Tranter tiptoes in. She moves to the window from which she can see the conservatory below.

INT. KITCHEN.

SAM
She's not going to turn him down, is she?

MARY
Never. She'd give her left arm. *And* all her dresses.

INT. CONSERVATORY.

CHARLES
I am here this morning to enquire if you would allow
me to ask your father . . . for your hand.

She looks at him.

ERNESTINA
Yes. I would allow it.

CHARLES
(*with a smile*)
Mind you, I don't know that he approves of me. After
all, I don't do what he considers to be work.

ERNESTINA
Are you suggesting that it is entirely Papa's decision?

CHARLES
Oh no. It is yours.

ERNESTINA
Yes. It is. Papa will do what I want.

CHARLES
In that case . . . might you take pity on a crusty old
scientist, who holds you very dear . . . and marry me?

Ernestina bursts into tears.

ERNESTINA
Oh Charles! I have waited so long for this moment.

He takes her hands.

INT. KITCHEN.

SAM

He's home and dry.

INT. ERNESTINA'S BEDROOM.

Mrs Tranter watching, delighted, her hand to her mouth.

INT. CONSERVATORY.

Charles under an overhanging branch.

CHARLES

This is not mistletoe, but it will do.

ERNESTINA

Oh Charles ...

They kiss chastely.

HOTEL ROOM. EARLY MORNING. PRESENT. 1979.

Dim light. A man and a woman in bed asleep. It is at once clear that they are the man and woman playing Charles and Sarah, but we do not immediately appreciate that the time is the present.

A telephone rings.

Mike turns, lifts receiver.

MIKE

Yes?

(Pause.)

Who is it?

(Pause.)

Yes, it is.

(Pause.)

I'll tell her.

Mike puts the phone down, turns on light, wakes Anna.

Anna.

ANNA

Mmmn?

MIKE

You're late. They're waiting for you.

ANNA

Oh God.
> (*She sits up.*)

What happened to the wake-up call?

MIKE

I don't know.

ANNA
> (*yawning*)

Who called?

MIKE

Jack.

She looks at him.

ANNA

Did you answer the phone?

MIKE

Yes.

ANNA

But then – they'll know you're in my room, they'll all
know.

MIKE

In your bed.
> (*He kisses her.*)

I want them to know.

ANNA

Christ, look at the time.

He holds her.

They'll fire me for immorality.

He embraces her.

They'll think I'm a whore.

MIKE

You are.

EXT. HOTEL. PRESENT.

Anna getting into car. It drives off.

INT. CAR.

Anna sitting.

CHAUFFEUR

Chilly morning.

INT. SMALL COTTAGE. LYME. DAY.

Two labourers are carrying a coffin down the stairs. They have difficulty manoeuvering it.

They pass the sitting figure of Sarah and carry the coffin into the street, leaving the door open.

Sarah is sitting by the window, drawing.

CLOSE-UP. THE DRAWING.

The drawing is of an old woman on her death bed.

INT. COTTAGE.

The Vicar's voice is heard giving instructions to the labourers. He comes into the room. He looks down at Sarah. She continues to draw.

> VICAR

You realize you cannot stay here any longer? I happen to know that Miss Duff has made no provision for you in her will. The place is to be sold.
> *(Pause.)*

How much money do you possess?
> *(Pause.)*

When did you last eat?
> *(Pause.)*

Miss Woodruff, I think I know someone who can help you. Mrs Poulteney from the Grange. She might take you in.

Sarah looks up.

> SARAH

Does her house overlook the sea?

> VICAR

It does. Yes.

> SARAH

Then I would be grateful for your good offices, Vicar.

EXT. MR FREEMAN'S WHARF. PORT OF LONDON. DAY.

A carriage draws up. Charles gets out of it and looks about him. A ship unloading. Tea chests, on pulleys, being deposited on the wharf. They are stamped: 'Freeman's Teas'. Men wheeling the tea chests towards the warehouse. Dray horses with carts standing by.

INT. MR FREEMAN'S OFFICE. WAREHOUSE. DAY.

The office looks over the wharf. Mr Freeman and Charles are sitting at his desk.

MR FREEMAN

Yes, indeed. I recognize, Charles, that you bring to
Ernestina not only your love and protection, but also . . .
in time . . . a considerable inheritance.

CHARLES

That is so.

MR FREEMAN

I know my daughter loves you. You seem to me an
upright man. Let us shake hands.

*They stand and shake hands. Mr Freeman clasps Charles's
shoulder warmly.*

I started here, Charles, with my dear wife at my side.

He looks up at a portrait of Mrs Freeman. Charles, too, looks up.

INT. MR FREEMAN'S WAREHOUSE. DAY.

*A large body of men stacking tea chests as they arrive from the
wharf. Mr Freeman and Charles walk through the warehouse.*

MR FREEMAN

We could have met at my office in the City, but I
thought you would be interested to see this place.

CHARLES

Indeed I am.

MR FREEMAN

In a few months we shall be opening depots in Bristol
and Liverpool.

They walk out on to the wharf.

EXT. THE WHARF. DAY.

The ship unloading.

Mr Freeman and Charles survey the scene.

MR FREEMAN

You know I have no son, Charles?

CHARLES

I do, sir, yes.

MR FREEMAN

This isn't the time to talk about it, but if you ever felt
disposed to explore the world of commerce, I would be
delighted to be your guide.

Charles looks at him.

CHARLES

Thank you.

MR FREEMAN

The times are on our side. This is the age of progress,
Charles. Progress is like a lively horse. Either you collar
it or you come a cropper. I am convinced that one day
an empire of sorts will come to Ernestina and yourself.
And thereafter to your children.

EXT. THE COBB. LOWER LEVEL. LYME. DAY.

Charles and Ernestina walking towards the camera.

ERNESTINA

Oh dear, don't tell me. Did he talk of his famous
'empire'?

CHARLES

He did.

ERNESTINA

And did he propose that you might one day join him in
the ruling of it?

CHARLES

He was most respectful of what he called my position as
a 'scientist and a gentleman'. In fact he asked me about

my ... my work. But as I didn't think fossils were his line exactly, I gave him a brief discourse on the Theory of Evolution instead.

ERNESTINA

How wicked of you!

CHARLES

Yes. He didn't seem to think very much of it, I must admit. In fact he ventured the opinion that Mr Darwin should be exhibited in a cage in the zoological gardens. In the monkey house.

Charles stops walking. A gust of wind. They are near the steps to the upper level of the Cobb.

The wind is very strong. Shall we return?

He suddenly sees Sarah standing at the very end of the Cobb, looking out to sea. The wind blows her shawl.

Good Lord! What on earth is she doing?

ERNESTINA

Who is it?

CHARLES

I don't know.

Ernestina peers at the woman.

ERNESTINA

Oh, it's poor 'Tragedy'.

CHARLES

Tragedy?

ERNESTINA

One of her nicknames. The fishermen have a grosser name for her.

CHARLES

What?

ERNESTINA

They call her the French Lieutenant's . . .
> (*She looks at him.*)

. . . Woman.

CHARLES

Do they?

A stronger gust of wind. The woman sways, clutches a cannon bollard.

I must speak to her. She could fall.
> (*To Ernestina:*)

Please wait for me.

ERNESTINA

She won't thank you. She's mad.

CHARLES

It's dangerous.

Charles climbs the steps to the upper ledge of the Cobb and runs towards Sarah.

Madam!

The woman does not turn.

Charles speaks loudly above the wind and sea.

Forgive me, I am alarmed for your safety. The wind –

She turns sharply, stares at him. He stops speaking.

CLOSE-UP. SARAH. STARING AT HIM.

EXT. THE COBB. LONG SHOT. DAY.

Charles and Sarah, staring at each other.

INT. MRS TRANTER'S HOUSE. KITCHEN. DAY.

Mary setting sandwiches and cakes on a tray.

Sam approaches her from behind, squeezes her waist.

The servants' bell rings.

> MARY
>
> They want their tea.

> SAM
>
> Let them wait.

> MARY
>
> Don't be silly.

> SAM
>
> You don't want to spoil them.

He tickles her. She giggles.

The bell rings again.

INT. ERNESTINA'S SITTING ROOM. DAY.

Ernestina at bell-pull. Charles is looking out of the window.

> ERNESTINA
>
> What *is* she doing? I'm dying for my tea.

> CHARLES
>
> Tell me, who is this French Lieutenant?

> ERNESTINA
>
> Oh . . . he is a man she is said to have . . .

> CHARLES
>
> Fallen in love with?

> ERNESTINA
>
> Worse than that.

CHARLES

Ah. And he abandoned her? Is there a child?

ERNESTINA

I think not. Oh, it's all gossip.

CHARLES

What is she doing here?

ERNESTINA

They say she is waiting for him to return.

Ernestina goes to the bell-pull and pulls it.

CHARLES

How banal.

INT. KITCHEN.

The bell ringing.

Mary trying to get away from Sam's embrace.

MARY

Stop it!

INT. SITTING ROOM.

ERNESTINA

Where *is* the girl? It's probably your man making eyes at her.

CHARLES

Out of the question. My man is a true gentleman's gentleman.

ERNESTINA

Huh!

CHARLES

But how does she live?

ERNESTINA

Who?

CHARLES

This . . . French Lieutenant's Woman.

ERNESTINA

She sews, or something. Oh, really, I don't want to talk about her.

EXT. MRS POULTENEY'S. EVENING.

Sarah walking alone on a country path towards Mrs Poulteney's house.

INT. MRS POULTENEY'S HOUSE. WINDOW IN HALL. DAY.

Sarah standing, looking out of window.

Servants on stairs watch her.

Mr Fairley passes her, without a glance.

From the landing the Vicar's voice.

VICAR

Miss Woodruff, would you please come up?

Sarah climbs the stairs, past the servants. The Vicar is waiting at the door of Mrs Poulteney's room.

Do come in.

INT. MRS POULTENEY'S SITTING ROOM.

Mrs Poulteney is sitting.

VICAR

Mrs Poulteney, this is Miss Woodruff.

MRS POULTENEY

Ah. I see.

(*She studies her.*)

I wish, as the Vicar has told you, to take a companion.
The Vicar has indicated to me that you might be a
suitable person for such a post. You are without
employment?

SARAH

I am, ma'm.

MRS POULTENEY

But you have education? You have been a governess?

SARAH

I have, ma'm.

MRS POULTENEY

The post of companion requires a person of
irreproachable moral character. I have my servants to
consider.

The Vicar coughs.

*Mrs Poulteney looks at him and then turns back to regard Sarah
in silence.*

You speak French, I believe?

SARAH

I do, ma'm.

MRS POULTENEY

I do not like the French.

The Vicar coughs again.

Perhaps you might leave us now, Mr Forsythe?

VICAR

Yes, of course, Mrs Poulteney.

He stands and bows.

Good afternoon.

He leaves the room.

MRS POULTENEY
Mr Forsythe informs me that you retain an attachment
to a ... foreign person.

SARAH
I do not wish to speak of it, ma'm.

Mrs Poulteney stares at her.

MRS POULTENEY
But what if this person returns. What then?
(*Sarah bows her head and shakes it.*)
You shake your head, but I have heard, from the most
impeccable witnesses, that you are always to be seen at
the same place when you are out. You stand on the
Cobb and look to sea.
(*Sarah looks at her.*)
I have been encouraged to believe that you are in a state
of repentance, but I must emphasize that such staring
out to sea is provocative, intolerable and sinful.

SARAH
Do you wish me to leave the house, Mrs Poulteney?

MRS POULTENEY
I wish you to show that this ... person is expunged from
your heart.

SARAH
How am I to show it?

MRS POULTENEY
By not exhibiting your shame.

Pause.

SARAH
I will do as you wish, ma'm.

MRS POULTENEY

I will not have French books in my house.

SARAH

I possess none.

MRS POULTENEY

I would like to hear you read from the Bible. If your expression is agreeable to me, you shall have the position.

She hands Sarah a Bible.

INT. DRESSING ROOM. PRESENT.

Anna is standing in her corset, her back to the camera. Her dresser is unlacing the corset. It comes off. Anna rubs her waist. She sighs with relief.

ANNA

Christ!

INT. MRS POULTENEY'S SITTING ROOM. EVENING.

Mrs Poulteney and Sarah, in different dresses, sitting. Sarah is reading from the Bible: Psalm 140.

SARAH

Deliver me, O Lord, from the evil man;
Preserve me from the violent man;
Which imagine mischiefs in their heart;
Continually are they gathered for war;
They have sharpened their tongues like a serpent;
Adders' poison is under their lip. Selah.
Keep me, O Lord, from the hands of the wicked;
Preserve me from the violent man,
Who have purposed to overthrow my goings.

Sarah looks at Mrs Poulteney, who has fallen asleep.

INT. MIKE'S HOTEL ROOM. LYME. DAY. PRESENT.

Anna, with glasses on, reading a book. Mike reading the sports page of a newspaper. She looks up.

                    ANNA

Wow!

                    MIKE

What?

                    ANNA
              (*referring to the book*)

Listen to this.
'In 1857 *The Lancet* estimated that there were eighty thousand prostitutes in the County of London. Out of every sixty houses one was a brothel.'

                    MIKE

Mmm.

Pause.

                    ANNA
                 (*reading*)

'We reach the surprising conclusion that at a time when the male population of London of all ages was one and a quarter million, the prostitutes were receiving clients at a rate of two million per week.'

                    MIKE

Two million!

                    ANNA

You know when I say – in the graveyard scene – about going to London? Wait.

She picks up her script of The French Lieutenant's Woman, *flips the pages, finds the page. She reads aloud:*

'If I went to London I know what I should become. I should become what some already call me in Lyme.'

MIKE

Yes?

ANNA

Well, that's what she's really faced with.
(*She picks up the book.*)
This man says that hundreds of the prostitutes were nice
girls like governesses who had lost their jobs. See what I
mean? You offend your boss, you lose your job. That's
it! You're on the streets. I mean, it's real.

Mike has picked up a calculator and starts tapping out figures.

MIKE

The male population was a million and a quarter but the
prostitutes had two million clients a week?

ANNA

Yes. That's what he says.

MIKE

Allow about a third off for boys and old men ... That
means that outside marriage – a Victorian gentleman
had about two point four fucks a week.

She looks at him.

EXT. LYME. DAY.

Near the Cobb. A helicopter takes off.

INT. HELICOPTER.

Mike sits beside the pilot.

*They speak, pointing at the ground but we do not hear their
words.*

EXT. UNDERCLIFF FROM HELICOPTER. DAY.

Travelling eye-line from helicopter.

The viewpoint, at first at sea level, swoops dramatically up from the rocks of the falling coastline to a high view of the vast wilderness of the Undercliff.

EXT. UNDERCLIFF. DAY.

The Undercliff is a great dense wood inland of the cliffs, looking over Lyme Bay. It has a very strange atmosphere, quite un-English in character. The terrain is abrupt, cut by deep chasms and towers of chalk and flint cliffs. The undergrowth is matted, the foliage lush. The ashes and beech trees are vast and tangled. Chasms are choked with ivy and wild clematis. The bracken is eight feet tall. Masses of wild flowers.

Charles, dressed in his fossil-hunting clothes, and carrying equipment, stands looking up at the vast trees above him.

CHARLES SEEN, FROM HIGH, THROUGH TREES.

HAMMER ON FLINT.

The camera tracks back to reveal Charles at the bottom of an inland flint cliff, hammering.

He puts hammer down, takes out chisel, begins to scrape the surface. He puts chisel down, drinks from water-bottle, cools his forehead with water. He is about to pick up chisel when he looks down sharply.

THE TREES. CHARLES'S P.O.V.

A figure glimpsed, moving through trees.

CHARLES LIFTING SMALL TELESCOPE.

THE TREES, MAGNIFIED.

Stillness.

UNDERCLIFF.

Charles leaves the flint cliff. He looks at the place where he had glimpsed the figure. He hesitates, and then goes towards the trees.

He tramps through the matted undergrowth, suddenly falls.

He stands. He goes on. Branches claw at him.

He suddenly finds a path. He follows it.

It opens on to a little green plateau, studded with wild flowers.

He is close to the edge of the Undercliff.

LYME BAY FAR BELOW.

CHARLES ON THE PLATEAU.

The plateau goes to a brink. He walks towards it and looks down.

THE LEDGE.

On the broad sloping ledge of grass Sarah is sitting.

The ledge is five feet below the plateau. Below it is a mass of brambles – beyond it the cliff falling to the sea.

THE PLATEAU.

Charles looking down.

THE LEDGE.

Sarah sitting on the ledge, looking out to sea.

She turns sharply, and sees Charles.

She stands quickly, stares at him.

CHARLES AND SARAH.

> CHARLES
> I am very sorry to disturb you.

He turns and climbs back towards the path.

CLOSE-UP. ANNA. CARAVAN. PRESENT.

She takes off her wig, puts it on a table. She shakes her hair loose. She stares at her face in the mirror.

EXT. THE DAIRY.

Charles seen emerging from trees. He walks towards the dairy. The dairy woman sitting by the door. She looks up as he approaches.

INT. MRS TRANTER'S HOUSE. DAY.

Mary opening the front door. Sam stands on the doorstep with a bunch of flowers.

> SAM
> For the lovely young lady upstairs.

He gives the flowers to Mary and brings a small posy from behind his back.

> And for the even more lovely one down.

He gives the posy to her. She smells the flowers and looks at him through them.

EXT. DAIRY.

The Dairywoman is ladling milk from a churn into a china bowl. Charles receives it and drinks.

The Dairyman comes out of the door; a vast bald man. The woman disappears. The man stares.

CHARLES

Very fine milk.

The man stares.

How much do I owe you?

DAIRYMAN

A penny.

Charles gives him a penny.

CHARLES

Thank you very much.

Suddenly a figure in black appears out of the trees walking on the path towards Lyme. It is Sarah. She glances in their direction and goes on. The two men watch her.

Do you know that lady?

DAIRYMAN

Aye.

CHARLES

Does she come this way often?

DAIRYMAN

Often enough. And she been't no lady. She be the French Loot'n'nt's Whore.

Charles glares at him.

INT. ERNESTINA'S ROOM. DAY.

A knock at the door. Mary comes in, with flowers.

MARY

From Mr Charles, Miss Tina. With his compliments.

ERNESTINA

Did he bring them himself?

31

MARY

No, miss.

ERNESTINA

Where is Mr Charles?

MARY

Don't know, miss. I didn't ask him.

ERNESTINA

Ask who?

MARY

His servant, miss.

ERNESTINA

But I heard you speak with him.

MARY

Yes, miss.

ERNESTINA

What about?

MARY

Oh just the time of day, miss.

ERNESTINA

You will kindly remember that he comes from London.

MARY

Yes, miss.

ERNESTINA

If he makes advances I wish to be told at once. Now
bring me some barley water.

Sullenly Mary bobs a curtsey and leaves the room.

Ernestina takes envelope from flowers and opens it.

THE LETTER.

'For my beloved. Charles.'

EXT. UNDERCLIFF.

Sarah walking.

Charles pursuing her. He catches her up.

CHARLES

Madam!

Sarah stops, turns to him.

He smiles.

I am very sorry to have disturbed you just now.

She inclines her head, moves on. He walks with her.

I gather you have recently become ... secretary to Mrs Poulteney. May I accompany you? Since we walk in the same direction?

She stops.

SARAH

I prefer to walk alone.

They stand.

CHARLES

May I introduce myself?

SARAH

I know who you are.

CHARLES

Ah ... then?

SARAH

Kindly allow me to go on my way alone.
(*Pause.*)

33

And please tell no-one you have seen me in this place.

She walks on.

He remains still, looking after her.

INT. CARAVAN. PRESENT. DAY.

Anna in her caravan. A knock on the door.

ANNA

Hello!

Mike comes in.

MIKE

May I introduce myself?

ANNA

I know who you are.

They smile. He closes the door.

MIKE

So you prefer to walk alone?

ANNA

Me? Not me. Her.

MIKE

I enjoyed that.

ANNA

What?

MIKE

Our exchange. Out there.

ANNA

Did you? I never know . . .

MIKE

Know what?

34

                    ANNA
Whether it's any good.

                    MIKE
Listen. Do you find me – ?

                    ANNA
What?

                    MIKE
Sympathetic.

                    ANNA
Mmn. Definitely.

                    MIKE
I don't mean me. I mean him.

                    ANNA
Definitely.

                    MIKE
But you still prefer to walk alone?

                    ANNA
Who? Me – or her?

                    MIKE
Her. You like company.
          (*He strokes the back of her neck.*)
Don't you?

                    ANNA
                 (*smiling*)
Not always. Sometimes I prefer to walk alone.

                    MIKE
Tell me, when you said that – outside – you swished
your skirt – very provocative. Did you mean it?

                    ANNA
Well, it worked. Didn't it?

                      35

Third Assistant's face at door.

> THIRD ASSISTANT
> We're going again.

EXT. UNDERCLIFF. DAY. ANOTHER ANGLE.

> CHARLES
> May I accompany you? Since we walk in the same
> direction?

She stops.

> SARAH
> I prefer to walk alone.

> CHARLES
> May I introduce myself?

> SARAH
> I know who you are.

She collapses in laughter. He grins.

> VOICE
> (*off screen*)
> Cut!
> (*with bewilderment*)
> What's going on?

INT. MRS POULTENEY'S SITTING ROOM. DAY.

*Mrs Poulteney is sitting. Sarah standing. Mrs Poulteney is
looking away from Sarah.*

> MRS POULTENEY
> I should never have listened to the Vicar. I should have
> listened to the dictates of my own common sense. You
> are a cunning, wicked creature.

Pause.

SARAH

May I know of what I am accused?

Mrs Poulteney turns sharply to her.

MRS POULTENEY

You have been seen walking on the Undercliff! Not
twice, but thrice!

SARAH

But what, pray, is the sin in that?

MRS POULTENEY

The sin! You, a young woman, alone, in such a place!

SARAH

It is nothing but a large wood.

MRS POULTENEY

I know very well what it is. And what goes on there – the
sort of person who frequents it.

SARAH

No-one frequents it. I go there to be alone.

MRS POULTENEY

Do you contradict me, Miss? Am I not to know what I
speak of?
(*Pause.*)
I will permit no-one in my employ to go to or to be seen
near that place. You will confine your walks to where it
is seemly. Do I make myself clear?

SARAH

Yes. I am to walk in the paths of righteousness.

Mrs Poulteney looks at her sharply.

INT. MRS TRANTER'S HOUSE. KITCHEN. DAY.

*Mary bustling about the kitchen. Sam, with his feet up, watching
her.*

SAM

Why don't you come with the young lady, when they're
married, as her maid?

MARY

I'm Mrs Tranter's maid.

SAM

She wouldn't mind.

He stands and moves to her.

I could show you around London, see the sights.

MARY

You wouldn't want to go walking out with me in
London, with all them fashionable London girls.

SAM

If you had the clothes, you'd do. You'd do very nice.

She moves away.

MARY

You're joking with me.

SAM

I'm dead serious. I'm not going to stay a servant all my
life. Not by a long chalk. I'm going to be a draper. I
want my own shop.

She looks at him wide-eyed.

All I need is one hundred pounds.

MARY

And where are you going to get that?

SAM

I'll get it.

He takes her face in his hands, kisses her, murmurs softly:

I'll get it.

INT. ERNESTINA'S SITTING ROOM. DAY.

Ernestina is lying on a chaise longue wearing a peignoir.

Charles is kissing her hand.

> ERNESTINA
> You shall not have a drop of tea until you have
> accounted for every moment of your day.

Charles brings from behind his back a fossil and gives it to her.

> CHARLES
> A gift – for you.

> ERNESTINA
> Good gracious! How pretty. What is it?

> CHARLES
> An echinoderm. It was once a sea urchin, of sorts.
> Micraster Coranguinium.

> ERNESTINA
> Where did you find it?

> CHARLES
> I have been exploring the Undercliff.

> ERNESTINA
> The Undercliff? But it's supposed to be dangerous and
> disreputable. The only people who go there ... are
> servants.

> CHARLES
> And why do they go there?

> ERNESTINA
> I hear they go there ... to dally.

CHARLES

Do they indeed? Well, I saw no dallying servants.

ERNESTINA

Nor dallying scientists?

CHARLES
(*smiling*)

No.

Pause.

ERNESTINA

You don't intend to take me there, I hope.

CHARLES

Certainly not. The place is full of wild and ferocious animals. I wouldn't want you eaten up.

She takes his hand.

ERNESTINA

Charles ... please tell me ... do you think me very foolish? You see, I'm so little educated. But I am a person of feeling.

He squeezes her hand.

CHARLES

You are a person of sweet feeling.

INT. HOTEL. EMPTY BILLIARD ROOM. NIGHT. PRESENT.

Mike and Anna rehearsing, holding scripts.

MIKE

Miss Woodruff!

ANNA

Just a minute, I've lost the place.

She turns pages of script.

MIKE

I suddenly see you. You've got your coat caught in
brambles. I see you, then you see me. We look at each
other, then I say: 'Miss Woodruff'.

ANNA

All right.

MIKE

Right. I see you. Get your coat caught in the bramble.

She mimes her coat caught in bramble.

Right. Now I'm looking at you. You see me. Look at
me.

ANNA

I am.

MIKE

Miss Woodruff!

ANNA

I'm looking at you.

MIKE

Yes, but now you come towards me, to pass me. It's a
narrow path, muddy.

She walks towards him.

You slip in the mud.

ANNA

Whoops!

She falls.

MIKE

Beautiful. Now I have to help you up.

ANNA

Let's start over again.

She goes back to the chair.

I've got my coat caught in the brambles. Suddenly you see me. Then I see you.

MIKE

Miss Woodruff!

She mimes her coat caught in brambles, tugs at it, walks along carpet towards him. He steps aside. She moves swiftly to pass him, and slips. She falls to her knees. He bends to help her up. She looks up at him. He stops a moment, looking down, and then gently lifts her. With his hand on her elbow, he leads her towards the window.

I dread to think, Miss Woodruff, what would happen if you should one day turn your ankle in a place like this.

She is silent, looking down.

He looks down at her face, her mouth.

ANNA

I must . . . go back.

MIKE

Will you permit me to say something first? I know I am a stranger to you, but –

Sharp cut to:

SARAH TURNING SHARPLY. A BRANCH SNAPPING.

UNDERCLIFF. DAY.

Men's low voices.

Charles standing. Sarah moving swiftly over the grass and disappearing behind a thicket of gorse.

The voices come nearer. Suddenly a dog and two men appear, in the undergrowth. The dog barks, the men stare at Charles and then withdraw hurriedly. Racing footsteps; a shrill whistle; the dog turns and disappears after the men. Silence.

THE THICKET OF GORSE.

Sarah stands, tensely.

Charles appears.

The gorse is in full bloom. He studies her standing against it.

> CHARLES
> It was not really necessary to hide.

> SARAH
> No gentleman who cares for his good name can be seen with the scarlet woman of Lyme.

> CHARLES
> Miss Woodruff, I know something ... about your circumstances. It cannot be ... any great pleasure to be in Mrs Poulteney's employ.

She does not respond.

> You should leave Lyme. I understand you have excellent qualifications.

> SARAH
> I cannot leave this place.

> CHARLES
> Why? You have no family ties, I believe, that confine you to Dorset?

> SARAH
> I have ties.

> CHARLES
> To this French gentleman?

43

She turns away.

> Permit me to insist. These matters are like wounds. If no-one dares speak of them, they fester. If he does not return, he was not worthy of you. If he returns –

SARAH

He will never return.

Pause.

CHARLES

You fear he will never return?

SARAH

I know he will never return.

CHARLES

I do not take your meaning.

She looks away, stays silent, looks back at him.

She speaks calmly, looking into his eyes.

SARAH

He is married.

MRS TRANTER'S HOUSE. KITCHEN. DAY.

The Cook and Undermaid preparing a tray of tea. Sam sitting. Mary enters.

SAM

Who is it?

MARY

It's that Mrs Poulteney. The one who kicked me out on to the street.

SAM

Is it? Poison her tea.

MARY

I'm not frightened of her. I work here now, where I'm
respected.

SAM

I'll say you are. Ugly old devil.

MARY

She is that.

SAM

Who's that with her?

MARY

Don't you know her? That's poor 'Tragedy'.

The servants' bell rings. They all look up.

MRS TRANTER'S HOUSE. GARDEN ROOM. DAY.

*Mrs Tranter, Mrs Poulteney, Sarah, Ernestina and Charles,
sitting.*

MRS TRANTER

Miss Woodruff, it is a pleasure to meet you. Are you
liking Lyme?

Charles looks at Sarah.

SARAH

Thank you ma'm. Yes.

MRS TRANTER

Were you born far from Lyme?

SARAH

In Dorchester ma'm. It is not very far.

*A knock on the door. Mary and the Undermaid enter with the
tea.*

MRS TRANTER

Ah, tea! Thank you Mary.

Mrs Poulteney glares at Mary. Mary ignores her. The maids set the tea.

MRS POULTENEY
(*to Ernestina*)

How long will you remain in Lyme, Miss Freeman?

ERNESTINA

Oh, for the summer. I must say, Mrs Poulteney, you look exceedingly well.

MRS POULTENEY

At my age, Miss Freeman, spiritual health is all that counts.

ERNESTINA

Then I have no fears for you.

MRS POULTENEY

With gross disorders on the streets it becomes ever more necessary to protect the sacredness of one's beliefs.

CHARLES

Gross disorders on the streets, Mrs Poulteney?

MRS POULTENEY

Certainly, Mr Smithson. Even a disciple of Darwin, such as I understand you to be, could not fail to notice the rise of the animal about us. It no doubt pleases you, since it would accord with your view that we are all monkeys.

CHARLES

I must look more closely into it, Mrs Poulteney, the next time I find myself on a street.

Mary and the Undermaid leave the room. Mrs Tranter begins to pour tea.

She passes a cup to Ernestina.

SARAH
(*to Mrs Tranter*)

Please allow me to help you, Mrs Tranter.

MRS TRANTER

Thank you.

Ernestina gives cup to Mrs Poulteney. Sarah gives cup to Charles.

MRS POULTENEY

Your maid, for example. I have been informed that she was seen only this morning talking with a person. A young person.

CHARLES

Then it was no doubt Sam. My servant.

Ernestina gives plate and napkin to Mrs Poulteney. Sarah gives plate and napkin to Charles.

Her hand opens the napkin slightly. He looks down.

Inside the napkin is the corner of an envelope.

CLOSE-UP. CHARLES.

He looks up quickly.

INT. THE ROOM.

ERNESTINA

Yes, I must say, Charles, your servant spends an inordinate amount of his time talking to Mary.

CHARLES

What is the harm in that?

ERNESTINA

There is a world of difference between what may be accepted in London and what is proper here.

47

CHARLES

But I do not understand what crime Mary and Sam, by talking, appear to commit.

MRS POULTENEY

Your future wife is a better judge than you are of these things, Mr Smithson. I know the girl in question, I had to dismiss her. If you were older you would know that one cannot be too strict in such matters.

CHARLES

I bow to your far greater experience, madam.

THE ROOM.

They all sip tea in silence.

EXT. MRS TRANTER'S HOUSE. DAY.

Mrs Poulteney and Sarah sitting in their carriage. Ernestina and Mrs Tranter stand by the carriage. Mrs Poulteney turns to Ernestina.

MRS POULTENEY

I am glad that you and I are of a mind, Miss Freeman.

The carriage drives out of the gate. Ernestina runs towards the house.

INT. GARDEN ROOM.

Charles, alone, tearing open envelope. He takes out a letter.

THE LETTER.

'I pray you to meet me at nine tonight. St Michael's Churchyard.'

INT. GARDEN ROOM.

Charles thrusts the envelope and letter into his pocket as Ernestina rushes in, slamming the door, bursting into tears. He takes her in his arms.

CHARLES

My dearest. What is it?

ERNESTINA

Oh Charles, she's a horrid old woman, and I took her part against you! How could I? I'm as horrid as she is.

CHARLES

You're sweet and silly. Aren't you?

ERNESTINA

Yes.

CHARLES

What if this wicked maid and my rascal Sam should fall in love? Are we to throw stones?

ERNESTINA

Only at Mrs Poulteney!

He laughs, kisses her eyes. She looks up at him, clings to him.

Eighty-eight days to our wedding. It's an eternity.

CHARLES

Let us elope – and go to Paris.

ERNESTINA

Oh Charles – what wickedness!

He kisses her lips quickly.

CHARLES

If only the worthy Mrs Poulteney could see us now!

She nuzzles into his chest, giggling.

CLOSE-UP. CHARLES. HIS FACE TENSE.

EXT. CHURCHYARD. NIGHT.

Sarah standing in the shadow of a large tombstone.

Footsteps approaching on gravel.

Charles approaching. He looks about.

Sound of organ suddenly from inside the church. (It continues in background throughout the scene.) Charles stops still.

Sarah's voice a swift whisper:

SARAH

Come here!

Charles turns, goes to her.

Thank you for coming. Thank you.

They both speak in low voices.

CHARLES

How did you dare to behave in so impertinent and presumptuous a manner? How dare you do such a thing in front of Miss Freeman?

SARAH

I had no-one else to turn to.

CHARLES

It must be obvious that it would be most improper of me to interest myself further in your circumstances.

SARAH

Yes. It is obvious.

She turns her face away. It is caught in moonlight.

CHARLES

Why do you not go to London? And find a new life?

SARAH

If I went to London I know what I should become. I should become what some already call me in Lyme.

CHARLES

My dear Miss Woodruff . . .

SARAH

I am weak. How should I not know it? I have sinned.

He stares at her.

You cannot imagine . . . my suffering. My only happiness is when I sleep. When I wake, the nightmare begins.

Footsteps. They freeze.

THE CHURCHYARD.

The Vicar walking towards the church.

THE TOMBSTONE.

She takes his hand, leads him to a darker place by a larger tombstone.

The organ grows louder. The church door closes. The organ dims.

They stand in the shadow of the tombstone.

CHARLES

This is highly –

SARAH

Why am I born what I am? Why am I not born Miss Freeman?

CHARLES

That question were better not asked.

SARAH

I did not mean –

CHARLES

Envy is understandable in your –

SARAH

Not envy. Incomprehension.
                    (*She looks at him.*)
You must help me.

CHARLES

It is not in my power – to help you.

SARAH

I do not – I will not believe that.

CHARLES

What in heaven's name do you want of me?

SARAH

I want to tell you of what happened to me eighteen
months ago.

The organ suddenly stops.

I beg you. You are my only hope. I shall be on the
Undercliff tomorrow afternoon and the next afternoon.
I shall wait for you.

CHARLES

I must go.

He walks away.

SARAH

I shall wait.

INT. HOTEL BEDROOM. NIGHT. PRESENT.

*Mike and Anna in bed. Moonlight. She is asleep. He is looking at
her.*

He quietly gets out of the bed, lights a cigarette, looks out of the window. He turns, looks back at the bed.

Anna's foot is exposed. He moves to the bed, tucks the foot in, carefully. Anna murmurs:

                    ANNA
        David . . .
                    (*She wakes, looks up at him.*)

                    MIKE
        It's not David. It's Mike.

                    ANNA
        What are you doing?

                    MIKE
        Looking at you.

                    ANNA
        Come back.

He gets back into the bed. She puts her arm around him, and folds him to her breast.

INT. DR GROGAN'S STUDY. NIGHT.

The room is bow-fronted and looks over the bay. A brass Georgian telescope rests on a table in the bow window.

Grogan is pouring brandy. Charles is examining the telescope.

                    GROGAN
        Like my telescope?

                    CHARLES
        It's most elegant, and indeed . . . most effective.

                    GROGAN
        I use it to keep an eye out for mermaids. I'm delighted
        you dropped in. It's about time we met. Here. The best

brandy in Lyme. I keep it for visitors from London, who
share a taste for the good life.

CHARLES

Your good health, Doctor.

GROGAN

Yours. I understand you're a scientist, a seeker after
fossils. Care for a cheroot?

CHARLES

Thank you. Yes, my interest is fossils.
(*He smiles.*)
I gather it is not yours.

GROGAN

When we know more of the living it will be time to
pursue the dead.

They sit back with their brandy and cheroots.

CHARLES

Yes. I was introduced the other day to a specimen of the
local flora that rather inclines me to agree with you. A
very strange case, as far as I understand it. Her name is
Woodruff.

GROGAN

Ah, yes. Poor 'Tragedy'. I'll tell you something. We
know more about the fossils out there on the beach than
we do about that girl's mind. There is a German doctor
called Hartmann who has recently divided melancholia
into several types. One he calls natural. By which he
means one is born with a sad temperament. Another he
calls occasional, by which he means springing from an
occasion. The third class he calls obscure melancholia.
By which he really means, poor man, that he doesn't
know what the devil it is that caused it.

CHARLES

But she had an occasion, did she not?

GROGAN

Oh, come now, is she the first young woman to be
jilted? No, no, she belongs to the third class – obscure
melancholia. Listen to me – I'll tell you – in the strictest
confidence – I was called in to see her – a ten-month
ago. She was working as a seamstress, living alone, well,
hardly living. Weeping without reason, unable to sleep,
unable to talk. Melancholia as plain as the pox. I could
see there was only one cure. To get her away from this
place. But no, she wouldn't have it. What does she do?
She goes to a house she knows is a living misery, to a
mistress who doesn't know the difference between a
servant and slave. And she won't be moved.

CHARLES

It's incomprehensible.

GROGAN

Not at all. Hartmann has an interesting thing to say
about one of his patients. 'It was as if her torture had
become her delight.'

Charles throws the stub of his cheroot into the fire.

CHARLES

And she has confided the real state of her mind to no-
one?

GROGAN

She has not.

CHARLES

But if she did . . . if she could bring herself . . . to speak?

GROGAN

She would be cured. But she does not want to be cured.

EXT. BEACH. DAY. PRESENT.

Anna barefoot in beach suit wanders along the shore picking up pebbles. She joins Mike who lies on the beach, eyes closed. She stands above him.

> MIKE
>
> Have a nice walk?

> ANNA
>
> Wonderful.

She stretches, looks up at the sky.

EXT. UNDERCLIFF. DAY.

A dell, high up, overlooking the sea.

Sarah and Charles emerge through trees into the dell. She sits. He sits. She looks out to sea.

> SARAH
>
> I was working as a governess. At the Talbots.
> His name was Varguennes.

EXT. BEACH. DAY. PRESENT.

Anna turns over suddenly on to her stomach and looks towards the Undercliff.

> MIKE
>
> What's the matter?

She is silent. He rolls over to look at her face.

> What's the matter? You look sad.

> ANNA
> (*softly*)
>
> No.

MIKE

Why are you sad?

ANNA

I'm not.

He lies under her, pulls her down gently, kisses her. Her eyes close, then open. She looks towards the Undercliff.

THE UNDERCLIFF. ANNA'S P.O.V.

EXT. THE UNDERCLIFF. DAY.

The dell. Sarah is sitting on a hummock. Charles is sitting on a flat-topped block of flint. She looks out to sea. Her face is in profile to him.

SARAH

His name was Varguennes. He was brought to the house after the wreck of his ship. He had a dreadful wound. His flesh was torn from his hip to his knee. He was in great pain. Yet he never cried out. Not the smallest groan. I admired his courage. I looked after him. I did not know then that men can be both very brave and very false.

(*Pause.*)

He was handsome. No man had ever paid me the kind of attentions he did, as he ... was recovering. He told me I was beautiful, that he could not understand why I was not married. Such things. He would ... mock me, lightly.

(*Pause.*)

I took pleasure in it.

(*Pause.*)

When I would not let him kiss my hand he called me cruel. A day came when I thought myself cruel as well.

CHARLES

And you were no longer cruel?

SARAH

No.

CHARLES

I understand.

SARAH
(*fiercely*)

You cannot, Mr Smithson. Because you are not a
woman. You are not a woman born to be a farmer's wife
but educated to be something . . . better. You were not
born a woman with a love of intelligence, beauty,
learning, but whose position in the world forbids her to
share this love with another. And you are not the
daughter of a bankrupt. You have not spent your life in
penury. You are not . . . condemned. You are not an
outcast.

CHARLES

Social privilege does not necessarily bring happiness.

SARAH

It brings the possibility of happiness.

EXT. DAY. BEACH. PRESENT.

*Mike and Anna lying side by side. Her eyes are closed. He is
looking at her.*

Over this, the voices of Sarah and Charles:

SARAH
(*VO*)

Varguennes recovered. He asked me to go back with
him to France. He offered me . . .

CHARLES
(*VO*)

Marriage?

Anna opens her eyes and looks at Mike.

EXT. UNDERCLIFF. DAY.

SARAH

Yes. He left for Weymouth. He said he would wait
there one week and then sail for France. I said I would
never follow him, that I could not. But . . . after he had
gone . . . my loneliness was so deep, I felt I would drown
in it.

(*Pause.*)

I followed him. I went to the inn where he had taken a
room. It was not . . . a respectable place. I knew that at
once. They told me to go up to his room. They looked
at me . . . and smiled. I insisted he be sent for. He
seemed overjoyed to see me. He was all that a lover
should be. I had not eaten that day. He took me . . . to a
private sitting room, ordered food.

(*Pause.*)

But he had changed. He was full of smiles and caresses
but I knew at once that he was insincere. I saw that I
had been an amusement for him, nothing more. He was
a liar. I saw all this within five minutes of our meeting.

(*Pause.*)

Yet I stayed. I ate the supper that was served. I drank
the wine he pressed on me. It did not intoxicate me. I
think it made me see more clearly. Is that possible?

CHARLES

No doubt.

Pause.

SARAH

Soon he no longer bothered to hide the real nature of
his intentions towards me. Nor could I pretend surprise.
My innocence was false from the moment I chose to
stay. I could tell you that he overpowered me, that he
drugged me. But it is not so.

(*She looks at him directly.*)

I gave myself to him.

(*Silence.*)

I did it . . . so that I should never be the same again, so
that I should be seen for the outcast I am. I knew it was
ordained that I could never marry an equal. So I
married shame. It is my shame . . . that has kept me
alive, my knowing that I am truly not like other women.
I shall never like them have children, a husband, the
pleasures of a home. Sometimes I pity them. I have a
freedom they cannot understand. No insult, no blame,
can touch me. I have set myself beyond the pale. I am
nothing. I am hardly human any more. I am the French
Lieutenant's Whore.

*Charles stands, walks over to her, looks down at her. For a
moment it seems that he will take her in his arms. He straightens.*

CHARLES

You must leave Lyme.

Suddenly voices, laughter, from below, ascending.

*Sarah stands. She beckons to him silently and moves to the trees.
He follows.*

The laughter comes closer.

*Sarah and Charles hide behind thick ivy. They look through it
down to an ashgrove.*

THE ASHGROVE. THEIR P.O.V.

A girl and a boy, coming up towards them. The boy has his arm round her waist. He turns her to him and kisses her. They fall to the grass. The girl lies back. The boy kisses her.

CLOSE-UP. SARAH SMILING AT CHARLES.

CHARLES.

He stares at her.

CHARLES AND SARAH.

They are looking at each other. Her smile fades. Silence.

> CHARLES
>
> Please go. We must never meet alone again.

She turns away.

A shrill laugh from below. Charles turns to look.

THE ASHGROVE

The girl running downhill. The boy chasing her. Their figures flash between trees; a laugh; a scream; silence.

> CHARLES
>
> Go. I will wait.

She moves past him, into the ashgrove.

CHARLES

He watches her walk downhill through trees.

EXT. THE DAIRY.

Mrs Fairley and the Dairyman outside the dairy. He is pouring milk. Mrs Fairley gasps and stares.

THE DAIRY FIELD. MRS FAIRLEY'S P.O.V.

Sarah walking openly downhill towards Lyme.

CLOSE-UP. SARAH. WALKING CALMLY.

INT. HOTEL ROOM. NIGHT. PRESENT.

Mike is lying on a sofa, staring at the ceiling. Jazz is playing from a transistor radio.

EXT. MRS POULTENEY'S HOUSE. NIGHT.

The house is dark.

A figure can be seen sitting by a dimly lit window.

INT. SARAH'S BEDROOM. NIGHT.

Sarah is sitting by the window. Candlelight. She is drawing.

The camera closes in on her and reveals that she is crying softly, as she draws.

THE DRAWING.

It is a self-portrait.

A sudden knock on the door. Sarah looks up.

MRS FAIRLEY
(*off screen*)

Miss Woodruff! Miss Woodruff! Mrs Poulteney wishes to see you!

EXT. STREET OUTSIDE WHITE LION HOTEL. NIGHT.

A small ragged boy running along the street.

He stops at the White Lion, looks in quickly, goes in.

INT. HOTEL. CHARLES'S SITTING ROOM. NIGHT.

Charles is lying on the sofa in dressing gown, staring at the ceiling.

An envelope slides under the door.

He looks at it, stands quickly, goes to door, opens it.

No-one.

He closes door, picks up envelope, opens it, takes out letter.

THE LETTER.

'*The secret is out. Am at the barn on the Undercliff. Only you stand between me and oblivion.*'

CHARLES SLOWLY PUTS THE LETTER IN HIS POCKET.

EXT. DR GROGAN'S HOUSE. NIGHT.

Charles knocking at the door. His carriage stands by the kerb.

Thunder.

Housekeeper opens the door.

> HOUSEKEEPER
>
> Yes?

> CHARLES
>
> Forgive me. I must speak to Dr Grogan.

> HOUSEKEEPER
>
> Dr Grogan is not here.

> CHARLES
>
> Not here?

> HOUSEKEEPER
>
> He is at the asylum. He was called to the asylum.

CHARLES

Thank you.

INT. ASYLUM. HALL AND CORRIDOR. NIGHT.

A long empty stone corridor.

Silence.

Distant thunder.

An echoing cry.

A heavy Man carrying keys comes towards camera, unlocks a door to the reception hall of the asylum.

Charles is waiting.

MAN

Dr Grogan is busy. He says to wait. Follow me.

He leads Charles down the stone corridor to a door. Charles goes in.

You wait there.

INT. ASYLUM. SMALL ROOM. NIGHT.

The room is bare. A table, two chairs.

Charles goes to the window, which is barred. He stares out at the rain.

He turns abruptly.

DOOR OF ROOM. HIS P.O.V.

Two female patients are at the open door, looking at him. One of them is smiling.

CLOSE-UP OF CHARLES.

He gasps with shock.

THE ROOM.

One of the women goes towards him. She speaks as if in fever. As she speaks, she touches his body. He recoils, tries to tear her hand away.

WOMAN
Help me – help me – help me – help me – help me – help me –

The Man comes in, seizes her, hits her, drags her out. Shouts along the corridor. A scream.

INT. CORRIDOR.

Charles goes into the corridor.

The Woman is being dragged along, screaming.

Various other sounds can be heard: moans, abrupt laughs, whimpers, sudden shouts.

At the far end of the corridor a line of patients shuffles across.

A man in a dark suit herds them.

Charles turns swiftly, goes back into the room, closes the door.

INT. ROOM.

Charles stands.

Sudden sound of footsteps approaching. The door opens – Grogan comes in, wiping his hands on a towel.

GROGAN
Smithson. Yes, I can guess what you've come about. Sorry I wasn't at home. I've been called to attend a breech birth. Well, the fact is we don't know where she is.

CHARLES

I'm sorry, I . . . I don't understand what you're saying.

GROGAN

You don't know what's happened?

CHARLES

No.

GROGAN

Then why are you here?

CHARLES

I need your advice.

GROGAN

I'm not sure I've any left to give.
Miss Woodruff has disappeared.
Mrs Poulteney dismissed her. There's a search party
out. I have offered five pounds to the man who brings
her back, or finds her body.

CHARLES

She is alive. I have just received a note from her.

Grogan stares at him.

A scream from another room.

GROGAN

I must attend to the mother. Go to my house and wait
for me.

EXT. THE UNDERCLIFF. NIGHT.

Sarah running up hill through the trees.

Thunder.

GROGAN'S STUDY. NIGHT.

Grogan pouring two glasses of brandy.

GROGAN

Tell me the facts.

CHARLES

She wants to see me.

He looks into Grogan's eyes.

GROGAN

I see.
                    (*He looks at his watch.*)
I must call off the search party. You know where she is?

CHARLES

Yes.

GROGAN

Mmn. Well, you can't go to her, can you?

CHARLES

I am in your hands.

GROGAN

You *are* engaged to be married?

Charles looks at him.

CHARLES

I am.

Grogan goes to a book shelf and takes down a copy of Origin of
Species. *He puts his hand on it, as on a Bible.*

GROGAN

Nothing that has been said in this room tonight or that
remains to be said shall go beyond these walls. Well,
now, you ask for my advice.

He paces up and down the room.

I am a young woman of superior intelligence and some
education. I am not in full command of my emotions.
What is worse, I have fallen in love with being a victim

of fate. Enter a young god. Intelligent. Good-looking.
Kind. I have but one weapon. The pity I inspire in him.
So what do I do? I seize my chance. One day, when I
am walking where I have been forbidden to walk, I show
myself to someone I know will report my crime to the
one person who will not condone it. I disappear, under
the strong presumption that it is in order to throw
myself off the nearest clifftop. And then – *in extremis*, I
cry to my saviour for help.

CHARLES

What in God's name are you talking about?

GROGAN

I have spoken to Mrs Poulteney's housekeeper. She was
at the dairy on the Undercliff. The girl walked out of the
woods under her nose. It was deliberate. She wanted to
be seen. Presumably to compromise you.

CHARLES

But why should she wish to harm me?

GROGAN

Listen to me. I have known many prostitutes. I hasten to
add – in pursuance of my own profession, not theirs.
And I wish I had a guinea for every one I have heard
gloat over the fact that a majority of their victims are
husbands and fathers.

CHARLES

But she is not a prostitute! Neither is she a fiend!

GROGAN

My dear man, you are half in love with her.

Charles stares at him.

CHARLES

On my most sacred honour nothing improper has
passed between us.

GROGAN

I believe you. But let me ask you this. Do you wish to
hear her? Do you wish to see her? Do you wish to touch
her?

Charles sits, covers his face.

CHARLES

Oh my dear Grogan, if you knew ... the confusion ...
my life is in.

GROGAN

You are not the first person to doubt his choice of bride.
(*Pause.*)
I will go to see the lady. I shall tell her you have been
called away. And you must go away, Smithson.

CHARLES

Yes.
(*He looks at Grogan.*)
I shall honour my vows to Miss Freeman.

GROGAN

I know of a private asylum in Salisbury. Miss Woodruff
... will be kindly treated ... and helped. Would you
bear the expense?

CHARLES
(*slowly*)
Yes. I would bear the expense.

EXT. WHITE LION. DAWN.

The storm has cleared. The growing dawn is still, clear.

INT. CHARLES'S SITTING ROOM.

Charles stands by the window. He looks out at the sky.

His expression is purposeful.

He turns, goes into his bedroom. Through the open door we see him dressing.

THE UNDERCLIFF. DAWN.

Charles striding swiftly through the woods. The sun slants through the trees.

Dense birdsong.

He climbs until he sees the sea stretched out below.

He stops.

The thatched roof of a barn.

EXT. BARN.

Charles approaches it. Silence.

He looks in at a small window, turns, looks about, opens door, enters.

INT. BARN.

Sunlight floods through the window.

He peers into the shadows, suddenly perceives a bonnet hanging on a nail, by a partition.

He goes to partition, looks over.

SARAH CURLED UNDER HER COAT, ASLEEP.

THE BARN.

Charles withdraws to the door of the barn, stands a moment, speaks.

CHARLES

Miss Woodruff.

*A rustle from behind the partition. Sarah looks over, sees him.
Her hand goes to her mouth. She goes back.*

He stands.

She comes out and walks towards him.

She stops a few feet away from him.

>Have you passed the night here?
>>(*She nods.*)
>
>Are you cold?
>>(*She shakes her head.*)
>
>Do not ... fear. I have come to help you.

He lays his hand on her shoulder.

She seizes his hand, raises it to her lips, kisses it.

He snatches his hand away.

>Pray control yourself, I –

>SARAH

I cannot.

She slips to her knees, cries softly.

>I cannot.

*He bends to her, slowly lifts her. She stands. His hands remain on
her arms. She looks up at him. He takes her into his arms. She
sways into his embrace. He kisses her deeply, crushing her body to
him.*

A giggle is heard, from outside the barn.

*Charles breaks away from Sarah, looks at the door, goes to it,
opens it.*

EXT. BARN. CHARLES'S P.O.V.

Sam and Mary, staring in astonishment.

71

EXT. THE BARN DOOR. THEIR P.O.V.

Charles standing. Behind him Sarah. She disappears from view.

EXT. BARN.

Charles walks towards them.

> CHARLES
>
> What are you doing here?

> SAM
>
> Out walking, Mr Charles.

> CHARLES
> (*to Mary*)
>
> Kindly leave us a moment.

Mary bobs and walks away.

> (*to Sam*)
>
> I have come here to help this lady. At the request of the physician who is treating her. He is fully aware of the circumstances.

> SAM
>
> Yes, sir.

> CHARLES
>
> Which must on no account be disclosed.

> SAM
>
> I understand.

> CHARLES
>
> Does she?

> SAM
>
> She won't say nothing. On my life.

They stare at each other.

> On my solemn oath, Mr Charles.

Sam goes to join Mary. Charles watches them walk away.

He turns and goes back into the barn.

EXT. THE WOODS.

Sam and Mary helpless in silent laughter.

INT. BARN.

Sarah is standing. He goes to her.

CHARLES

I have taken unpardonable advantage of your situation. I am wholly to blame.

(*Pause.*)

You must go to Exeter. There is talk in the town of committing you to an institution. You need not take it seriously. But you will save yourself ... embarrassment if you do not return to Lyme. Where are your belongings?

SARAH

At the coach depot.

CHARLES

I will have them sent to the depot in Exeter. Walk to Axmouth Cross. Wait for the coach there. Take the money in this purse.

He gives her the purse.

SARAH

Thank you.

He gives her a card.

CHARLES

Here is my lawyer's address. Let him know where you are. I will instruct him to send you more money.

                    SARAH
Thank you.

They look at each other.

I shall never see you again.

                    CHARLES
No.
                    (*Pause.*)
You are a remarkable person, Miss Woodruff.

                    SARAH
Yes, I am a remarkable person.

EXT. UNDERCLIFF. DAY. PRESENT.

*Anna, wearing jeans, weaves her way through the crowd towards
Mike. Mike is in costume, eating salad. She sits beside him.*

*In the background a mobile canteen – the unit eating lunch at
trestle tables: some playing football. 'Ernestina' and 'Mary' in
costume at a table.*

                    ANNA
I'm going. To London.

                    MIKE
Yes.
                    (*Pause.*)
Do you have to?

                    ANNA
I don't have any more scenes to do in Lyme.

                    MIKE
Yes. Well, have a good time.

She looks at him.

                    ANNA
David's coming in from New York.

MIKE

How nice for you.
(*He takes her hand.*)
No, it will be nice for you. Nice for him, too.

ANNA

I'll miss you.

The Third Assistant approaches.

MIKE

When do we go to London?

THIRD ASSISTANT
(*to Mike*)

Tuesday or Wednesday.
I'll drive you up to The Cups straight after lunch. Okay?

MIKE

Right.

THIRD ASSISTANT
(*to Anna*)

See you in Exeter, Anna. Think of us slogging away.

ANNA

I will.

Third Assistant goes.

MIKE

I must see you in London.

ANNA

We'd have to be careful.

MIKE

I must see you.

ANNA

Yes. Yes.

Voice on loud hailer: 'Right everybody. We're moving up to The Cups.'

INT. THE CUPS. SITTING ROOM.

Sam folding shirts. Charles comes in.

CHARLES
Sam, I want you to go to London today.
Open up the house. I'll be leaving myself tomorrow.
Change of plan.

SAM
I see, sir.
                    (*He clears his throat.*)
This doesn't have any bearing on your future plans, I . . .
uuh . . . I trust, sir?

CHARLES
My future plans? What are you talking about?

SAM
Well . . . I've got to think about my future, sir.

Charles glares at him.

CHARLES
Have you? Well, your immediate future is to go to
London today. Is that clear?

SAM
Yes, Mr Charles.

INT. MRS TRANTER'S HOUSE. HALL. DAY.

Mary opening front door. Charles.

CHARLES
Ah. Good afternoon.

MARY

Good afternoon, sir. Miss Ernestina is in the garden.

CHARLES

Thank you.

He enters, takes off his hat and gloves and gives them to her. He clears his throat, speaks quietly.

Sam ... has explained the circumstances of this morning?

MARY

Yes, sir.

CHARLES

You ... understand?

MARY

Yes, sir.

He feels in his waistcoat pocket and brings out a golden coin. He presses it into her hand.

Oh sir, I don't want that.

He moves down the hall.

She looks at the coin.

INT. GARDEN ROOM.

Charles walks through the room to the window. He looks out into the garden.

Ernestina is sitting with tea, reading a book.

Charles stands, heavy and pensive, looking out on the scene.

He walks into the garden.

EXT. MRS TRANTER'S HOUSE. GARDEN. DAY.

Charles strides across the lawn.

CHARLES

Good afternoon!

ERNESTINA

Charles!

He takes her hand.

So you have actually deigned to desert the world of the
fossil for me. I am honoured.

CHARLES

I assure you, the true charm of the world resides in this
garden.

ERNESTINA

Honeyed words.

She squeezes his hand.

CHARLES

My dearest, I am afraid I must leave you for a few days.
I must go to London.

ERNESTINA

To London?

CHARLES

To see Montague – my lawyer.

ERNESTINA

Oh Charles!

CHARLES

It's unavoidable, I'm afraid. Apparently there are
matters outstanding – to do with the marriage
settlement. Your father is a most scrupulous person.

ERNESTINA

What does he want?

CHARLES

Justice for you.

ERNESTINA

Sweet justice, that takes you away from me.

CHARLES

Ernestina, I know our private affections are the
paramount consideration, but there is also a legal and
contractual side to matrimony which is –

ERNESTINA

Fiddlesticks!

CHARLES

My dearest Tina –

ERNESTINA

I am weary of Lyme. I see you so little.

CHARLES

I shall be back in three days.

ERNESTINA

Kiss me then. To seal your promise.

He hesitates for a second, then kisses her.

EXT. ENDICOTT'S HOTEL. EXETER. EVENING.

Sarah walks slowly up the hill from the railway station.

She carries two suitcases.

She stops for a rest.

She sees Endicott's Hotel.

INT. REAL TENNIS COURT. LORDS. LONDON. DAY.

(N.B. Real tennis is the old English game of tennis, played in an indoor court.)

Charles and Montague in the middle of a rally.

The rally is violent, intense. Charles hits the ball savagely and wins the point.

INT. DRESSING ROOM. LORDS. DAY.

Montague dressing. Charles comes in, dressed.

> MONTAGUE
> Goodness, Charles, you were in cracking form. Sharp as a razor. What's the answer? Country grub?

Charles laughs shortly.

> CHARLES
> It's good to ... hit a ball.

> MONTAGUE
> You were hitting it as though you hated it.

Charles closes the door.

> CHARLES
> Harry ... a word ... you will be hearing from a person. A Miss Woodruff – from Exeter. She will give you her address. I'd like you to send her some money for me.

> MONTAGUE
> Of course. How much?

> CHARLES
> Fifty pounds.

> MONTAGUE
> Of course.
> (*Pause.*)

Miss Woodruff.

CHARLES

Yes.

(*Pause.*)

And I want to hear . . . nothing more about it.

Montague looks at him.

MONTAGUE

You shan't.

INT. HOTEL ROOM. EXETER. EVENING.

Sarah is alone in the room.

She is taking parcels from a canvas bag.

She unwraps the first and takes from it a nightgown.

She lays it on the bed.

She unwraps the second parcel. It is a dark green merino shawl. She holds it, feels it, brings it to touch her cheek. She shakes the shawl out and then arranges it round the shoulders of the laid-out nightgown.

She studies the image for a moment, goes through the open door into her small sitting room, where a fire burns, and puts a kettle on the hearth.

EXT. CHARLES'S KENSINGTON HOUSE. EVENING.

Lamplight.

A carriage draws up. Charles jumps out, walks quickly up the steps to his house and knocks on the door.

He waits.

He knocks again, violently.

INT. KENSINGTON HOUSE. HALL. EVENING.

Sam walking towards front door.

He opens it. Charles strides in.

> CHARLES
> Where the devil have you been?

> SAM
> I'm sorry sir.

> CHARLES
> Are you deaf?

Charles walks up the stairs.

> Lay out my clothes. I'm dining at my club.

> SAM
> Yes, sir. Can I have one word with you, sir?

> CHARLES
> No. You can't.

INT. LONDON CLUB. EVENING.

Charles enters the smoking room.

Two men of Charles's age, Nathaniel Dyson and Sir Tom Burgh, drinking at a table.

> SIR TOM
> Charley! What the devil are you doing out of the
> matrimonial lock-up?

> CHARLES
> Good evening, Tom. Nathaniel, how are you?

Nat raises a languid hand.

> On parole, you know. The dear girl's down in Dorset
> taking the waters.

SIR TOM

I hear she's the rose of the season. Nat says: 'Damned Charley. Best girl and best match.' Ain't fair, is it, Nat?

CHARLES

Would you discuss a punch and bubbly?

SIR TOM

We would certainly discuss a punch and bubbly. James! Punch and bubbly!

Charles sits.

How goes the hunting in Dorset, Charles? And how go you for hounds? I can offer you a brace of the best Northumberland. Real angels. Do you know who their granpapa was? Tornado. You recall Tornado – at Cambridge?

CHARLES

I recall him. So do my ankles.

Servants bring a bowl of punch and champagne.

SIR TOM

Aye, he took a fancy to you. Always bit what he loved.

Servants pour champagne.

What a profoundly good idea this was, Charley.

He raises his glass.

Dear old Tornado – God rest his soul.

Charles and Nat raise their glasses, and murmur: 'God rest his soul.'

INT. CLUB. DINING ROOM.

The three men at a table.

Waiter approaching the table with two decanters of port.

He places them.

SIR TOM

Bravo! Port is essential to wash down the claret.

NAT

As claret was essential to wash down the punch.

SIR TOM

As punch was essential to sluice the champagne.

They are all drunk, Charles the most drunk.

NAT

What follows?

SIR TOM

What follows? A little drive round town follows. That most essentially follows.

He pours more port for them all.

CHARLES

Tom, dear old fellow, you're a damn good fellow.

SIR TOM

So are you, my Charley boy. We're all damn good fellows.

Sir Tom stands.

On we go gentlemen.

Nat stands.

The dining room is empty.

CHARLES

Where are we going?

NAT

Where damn good fellows always go of a jolly night. Eh, Tom? To Kate Hamilton's. Bless her heart.

SIR TOM
The Bishop's son has hit it, Charley.
          (*He puts a finger to his lips.*)
But not a word to his old man.

Charles stands and collapses. They catch him, and hold him up between them.

The group staggers across the room and crashes into a table, knocking it over. They ricochet into another table.

With cries from Sir Tom and Nat of 'Whoops!' 'Steady there!' and finally 'Charge!' the group crashes into table after table along the length of the dining room.

Three expressionless waiters watch them.

They all collapse in a heap on the floor. Charles's eyes closed.

SIR TOM
I don't think our dear Charley is going anywhere tonight, old boy, do you?

EXT. CHARLES'S KENSINGTON HOUSE. MORNING.

A Messenger walking along the street. He goes up the steps of Charles's house, knocks at door. Sam opens it. Messenger hands Sam an envelope.

MESSENGER
For Mr Smithson from Mr Montague.

SAM
Thank you very much.

He shuts the door.

INT. CHARLES'S KENSINGTON HOUSE. HALL. MORNING.

Sam is looking at the envelope.

INT. KENSINGTON HOUSE. KITCHEN. MORNING.

Sam steaming open the envelope. He takes out a letter. He reads is. He replaces it, picks up some gum, begins to seal the envelope.

INT. KENSINGTON HOUSE. STUDY. MORNING.

Charles lying, half-dressed, asleep, on a Chesterfield. Sam enters, goes to Charles, bends over him.

SAM

Mr Charles ... Mr Charles ...

Charles opens his eyes.

A letter's just come for you, sir.
Special messenger, from Mr Montague.

He gives the letter to Charles.

Charles looks at the handwriting on the envelope.

THE ENVELOPE.

In Sarah's handwriting: For the Personal Attention of Mr Charles Smithson.

His hands tear open the envelope. He opens the letter.

The letter: 'Endicott's Family Hotel, Exeter.'

INT. KENSINGTON HOUSE. THE STUDY. MORNING.

Charles looks up from the letter to Sam.

CHARLES

Bring me tea.

INT. KENSINGTON HOUSE. THE STUDY. MORNING.

Later.

Charles at desk, in dressing gown, writing a letter.

Sam comes in, places tray of tea on side table, remains standing.
Charles continues to write.

THE WRITING PAPER. CHARLES'S HAND.

'There can be no question of further communication between us – '

Charles's hand stops writing.

CHARLES AND SAM.

Charles turns to Sam.

CHARLES

What is it?

SAM

I would like your advice, sir.

CHARLES

On what subject?

SAM

My ambition is to go into business, sir – in due course.

Charles turns back to his letter and continues to write.

CHARLES

Business?

SAM

Yes, sir.

CHARLES

What sort of business?

SAM

Drapers and haberdashers. I've set my heart on a little
shop.

CHARLES

Would that not be a somewhat expensive undertaking?

SAM

It would cost two hundred and eighty pounds.

CHARLES

And how much have you put by?

SAM

Thirty pounds. Over the last five years. So I was
wondering if you could help me.

*Charles turns to look at him, as he picks up the letter from his
desk, calmly tears it into pieces and puts the pieces into the pocket
of his gown.*

CHARLES

I can't say it sounds a very practical idea to me, Sam.

Sam stares at him coldly.

SAM

I am very enthusiastic about the idea myself, sir. Very.

CHARLES

I see. Well, let me think about it. I shall certainly be
happy to think about it.
Pack, will you? We're going to Lyme today.

SAM

To Lyme, sir?

CHARLES

To Lyme. Yes.

INT. BAR IN LONDON. PRESENT.

Anna and Mike at table with drinks.

ANNA

How are you. How's it going?

> MIKE

All right. Bloody hard. I'm exhausted. I've been dying for you.

> ANNA

Mmmn.

> MIKE

How's it been? Have you been having a good time?

> ANNA

I don't know ... it's all so unreal ...

> MIKE

What do you mean?

> ANNA

The world isn't real ... up here.

> MIKE

What about your boyfriend? Isn't he real?

> ANNA

I miss Sarah. I can't wait to get back. I can't wait to be in Exeter.

> MIKE

You know what's going to happen in Exeter? I'm going to have you in Exeter.

> ANNA

Are you now?

> MIKE

Yes.

> (*He smiles.*)

I am.

TRAIN ARRIVING AT STATION. AFTERNOON.

Large signs: Exeter.

The train stops. Sam runs along platform to meet Charles, who descends from a first-class compartment.

SAM

Carriage to Lyme, sir?

Charles looks up at the sky.

CHARLES

It's going to rain – badly.

They both look up.

We had better stay the night. We'll put up at The Ship.

SAM

But we're expected in Lyme, sir.

CHARLES

We'll be there in the morning. I think I'll stretch my legs. You go on with the baggage.

SAM

Shall I order dinner, sir?

CHARLES

I'll decide when I come in. I may attend Evensong at the Cathedral.

Charles walks down the platform.

EXT. BACK STREET. EXETER. DUSK.

Charles appears in the street. He looks about him. A small boy passes. Charles stops him, asks him a question.

The boy leads Charles to a corner and points.

Charles gives him a coin and disappears round the corner.

EXT. ENDICOTT'S FAMILY HOTEL.

Charles approaching. He enters.

INT. HOTEL. THE HALL.

Charles in the hall. The door of a room is ajar. He knocks and goes in. Mrs Endicott rises.

MRS ENDICOTT

A room, sir?

CHARLES

No, I ... that is, I wish to speak to one of your ... a Miss Woodruff?

MRS ENDICOTT

Oh the poor young lady, sir, she was a-coming downstairs yesterday morning and she slipped, sir. She's turned her ankle terrible. I wanted to ask the doctor, sir, but she won't hear of it.

CHARLES

I have to see her ... on a business matter.

MRS ENDICOTT

Ah. A gentleman of the law?

CHARLES

Yes.

MRS ENDICOTT

Then you must go up, sir.
(*shouting*)
Betty Anne!

The maid, Betty Anne, appears.

Take this gentleman to Miss Woodruff's room.

INT. LANDING.

Betty Anne leads Charles to a door. She knocks and opens it.

BETTY ANNE

A gentleman to see you, Miss.

Charles steps into the room. Betty Anne closes the door behind him.

INT. SARAH'S SITTING ROOM.

Sarah is sitting in a chair by the fire, her naked feet on a stool. One ankle is bandaged. A blanket over her knees. She is wearing her green shawl over a long-sleeved nightgown. Her hair is loose.

She looks up at him, swiftly, then down.

> CHARLES
>
> I was passing through Exeter.
> > (*Pause.*)
> Had I not better go at once and fetch a doctor?

> SARAH
>
> He would only advise me to do what I am already doing.

> CHARLES
>
> You are not in pain?

She shakes her head.

> At any rate be thankful that it did not happen on the Undercliff.

> SARAH
>
> Yes.
> > (*Silence.*)
> Do sit down.

Charles sits by the table. He looks at her. The firelight flickers over her white nightgown, her face, her hair.

Rain patters on the window.

Sarah raises her hands suddenly to her mouth, bends her head, begins to cry quietly.

CHARLES

Miss Woodruff ... please ... I should not have come ...
I meant not to ...

She shakes her head violently. She stops crying, looks at him.

SARAH

I thought never to see you again.

She looks down. He closes his eyes.

Silence.

*Suddenly a cascade of coal falls from the fire. One or two bounce
out of the grate and on to the edge of Sarah's blanket. She jerks
the blanket away.*

*Charles stands quickly and shovels the coals back into the fire. He
snatches the blanket, which is smouldering, throws it on the floor
and stamps on it. He picks it up, slaps it and then carefully places
it across her legs, bending over her. As he is doing so, her hand
rests on his.*

They look at each other. Their fingers interlace.

*He drops to his knees. They kiss violently. He half withdraws.
She presses him back to her mouth. They kiss again. He raises her
head and looks at her. They kiss again. The chair rolls back. He
turns to look at the bedroom door, which is open.*

*He stands, pulls her up. She falls towards him. He picks her up in
his arms. The shawl falls. He kisses her mouth and her breasts as
she lies back in his arms. He carries her into the bedroom.*

*In the dim light of the bedroom he throws her across the bed. She
lies, one arm flung back.*

*Sound of stripping clothes. He appears, goes to the bed. His body
covers her. He moves upon her.*

*He enters her. She cries out with pain. He stops. She draws him to
her. He makes love to her.*

CHARLES

Oh, my dearest . . . my sweetest angel . . . my sweetest
angel . . . oh, Sarah.

Gasps. A long groan.

They are still.

EXT. ENDICOTT'S HOTEL. EVENING.

*Sam looking at hotel. He goes in the door. Camera pans to see
through window Sam talking to Betty Anne. He gives her a coin.*

INT. SARAH'S BEDROOM. EVENING.

*Sarah and Charles on the bed. They lie in silence. Her hand
touches and caresses his. He looks at her.*

CHARLES

I was . . . the first.

SARAH

Yes.

CHARLES

Why did you lie to me – about the Frenchman?

SARAH

I don't know.

CHARLES

Does he exist?

SARAH

Oh, yes. He exists. I did follow him to Weymouth, to
the Inn. As I drew near I saw him come out, with a
woman. The kind of woman one cannot mistake. When
they had gone, I walked away.

CHARLES

But then – why did you tell me – ?

SARAH

I don't know. I cannot explain.
            (*She puts a finger on his mouth.*)
Not now.

CHARLES

I must make myself free.

SARAH

I ask nothing of you.

CHARLES

I am to blame. I knew when I came here –

SARAH

I wished it so. I wished it so.

He strokes her hair.

CHARLES

Sarah – it is the sweetest name.

SARAH

I have long imagined a day such as this. I have longed
... for it. I was lost from the moment I saw you.

CHARLES

I ... too.
            (*Pause.*)
I must go to Lyme, to see her, to tell her. You must give
me a day's grace. You will wait for me? Won't you? I
shall come back for you, my sweet ... mystery.

He takes her in his arms, kisses her.

EXT. ENDICOTT'S HOTEL. EVENING.

Sam standing at a doorway, looking up at a dimly lit window.

INT. SARAH'S SITTING ROOM. EVENING.

Charles has dressed. They stand at the door of the room. She smiles. He kisses her. She holds him.

> SARAH
>
> Do what you will. Or what you must. Now I know there was truly a day upon which you loved me, I can bear anything. You have given me ... the strength to live.

EXT. EXETER STATION. PLATFORM. NIGHT. PRESENT.

The London train is standing at the platform. Mike runs up the platform with a sandwich to the open window of a carriage. Anna is at the window looking out. Porters banging doors. He gives her the sandwich.

> MIKE
>
> Cheese and onion.

> ANNA
>
> Perfect.

She bites into sandwich.

> MIKE
>
> I'm losing you.

> ANNA
>
> What do you mean?

> MIKE
>
> I'm losing you.

> ANNA
>
> What are you talking about? I'm just going to London for –

> MIKE
>
> Stay tonight.

ANNA

I can't.

MIKE

Why not? You're a free woman.

ANNA

Yes. I am.

MIKE

I'm going mad.

ANNA

No you're not.

She leans through the window and kisses him.

MIKE
(*intensely*)

I want you so much.

ANNA
(*with mock gravity*)

But you've just had me. In Exeter.

She burst into laughter. He grins slowly. A woman looks up at them.

The train moves out of the station. She remains at the window. He remains on the platform.

CLOSE-UP. ERNESTINA.

She is listening. Sound of front door closing, of Mary's and Charles's voices. Her face lights up.

Sound of quick knock on her door and it opening.

ERNESTINA

Charles!

Sound of door closing. Silence. She frowns.

What is it? Charles? What is it?

ERNESTINA'S SITTING ROOM. DAY.

Charles stands by the door.

CHARLES

Please sit down.

She does so, slowly.

ERNESTINA

What has happened?
Why do you look at me like that?

CHARLES

I do not know how to begin to say what I must. I have
come to tell you the truth.

ERNESTINA

The truth? What truth?

CHARLES

That I have, after many hours of the deepest, the most
painful consideration, come to the conclusion that I am
not worthy of you.

ERNESTINA

Not *worthy* of me?

CHARLES

Totally unworthy.

She laughs.

ERNESTINA

You are joking.

CHARLES

No.

Pause.

ERNESTINA

Will you kindly explain to me what you are saying?

CHARLES

The terms your father offered in the settlement were more than generous –

ERNESTINA

But you despise the idea of marrying into trade.

CHARLES

I do not despise it – I –

ERNESTINA

Then what are you saying?

Pause.

CHARLES

Ernestina, I have realized, in these last days, that too great a part of my regard for you has always been ignoble. I was far more tempted by your father's fortune than I have cared to admit. Now I have seen that to be the truth –

ERNESTINA

Are you saying you have never loved me?

CHARLES

I am not worthy of you.

ERNESTINA

Charles ... I know I am spoiled. I know I am not ... unusual. But under your love and protection ... I believed I should become better. I would do anything ... you see ... I would abandon anything ... to make you happy ...

She covers her face.

He stands still.

She suddenly looks at him.

You are lying. Something else has happened.

Pause.

CHARLES

Yes.

ERNESTINA

Who?

CHARLES

You do not know her.

ERNESTINA
(*dully*)

I don't know her?

CHARLES

I have known her ... many years. I thought the attachment was broken. I discovered in London ... that it is not.

Pause.

ERNESTINA

Why did you not tell me this at the beginning?

CHARLES

I hoped to spare you the pain of it.

ERNESTINA

Or yourself the shame of it. Who is she? What woman could be so vile as to make a man break his vows? I can guess. She is married.

CHARLES

I will not discuss her. I came to tell you the truth, the most terrible decision of my life –

ERNESTINA

The truth! You are a liar. My father will drag your name
– both your names – through the mire. You will be
spurned and detested by all who know you. You will be
hounded out of England, you will be –

Ernestina sways, slumps to the floor.

INT. ENDICOTT'S HOTEL. BEDROOM WINDOW. DAY.

*Sarah sitting on the bed, which is made. She covers her face,
begins to cry. She stands, goes to the window, looks out.*

EXT. EXETER STATION. HER P.O.V.

A goods train going out.

INT. BEDROOM WINDOW.

Sarah at the window, crying.

INT. CHARLES'S HOTEL ROOM. LYME. DAY.

Charles comes in and slams the door.

He opens the window and takes in a long breath of air.

*He goes to writing table and nervously sets out writing materials.
He begins to write 'Dear Mr Freeman – '*

A sharp knock on the door. Sam enters with brandy.

CHARLES

What the devil do you want? I didn't ring.

SAM

I brought you a glass of brandy, sir. I thought you might
want it.

Charles takes brandy and sips.

It's never true, sir.

Charles looks at him.

CHARLES

Yes, it is true. Miss Freeman and I are no longer to marry. Now go. And keep your mouth shut.

He bends to the paper. Sam does not move. Charles looks up.

Did you year what I said?

SAM

Yes, sir. Only, with respect, I have to consider my own situation.

CHARLES

What?

SAM

Will you be residing in London from now on, sir?

CHARLES

We shall probably go abroad.

SAM

Ah. Well, I beg to advise you that I won't be accompanying you. And I'm not coming back to Exeter either. I'm leaving your employ. As I ought to have done weeks ago, when all this started.

Charles stands.

CHARLES

Go to hell!

They glare at each other. Sam opens the door. He turns.

SAM

I don't fancy nowhere, *sir*, as I might meet a friend of yours.

Sam goes out slamming the door. Charles rips it open.

CHARLES

Sam!

SAM

If you wish for attention, ring for one of the hotel domestics.

He goes down the stairs. Charles slams the door and stands.

He picks up the brandy glass and hurls it into the fireplace.

INT. SARAH'S SITTING ROOM. EXETER. DAY.

Sarah is dressing. She puts the shawl around her shoulders and looks at herself in the mirror. She hears sounds of children in the street, goes to the window and looks down at them.

She turns back into the room, picks up a kerchief which Charles has left behind him. She fondles it, puts it down.

INT. HOTEL. LYME. LANDING. DAY.

CHARLES

Mr Barnes! Make up my bill! I'm leaving.

VOICE

Rightaway, Mr Smithson.

Charles goes back into his room and slams the door.

INT. HOTEL ROOM.

The room is in chaos. Wardrobe doors and cupboard drawers wide open, clothes spilling out. Charles is trying to pack his belongings into two large trunks. He flings the clothes in.

A quick knock at the door. Grogan comes in. Charles looks at him, continues packing, moving from wardrobe to trunk.

GROGAN

I await your explanation, my friend.

CHARLES

I am leaving Lyme.

He pulls at a drawer in a chest of drawers. The drawer comes out and falls with a crash.

Damn!

GROGAN

I have come from Miss Freeman. I have put her to sleep. When she wakes you could be by her. It is not too late – to mend the matter.

CHARLES

It is far too late.

Grogan watches him.

GROGAN

I have been told by Mrs Tranter that there is another woman.

CHARLES

I must ask you not to reveal her name.

GROGAN

You ask me to follow your example in deceit?

CHARLES

I believed the deceit to be necessary.

GROGAN

As you believed the satisfaction of your lust to be necessary.

CHARLES

I will not accept that word.

GROGAN

You had better learn to. It is the one the world will use.

CHARLES

Let it do so.

He continues to pack.

GROGAN

You will marry the lady?

CHARLES

That is my deepest wish.

GROGAN

You have committed a crime. It will fester in you all your life.

Charles stops packing and looks at him.

CHARLES

No ... Grogan. You do not understand. She is remarkable. She is free. I am free also. She has given me this freedom. I shall embrace it.

Silence.

GROGAN

So be it.

EXT. ENDICOTT'S HOTEL. EXETER. NIGHT.

A carriage comes down the street and draws up. Charles gets out and goes into the hotel.

INT. ENDICOTT'S HOTEL. EXETER. HALL. NIGHT.

Charles comes in the front door. Mrs Endicott looks out of her room. Charles gives her a coin.

CHARLES

Miss Woodruff expects me. I'll find my own way.

He turns to the stairs.

MRS ENDICOTT

The young lady's left, sir.

CHARLES

Left? You mean gone out?

MRS ENDICOTT

No, sir. I mean left.

He stares at her.

She took the London train this afternoon.

CHARLES

What?

MRS ENDICOTT

She took the three o'clock to London. Didn't leave no address.

CHARLES

You're a liar.

He turns and bounds up the stairs.

Sarah!

MRS ENDICOTT

Where are you going?

INT. SARAH'S ROOM.

Charles bursts in.

MRS ENDICOTT
(*off screen*)

What are you doing? You can't do that.

Charles goes to the writing table, shelves, etc., lifts objects, table cloth, goes into bedroom through open door.

Mrs Endicott comes into the room.

MRS ENDICOTT

You've no right! You're trespassing.

Charles stares at the unmade bed.

Did you hear what I said?

Charles turns to her, speaks with great violence.

CHARLES

Get out!

She retreats to the door.

Charles follows her and slams it.

He looks about the room, silent in the moonlight.

He sits down and stares at the window.

INT. ANNA'S LONDON HOTEL. SUITE. DAY. PRESENT.

A waiter serving a tray of tea. He leaves the room.

Anna in foreground on sofa reading the last few pages of her script of The French Lieutenant's Woman. *David sitting at a desk, using a calculator and making notes.*

The phone rings. He picks it up.

DAVID

Hello.

(*Silence.*)

Hello.

INT. MIKE'S LONDON HOUSE. DAY.

Mike holding the telephone.

Children's voices from the garden.

DAVID
(*VO*)

Room 206.

Mike puts the phone down.

INT. ANNA'S HOTEL. SUITE.

David listening to dialling tone.

He replaces the receiver.

ANNA

Who was that?

DAVID

Don't know. He put the phone down.

ANNA

Who did?

DAVID

I don't know. He didn't say.

ANNA

Maybe it was a wrong number.

David looks at her.

INT. MIKE'S LONDON HOUSE.

Mike sitting by the phone. In background, in the garden, children are playing. Sonia comes into the room. She looks at him.

SONIA

You all right?

MIKE

What? Yes. Fine.

She moves to the garden door.

Listen. What about asking a few people to lunch on Sunday?

SONIA

What people?

MIKE

Oh ... some of the cast.

SONIA

Fine.

MIKE

Well ... you know ... the film's nearly over, Anna's got to get back to the States ... you know ...

SONIA

Fine. Fine. As long as it's not the whole unit.

MIKE

No, no, just ... you know ...

SONIA

All right. Fine.

She goes into the garden.

INT. ANNA'S LONDON HOTEL. SUITE.

The phone rings. David picks it up.

DAVID

Hello.

MIKE
(*VO*)

Hello David. It's Mike here. Listen. We're having a little lunch party here on Sunday. Can you both come?

DAVID

Uuh ... well ... here's Anna.

He passes the phone to Anna, his hand over the receiver.

> (*whispering*)
> Lunch on Sunday.

Anna lies back on the sofa.

> ANNA
> (*into phone*)
> Hi!

> MIKE
> (*VO*)
> You've gone. Where are you? You weren't in your room.

> ANNA
> (*laughing*)
> What?

> MIKE
> (*VO*)
> In Exeter. Listen, come to lunch on Sunday. Oh, by the way, I love you.

> ANNA
> How lovely. Yes. We'd love to come. See you then.

> MIKE
> (*VO*)
> Great.

She puts the phone down, looks at David.

> ANNA
> Lunch on Sunday.

> DAVID
> I know.

She picks up her script. He looks at her.

Weren't you going down to do the last scene on
Sunday?

ANNA

No. They're behind schedule. It's Wednesday.

DAVID

Ah. Have they decided what they want to do with the
end?

ANNA

I've decided.

DAVID

What have you decided?

ANNA

I want to play it exactly as it's written.

DAVID

Is there going to be a fight about it?

ANNA
(*grimly*)

I hope not.

HAND HOLDING NEWSPAPER.

The newspaper is opened at an advertisement.

GRIMES
(*VO*)

'Will Miss Sarah Woodruff urgently communicate her
whereabouts to Montague and Montague, 180 Chancery
Lane, London.'
Yes. Very well worth it, I would say.

INT. GRIMES'S OFFICE. DAY.

Grimes and Charles sit at a desk.

III

*On desk various cups with tea dregs, glasses, ashtrays with cigar
stubs.*

GRIMES

Well, Mr Smithson, I'm not going to pretend to you
that it will be an easy task. But I have four good men
who will go on to the job at once. We shall try the
Educational Boards of all the Church Schools. We shall
also investigate these new female clerical agencies.
They're everywhere, growing like wildfire. And we'll
investigate all the girls' academies in London.

CHARLES

Yes.

GRIMES

I shall also be examining the register of deaths.
(*Pause.*)
One last question, sir, for the moment.

CHARLES

Yes?

GRIMES

Does the young lady wish to be found, would you say,
or not?

Pause.

CHARLES

I cannot say.

INT. CHARLES'S KENSINGTON HOUSE. DAY.

Montague leans back in his chair, reading aloud from a letter.

MONTAGUE

'We are instructed by Mr Ernest Freeman, father of
Miss Ernestina Freeman, to request you to attend at
these chambers at 3 o'clock this coming Friday. Your

failure to attend will be regarded as an
acknowledgement of our client's right to proceed.
Aubrey and Baggott.'

CHARLES

What does it mean?

MONTAGUE

It means they have cold feet. But they're not letting us
off altogether. My guess is we will be asked to make a
confessio delicti.

CHARLES

A statement of guilt?

MONTAGUE

Just so. I am afraid we must anticipate an ugly
document. But I can only advise you to sign it. We have
no case.

EXT. FACTORY. LONDON. DUSK

Dozens of women emerging from the factory.

*Charles stands at a street corner, his eyes searching the crowd.
Some of the women look at him and laugh. He turns away.*

INT. AUBREY'S CHAMBERS. DAY.

*Piles of legal volumes on the desk and the floor. Box files of cases
ranged high around the room.*

Charles and Montague sit side by side opposite a desk.

Aubrey is addressing them from behind the desk.

Mr Freeman stands by the window with his back to the others.

*Serjeant Murphy, a very tall, thin man, stands, arms folded,
leaning against a bookcase.*

AUBREY

I now come to your client's sordid liaison with another
woman.

(*He glowers at Charles.*)

You may, sir, have thought Mr Freeman not to be fully
cognisant of your amours. You are wrong. We know the
name of the female with whom you have entered into
such base relations. We have a witness to circumstances
I find too disgusting to name. Circumstances which
took place in the town of Exeter three months ago, in
June of this year.

Charles flushes. Mr Freeman is now looking at him.

Murphy's eyes never leave him.

MONTAGUE

My client did not come here to defend his conduct.

MURPHY

Then you would not defend such an action?

MONTAGUE

With respect, sir, I must reserve judgement on that matter.

MURPHY

The judgement is hardly at issue, Mr Montague.

AUBREY

Our advice to Mr Freeman has been clear. In my very
long experience this is the vilest example of
dishonourable behaviour I have ever had under my
survey. I believe firmly that such vicious conduct should
be exhibited as a warning to others.

Charles suddenly looks at Murphy. They hold each other's gaze.

However, it is your client's good fortune that Mr
Freeman has elected to show a mercy the case in no way
warrants.

(Pause.)

I have, with esteemed advice –
            (He glances at Murphy.)
– prepared an admission of guilt. But I should instruct
you that Mr Freeman's decision not to proceed
immediately is contingent upon your client's signing
this document in our presence – today.

*Murphy extends his hand for the document. Aubrey passes it to
him.*

MURPHY

'I, Charles Henry Smithson, do fully, freely and solely
by my desire to declare the truth admit that:

1. I contracted to marry Miss Ernestina Freeman.
2. I was given no cause whatsoever to break my solemn
    contract with her.
3. I was fully and exactly apprised of her rank in society,
    her character, her marriage portion, and future
    prospects, before my engagement to her hand.
4. I did break that contract without any justification
    whatsoever beyond my own criminal selfishness and
    lust.
5. I entered into a clandestine liaison with a person
    named Sarah Woodruff.
6. My conduct throughout this matter has been
    dishonourable. By it, I have forever forfeited the right
    to be considered a gentleman.
                (Pause.)
I hereby acknowledge that the injured party may make
whatever use she desires of this document.'

Silence.

MONTAGUE

Mr Smithson, you are entitled to withdraw with me into
another room . . .

> CHARLES
> (*interrupts*)

That will not be necessary.

> (*He looks at Aubrey.*)

But I should like to ask one question. What does 'the injured party may make whatever use she desires of this document' mean?

> AUBREY

It means precisely what it says.

> MURPHY
> (*smiling*)

She might for instance wish to have it published in *The Times*.

> CHARLES

And she would be free to do that?

> MURPHY

She would indeed.

Charles nods.

> CHARLES

I will sign.

All stand. Charles signs the document. He does not wait for the others to follow as he turns and leaves the room.

EXT. LONDON MEWS. DAY. PRESENT.

A white Mercedes draws up. Anna jumps out, runs towards the door. The chauffeur gets out, stretches.

INT. COSTUME SHOP. DAY.

Anna draping a length of material across her. She looks at herself in a long mirror.

ANNA

Yes, I think I'm going to like her in this.

INT. GRIMES'S OFFICE. DAY.

Grimes and Charles standing.

CHARLES

Nothing at all?

GRIMES

Nothing. I am sorry.

Pause.

CHARLES

Don't give up.

He leaves the room.

EXT. MEWS. DAY. PRESENT.

Anna comes quickly out of the costume shop into the Mercedes.
The Mercedes drives off.

INT. CHARLES'S HOUSE. DRAWING ROOM. NIGHT.

Charles and Montague sit at a distance from each other. Silence.

CHARLES

I don't understand. To give herself to me ... and then
to dismiss me ... as if I were nothing to her.

MONTAGUE

Perhaps you were nothing to her.

Pause.

CHARLES

I cannot believe it.

                              MONTAGUE
    But on the evidence you must believe it.

Pause.

                              CHARLES
    No. I do not.

EXT. LONDON STREET. NIGHT.

Charles walking along the street. He passes a public house. Loud singing from within. He looks through the windows.

INT. PUBLIC HOUSE. NIGHT.

Charles comes in and stands, watching. A group of men surround a girl who is dancing on a table. Old ladies, at a table near the window, drinking stout, cackling. A group of young women at the bar.

Charles's glance swings from one female face to another. He goes out.

EXT. LONDON STREET. NIGHT.

Charles passes a blind beggar, a group of urchins, whores standing in doorways. An old lady, sitting at a window, taps loudly to draw his attention. The whores call out after him. He crosses the street and gets into a hansom cab.

STREET OFF THE HAYMARKET.

The hansom goes down the street, and turns the corner.

ANOTHER STREET.

This street is narrow and silent.

A solitary Girl stands under a gas lamp.

Charles cranes forward. She has a faint resemblance to Sarah. He knocks with his stick on the roof of the cab. It stops.

                                118

Footsteps. The Girl looks in the window.

GIRL

Hullo, sir.

THE GIRL'S HOUSE, STAIRS, AND ROOM. NIGHT.

The Girl leads. Charles follows.

GIRL

Is it for all night, sir?

CHARLES

Yes. How much will that be?

GIRL

A sovereign, sir.

They enter the room. Charles gives her a sovereign.

Thank you, sir. Make yourself at home. I shan't be a minute.

She goes through a door into another room.

He stands by the fire.

Through the door sounds of a child, a low murmur.

The door opens. The Girl comes in.

It's my little girl, sir. She'll be all right. She's as good as gold.

The Girl has undressed and now wears only a peignoir over her naked body.

I've got some wine, sir. Would you like a glass of wine?

CHARLES

What wine is it?

GIRL

It's German wine.

CHARLES

Thank you. A glass.

She goes to a cupboard, takes out a bottle, half empty, and pours a glass, takes it to him.

GIRL

Sit down by the fire, sir, go on, for a minute, warm yourself. I'll see if I can get it going better.

He sits, with glass. She kneels at his feet and pokes the fire.

It's best quality coal, but it's the cellar. It's so damp down there.

Charles looks at her breasts. He swallows wine and grimaces. The Girl stops poking the fire.

That's got a bit more life to it.

She stands.

Like the wine, sir? Go on, have some more.

The baby begins to cry in the other room.

The Girl pours some more wine.

Drink up. It's good for your muscles.

The cries grow louder. The Girl stands uncertainly.

CHARLES

Go to her.

GIRL

Yes, I'll just . . .

She goes into the other room. The door remains open.

Charles drinks. Sounds of Girl attempting to soothe the baby. The baby is not soothed.

The Girl comes back into the room. She sits, pulls on some boots.

GIRL

I can't quieten her. I've got a friend – next door. She'll take her. Oh, I'm sorry, sir.

She stands, puts on cloak over her peignoir.

Could you just ... keep an eye on her, sir ... for a minute?

CHARLES

Yes, yes.

GIRL

I won't be a minute.

She goes out.

Charles sits with drink. A moment's silence from the other room, then a prolonged cry. Charles stands, goes to the open door and looks into the room.

OTHER ROOM.

In dim light, the baby in a small truckle bed.

CHARLES

Hush, hush. Your mother will return soon.

At this the child screams. Charles goes to her, pats her head. This has no effect. He suddenly gropes for his watch, frees the chain from his waistcoat and dangles it over her. The cries stop. She reaches up, grabs the watch. She plays with it. He gently takes it from her and dangles it in front of her, like a pendulum. She watches this with delight, then grabs it, gurgling with laughter.

Yes, yes, isn't it a pretty watch? ... That's a good little girl ... isn't it a pretty watch?

The door of the other room opens. The Girl comes through and stands in the doorway.

GIRL

She wasn't there.

She looks at the gurgling baby and then at Charles.

Oh ...

CLOSE-UP. BABY WITH WATCH.

SITTING ROOM.

Charles walks in, drains his glass, grimaces.

The Girl comes in from the other room, closing the door.

She slips out of her boots and cloak.

GIRL

You like little baby girls, sir?

Charles grunts.

Would you like me to sit on your lap?

CHARLES

Do.

The Girl does.

GIRL

You're a very handsome gentleman.

CHARLES

You're a very pretty girl.

GIRL

You like us wicked girls? You like wickedness, do you?

She slips his hand under her peignoir onto her breasts.

She kisses him. His hand wanders over her body. Her robe falls away. She stands.

Come on. It's a nice soft bed.

He stands. She drops her robe, shows him her body.

Like me?

The baby begins to cry in the other room.

The Girl gets into the bed. He suddenly sways, closes his eyes, puts his hand to his head.

You all right?

The baby continues to cry. He walks to the bed and looks down at the Girl.

CHARLES
I don't know your name.

GIRL
Sarah. What's yours?

He is racked by a sudden spasm.

What's the matter?

The Girl jumps out of bed. She puts her hand on his shoulder.

CHARLES
(*violently*)
Go to your baby!

He rushes from the room.

EXT. HOUSE. ALLEY. LONG SHOT.

Charles vomiting.

EXT. VICTORIAN HOUSE. DAY. PRESENT.

The house is double fronted, with a portico.

The door opens, suddenly. A Girl of nine stands in the doorway. She looks down the steps.

GIRL

Hullo! I saw you through the window!

REVERSE SHOT.

Anna and David walking up the steps of the house.

ANNA

Hullo! Are you Lizzie?

LIZZIE

Yes. I am.

MIKE'S HOUSE. THE GARDEN.

Food and drink on tables.

In the background Sonia talking to David, 'Grogan' to 'Ernestina', Mike to 'Sam'.

'Mrs Poulteney' and Anna.

'MRS POULTENEY'

I must say they have a lovely garden, don't they?

ANNA

Yes.

'MRS POULTENEY'

Well, it's a lovely house. Don't you think? So serene. Of course, she seems so serene, doesn't she, the wife?

ANNA

Mmn. Yes.

'MRS POULTENEY'

Look at their little girl. Isn't she lovely? Such a pretty little thing.

Lizzie passes. 'Mrs Poulteney' stops her.

Aren't you a pretty little thing? Who made that dress for you?

LIZZIE

I don't know.

'MRS POULTENEY'
(*to Anna*)

I made all my own dresses once upon a time. Everyone admired them. I honestly have no idea why I took up acting.

ANOTHER PART OF THE GARDEN.

Mike and David.

DAVID

Have they decided how they are going to end it?

MIKE

End it?

DAVID

I hear they keep changing the script.

MIKE

Not at all. Where did you hear that?

DAVID

Well, there are two endings in the book, aren't there? A happy ending and an unhappy ending?

MIKE

Yes. We're going for the first ending – I mean the second ending.

DAVID

Which one is that?

MIKE

Hasn't Anna told you?

INT. MIKE'S HOUSE.

'Sam' and 'Ernestina' playing a duet on the piano.

ANOTHER PART OF THE GARDEN.

Anna and Sonia.

> ANNA
>
> It's a great garden. Who looks after it for you?

> SONIA
>
> I do.

> ANNA
>
> What, all on your own?

> SONIA
>
> Mmn. More or less.

> ANNA
>
> What about Mike? Doesn't he help?

> SONIA
>
> Oh, when he's here. A bit. He's pretty lazy actually.

Anna smiles.

> ANNA
>
> I really envy you.

> SONIA
>
> Envy me? Why?

> ANNA
>
> Well, for being able to create such a lovely garden.

> SONIA
> (*laughing*)
>
> Oh, I wouldn't bother to envy me, if I were you. Have
> some more wine.

Sonia goes towards a table for a bottle.

INT. MIKE'S HOUSE. LANDING.

Mike rushing up stairs.

The bathroom door opens.

Anna comes out, wearing a coat.

He grasps her arm, speaks in a low voice.

> MIKE
> This is pure bloody hell.

> ANNA
> For Christ's sake! Anyone could . . .

> MIKE
> We've got to talk. Properly. At Windermere.

> ANNA
> What are we going to say?

> MIKE
> We've got to decide – what we want.

> ANNA
> Yes. Yes.

Voice of Sonia from below:

> SONIA
> I think she's getting her coat.

Anna, breaks away, looks down.

Sonia, David and Lizzie looking up from the hall.

> ANNA
> Coming!

She turns to Mike and kisses him on the cheek.

> See you at Windermere.

She goes down the stairs to David and Sonia. Lizzie opens the front door. They walk towards it.

CLOSE SHOT. MIKE.

Voices over:

> ANNA
>
> It's been a lovely afternoon. I've had a great time. It's such a beautiful house.

> SONIA
>
> Thank you.

> DAVID
>
> Very good to meet you.

> SONIA
>
> And you.
> > (*To Anna.*)
> Good luck for the last scene.

> ANNA
> (*laughing*)
>
> We'll need it.

The door closes.

EXT. HOTEL GARDEN. DAY.

The following title appears on the screen.

SOME YEARS LATER

Charles, with a beard, walks along the terrace of a hotel by the sea. He sits down.

A porter descends the steps of the hotel and gives Charles a telegram. He opens it.

THE TELEGRAM.

'*She is found. Under name Mrs Roughwood. Montague.*'

EXT. LAKE WINDERMERE. DAY.

Calm water.

A small steam-powered vessel is puffing slowly across the lake.

Charles, bearded and gaunt, sits in the prow searching for something on land. He raises his pocket telescope to his eye.

EXT. LAKE. CHARLES'S EYE-LINE.

High above the shore stands a white house with bow windows and green slate roof.

CLOSE-UP. CHARLES.

His interest quickens. He pulls a note out of his pocket.

THE NOTE.

'MRS ROUGHWOOD'
THE NEW HOUSE
WINDERMERE

LAKE SHORE. DAY.

Charles ascending a wooded bank. Behind him, the lake.

Piano music.

Charles looks through shrubbery at the white house.

He begins to skirt it. He waits for signs of life.

THE NEW HOUSE. DAY.

Charles's view – a glimpse of white walls through dense shrubbery.

The sound of playing children.

NEW HOUSE. DAY.

Charles cautiously circles the house from a distance. He reaches a lawn, at a higher level above the house.

The house comes into full view.

Charles approaches it.

EXT. THE HOUSE.

Charles knocks at front door, waits.

The door is opened by a Boy of twelve.

> BOY
>
> Good morning.

> CHARLES
>
> Good morning.

> BOY
>
> I'm Tom Elliott. Who are you?

> CHARLES
>
> My name is Smithson.

> BOY
>
> Mama and Papa are abroad.

> CHARLES
>
> I . . . I'm looking for a Mrs Roughwood.

> BOY
>
> Oh! Yes. Please come in.

Charles goes in.

INT. HOUSE.

The interior of the house is white, full of light. A piano is playing, haltingly. Laughter from another room.

The Boy goes to the foot of the stairs and shouts up.

                    BOY
Mrs Roughwood! Someone to see you.
          (*The Boy turns to Charles.*)
I think she's working. But she doesn't mind being interrupted.

Sarah's voice from above: 'What is it?'

She appears on the landing and looks down into the hall.

She sees Charles.

He stands still, looking at her.

                    BOY
Please go up.

Charles walks up the stairs towards her. She waits. He reaches her. They look at each other.

She turns, goes towards room. He follows.

INT. STUDIO.

Pictures on walls. A trestle table. Piles of drawings. A drawing in progress on a small table.

She closes the door.

                  CHARLES
Mrs Roughwood.

                  SARAH
Mr Smithson.

Pause.

CHARLES

My solicitor was told you lived at this address. I do not know by whom.

SARAH

By me.

Pause.

CHARLES

By you?
(Pause.)
I have been looking for you for three years.
(Pause.)
I broke off my engagement. I came back for you, to take you with me, to marry you. You had gone.
(Pause.)
And now ... all these years later ... you choose to let me know that you are alive. Why?

SARAH

I could not do so before this.

Pause.

CHARLES

You have married.

SARAH

No. I have not. I pass as a widow ... in the world.

Pause.

CHARLES

What is this house.

SARAH

He is an architect. His name is Elliott. They gave me shelter – a long time ago. I am tutor to their children, but I ... I am free to do my own work. They have encouraged it.

He looks at the drawings. They are of children.

CHARLES

These are yours?

SARAH

Yes.

CHARLES

You have found your gift.
(*He looks at her.*)
Why did you leave Exeter? You told me you loved me.
You showed ... your love.
(*Pause.*)
Answer me.

SARAH

There was a madness in me ... at the time, a bitterness,
an envy. I forced myself on you, knowing that you had
... other obligations. It was unworthy. I suddenly saw,
after you had gone, that I had to destroy what had
begun between us.

CHARLES

Are you saying you never loved me?

SARAH

I could not say that.

CHARLES

But you must say that! You must say: 'I am totally evil. I
used him as an instrument. I do not care that in all this
time he has not seen a woman to compare with me, that
his life has been a desert without me, that he has
sacrificed everything ... for me!' Say it!

SARAH

No.

133

CHARLES

Why did you ask me here? What do you want of me?

SARAH

I saw the newspaper advertisements long ago –

CHARLES

You *saw* them? You *read* them? And did nothing?

SARAH

Yes. I changed my name.

CHARLES

Then you have not only caused my ruin. You have
taken pleasure in doing so.

SARAH

You misjudge me. It has taken me this time to find my
own life. It has taken me this time ... to find my
freedom.

CHARLES

Freedom!

SARAH

Yes.

CHARLES

To make a mockery of love, of all human feeling. Is that
all Exeter meant to you?
One brief transaction of the flesh? Only that? You have
planted a dagger in me and your 'damned freedom'
gives you licence to twist it in my heart. Well, no more!

He strides to the door. She seizes his arm.

SARAH

No!

He flings her away, violently.

CHARLES

Yes!

She falls to the floor, hitting her head. He stops.

She sits up, holding her head. He stares down at her. She looks at him. She smiles.

SARAH

Mr Smithson ... I called you here ... to ask your forgiveness.
> (*Pause.*)

You loved me once.
> (*Pause.*)

If you still love me, you can forgive me.
> (*She stands.*)

I know it is your perfect right to damn me.
> (*Pause.*)

But if you do ... still ... love me ...

They look into each others' eyes.

CHARLES

Then I must ... forgive you.

Pause.

SARAH

Yes. You must.

A piano is heard.

Sunlight falls across the room.

Charles and Sarah move towards each other.

The camera tracks closer and stops.

They are embracing.

They kiss.

CHARLES
(*softly*)

Sarah.

Slow dissolve to:

EXT. LAKE BOATHOUSE. EVENING.

A rowing boat is emerging from the darkness of a boathouse on to the lake. Sarah sits in the prow, Charles is by the oars.

As the boat glides out into the calm evening water Charles begins to row slowly.

Rock music.

EXT. THE NEW HOUSE GARDEN. NIGHT. PRESENT.

The unit party in full swing. A three-piece band on a platform. All the actors we have seen in the film are present, in modern clothes, apart from Mike and Anna, who still wear their costumes of the previous scene.

'Grogan' lurches by, drunk, dancing with 'Mary'. 'Sam' is dancing with 'Mrs Poulteney'; the 'Prostitute' with 'Mr Freeman'; 'Mrs Fairley' with 'Serjeant Murphy'; 'Aunt Tranter' with 'Mr Aubrey'; the 'Dairywoman' with 'Montague'; 'Mrs Endicott' with 'Sir Tom'. 'Nat', the 'Dairyman' and members of the crew stand around. Anna is dancing with a member of the crew. Mike is standing aside, drinking.

CLOSE-UP. MIKE.

He looks at his watch, signals to Anna.

CLOSE-UP. ANNA.

She responds to Mike's signal, kisses her partner on the cheek, turns.

THE PARTY. LONG SHOT.

Anna walking towards the house.

'Ernestina' comes into the garden, wearing a fur coat and boots. She goes up on a small platform, opens her coat and, to applause and whistling, reveals that she is dressed in a Victorian corset. She starts to do a kind of fan dance, opening and closing her coat. Great enthusiasm.

INT. THE NEW HOUSE. ANNA'S DRESSING ROOM.

Anna at her dressing table.

She has changed her clothes.

She stares at herself in the mirror.

THE PARTY.

Mike moves towards the house. He is stopped by the 'Prostitute', who kisses him, and then by 'Grogan', who hugs him. In background 'Ernestina' being carried off the platform. Laughter. She is thrown about between a number of men, who dance with her in turn.

INT. NEW HOUSE.

Mike runs into the hall and up the stairs on which he first saw 'Mrs Roughwood'.

ANNA'S DRESSING ROOM. EMPTY.

Mike rushes in. The room is empty.

Sarah's long red wig hangs from a block.

He quickly opens another door, which leads into the white room.

INT. THE WHITE ROOM.

Moonlight falls across the room.

Sounds of the party from below. Suddenly the sound of a car starting up. Mike runs to the window, looks out.

EXT. HOUSE.

Anna's white car driving towards the gate.

EXT. HOUSE. WINDOW.

Mike at window. He calls out:

MIKE

Sarah!

The Heat of the Day

The Heat of the Day was produced by Granada Television in 1989. The cast was as follows:

HARRISON Michael Gambon
STELLA Patricia Hodge
ROBERT Michael York
FRANCIS Ralph Michael
PARLOUR MAID Tina Earl
MRS TRINGSBY Hilary Mason
NETTIE Peggy Ashcroft
DR TRINGSBY John Gill
TAXI DRIVER Aubrey Phillips
BLYTHE Stephen Hancock
LOUIE Imelda Staunton
RODERICK Grant Parsons
ERNESTINE Anna Carteret
MRS KELWAY Heather Chasen
PETER Rafael Pauley
ANNE Jessica Simpson
DONOVAN David Kelley
HANNAH Pat O'Toole
MARY Grace Kinirons

Lighting Cameraman Jon Woods
Production Designer Christopher J. Bradshaw
Costume Designer Jane Robinson
Editor Andrew Sumner
Music Ilona Sekacz
Producer June Wyndham-Davies
Director Christopher Morahan

INT. A ROOM. NIGHT.

A man sitting at a table. One lamp is lit over the table.

The man is sifting through photographs.

The back of his head. His hands.

The photographs:
> *Robert in officer's uniform with fellow officers emerging from a London club.*
> *Robert alone on station platform.*
> *Robert and Ernestine at bus stop.*
> *Robert alone at bus stop.*
> *Robert and civilian at bus stop.*
> *Civilian alone at bus stop.*
> *Robert and Stella in Regent's Park, arm in arm.*

Hand puts this photograph aside and continues sifting.
> *Robert in phone box.*
> *An empty station platform. Dawn.*
> *A stationary car. Country lane.*
> *Robert and Stella hailing taxi.*
> *Stella in taxi at window. Robert waving.*

Hand puts these last two aside.
> *Robert with two men at a street corner. Umbrellas.*
> *Robert and Stella lying on grass, asleep. She in summer dress. He with open shirt.*
> *Stella lying on the grass. Eyes open.*

Hand puts the first of these two photographs aside, takes single photograph of Stella and pins it on to the wall.

EXT. REGENT'S PARK. SUMMER. DAY.

Robert and Stella walking towards trees.

They pass a man sitting on a bench. It is Harrison.

Robert and Stella disappear into the trees.

INT. ROOM.

The man at the table stands abruptly. Switches out the light.

EXT. WISTARIA LODGE. MAY. DAY.

A taxi arriving.

Cousin Francis gets out. He wears tweeds. He goes to house, rings brass bell. Silence. Wistaria frames the white pillared porch. The doors open. A Parlour Maid.

> PARLOUR MAID
>
> Yes?

> FRANCIS
>
> Mrs Tringsby?

In background in the hall a woman speaks.

> MRS TRINGSBY
>
> Yes, yes? Oh yes. Do come in. Do come in.

He goes in.

INT. HALL. DAY.

> FRANCIS
>
> Mrs Tringsby? I'm Francis Morris.

He shakes her hand.

> MRS TRINGSBY
>
> Oh dear. Yes, yes. Please, will you come into the drawing room?

FRANCIS

Is my wife in there?

MRS TRINGSBY

No, oh dear no. She likes to be cosy in her room.

FRANCIS

She expects me, I trust?

Mrs Tringsby puts her fingers to her lips.

MRS TRINGSBY

Ssshh. There are other people . . .

She leads him into the drawing room.

INT. DRAWING ROOM. DAY.

Mrs Tringsby closes the door.

MRS TRINGSBY

I told her, of course, that you were coming . . . but
whether she remembers . . . She loves her wool . . . This
is such a quiet house, you see . . . a true home of rest . . .
our task is to protect and reassure . . . She loves her wool
. . . She's so quiet and content and you haven't of course
seen her for . . .

*During this she has been staring at him with growing alarm and
bewilderment. His eyes are blinking rapidly. He holds on to the table.*

. . . and you haven't of course seen her for . . .

*He clutches the table, groans, falls, bringing table and vase of
flowers over.*

Mrs Tringsby screams.

INT. NETTIE'S ROOM. DUSK.

*Nettie sitting with wool. Sound of ambulance arriving. Nettie
continues knitting.*

EXT. WISTARIA LODGE. DUSK.

Ambulance men bringing stretcher from the house, body covered in a sheet.

Dr Tringsby. Mrs Tringsby with hands clasped. Faces at the windows. The stretcher is placed in the ambulance.

Taxi drives into the forecourt and comes to a halt. The Driver looks out of the window. He speaks to Dr Tringsby.

DRIVER

Mr Morris?

DR TRINGSBY

What? Who?

DRIVER

Mr Morris. I'm picking him up for the six o'clock train.

DR TRINGSBY

No, no . . . I'm Dr Tringsby.

DRIVER

I brought him here a couple of hours ago.

The ambulance drives off.

DR TRINGSBY

Yes, yes! He's gone away! He's not here!

DRIVER

But he told me to come and pick him up.

DR TRINGSBY

Yes, but he's gone!

DRIVER

But what about my ten bob? He owes me ten bob.

DR TRINGSBY

He's taken it with him!

144

Mrs Tringsby howls, runs into the house.

INT. COUNTRY CHURCH. DAY.

*Stella comes into the church. She wears a dark suit. People are
seated. Heads turn as her heels clip up the aisle. She carries a
bouquet of tulips and white lilac. Harrison is sitting alone at the
back of the church. She sits and looks at the coffin. An organ
plays.*

EXT. GRAVEYARD. DAY.

*In long shot a group is turning from a grave and walking towards
the road. Stella walks alone. She looks back and glimpses
Harrison 'stepping cranelike' over the graves.*

A man catches up with Stella.

> BLYTHE

Mrs Rodney?

> STELLA

Yes?

> BLYTHE

My name is Blythe. I am – I was – Mr Morris's lawyer.

> STELLA

Ah.

> BLYTHE

Your son wasn't able to come?

> STELLA

He's in the army.

> BLYTHE

Yes, quite. When we get to the hotel – I should be
obliged if you would give me a few minutes of your time
for a private word?

STELLA

Yes ...

BLYTHE

Have you any idea who that man is, by the way?

STELLA

No.

BLYTHE

Nobody knows him.

EXT. VILLAGE: MAIN STREET. DAY.

The group walking along the pavement past empty shop windows.
Mrs Tringsby shepherds two elderly ladies, precisely dressed, who
walk arm in arm.

A fishmonger's slab empty; a baker's shop empty; a greengrocer's
shop with fans of cardboard bananas and a DIG FOR VICTORY
placard; a butcher's shop with a few joints of purplish meat; sign
on window of empty newspaper shop: NO MATCHES.

The group enters the hotel.

INT. HOTEL: LADIES' CLOAKROOM. DAY.

Mrs Tringsby and Stella taking off coats.

MRS TRINGSBY

Are you a relation of Mr Morris?

STELLA

He was my husband's cousin.

MRS TRINGSBY

He dropped dead in my house. Can you believe it?
We'd hardly been introduced. I mean, he had only been
in the house five minutes. Can you imagine?
                    (*She indicates the Ladies.*)
These are two of my oldest house-guests. I've brought

them out for a little treat. Are you having a nice little
treat?

The Ladies smile.

INT. HOTEL: LANDING. DAY.

They emerge from the cloakroom. Blythe approaches.

> BLYTHE

Mrs Rodney, might I have that word?

He takes Stella into a recess.

I thought you should know straightaway that in his will
Mr Morris left all his estate to your son Roderick. There
is an existing trust for his widow, of course. But apart
from that, his house, land and capital go to your son.

> STELLA

Good gracious.

> BLYTHE

This is a copy of the will. As he is still under twenty-
one, you are of course his guardian.

Stella takes the envelope, looks at it, looks at Blythe.

> STELLA

But I can't ... They never met ... Why do you
think ... ?

> BLYTHE

He knew no other young person. I believe he wanted to
leave his estate to a young person – in the hope that he
may care in his own way to carry on the old tradition.
And they were, of course, cousins.

> STELLA

Yes. Yes, they were.

INT. HOTEL: LUNCHROOM. DAY.

A table with a simple buffet. Blythe and Stella come into the room. People turn, look curiously at Stella. Some whisper.

Harrison stands alone at the window.

Blythe gives Stella a cup of coffee. Someone calls his name. He turns.

> BLYTHE
> (*to Stella*)

Excuse me.

She sips her coffee. Suddenly Harrison is at her side.

> HARRISON

Can I get you some port?

She turns to him.

They do have port here – or at least they call it port.

> STELLA

No thank you, I –

> HARRISON

Or there's a bar downstairs.

> STELLA

Don't let me stop you.

> HARRISON

My name's Harrison. You're Mrs Rodney – am I right?

> STELLA

Yes. I'm sorry . . . but how do you know my name is Rodney?

> HARRISON

Well, there's no one else here who could be you, is there? I've heard your praises sung a good deal, you see.

STELLA

Who by?

HARRISON

Your cousin, Frankie.

STELLA

Oh, you knew him?

HARRISON

Oh yes. Very well. I used to go to see him in Ireland. Great old house. Do you remember it?

STELLA

I haven't been there for ... many years.

HARRISON

On your honeymoon, wasn't it? It's to go to your son – I seem to remember?

STELLA

Yes, I –

HARRISON

Yes, he told me all about you, old Frankie. Told me you were a widow – had a boy – everything. He was really very fond of you. Used to talk about you a lot.

STELLA

Did he? But ... if I'd known that ... If I'd known he remembered me I could have gone to see him ... taken my son. I didn't know, you see.

HARRISON

Yes. Pity. One so often thinks of things too late.

STELLA

Excuse me.
        (*She turns away, calls:*)
Mr Blythe? Mr Blythe, can I have a word?

EXT. COUNTRY ROAD. DAY.

Stella walking alone towards the station.

EXT. COUNTRY STATION: PLATFORM. DAY.

*Stella standing alone at the end of the platform. A voice: 'First
smoker?' She turns sharply. It is Harrison.*

> STELLA
>
> I'm travelling third.

> HARRISON
>
> Oh, come on! Let's blow the expense – in honour of
> Frankie. It's on the house anyway.

The train comes in.

INT. TRAIN: FIRST-CLASS COMPARTMENT. DAY.

Stella and Harrison come in and sit facing each other.

> HARRISON
>
> It's not every day, you know, that one runs into someone
> one's been wanting to meet for so long. It's quite an event.

> STELLA
>
> What do you do?

> HARRISON
>
> What do I do?

> STELLA
>
> Yes.

> HARRISON
>
> Government work.

EXT. COUNTRY STATION: PLATFORM. DAY.

*The stationary train. Two RAF Officers run up the platform and
jump on.*

INT. TRAIN: FIRST-CLASS COMPARTMENT. DAY.

Harrison smiles, leans forward.

> HARRISON
>
> Yes, I'd like to meet your son.

> STELLA
>
> Really? Why?

> HARRISON
>
> Well, somehow he seems . . . all that's left of old
> Frankie.

> STELLA
>
> Oh.

> HARRISON
>
> I'd like to get to know you both as a matter of fact – as a
> family.

> STELLA
>
> I'm sorry, I don't understand –

*The door opens. The two RAF Officers enter, sit, lean back, close
their eyes.*

Stella speaks in a lower voice.

> I don't understand your . . . interest . . . in us.

> HARRISON
>
> Well, I could explain it – I could explain one aspect of it –
> if you like. I'll tell you what – when we get to town – why
> don't I take you home in a taxi and we could have a chat?

> STELLA
> (*non-committal*)
>
> Mmmn-hmmn.

*She looks out of the window. The platform is empty. The train
does not move. She closes her eyes.*

Harrison watches her, lights a cigarette.

INT. KING'S CROSS STATION: PLATFORM. DAY.

Harrison and Stella walking along the platform.

HARRISON
Listen. I'll dash ahead to the rank and grab a taxi. All right? See you there.

He runs on. She turns right out of the platform and goes down the stairs to the Underground.

INT. ROOM.

Hand sifting photographs:
  Long shot of Stella at the entrance to the King's Cross Underground.
  Robert going up steps to Stella's front door.
  Robert and two men at the bar of a pub.
  Robert and Stella at a restaurant table.

Hand puts this photograph aside.
  Stella in the graveyard.
  Stella on the Underground platform.

The hand pins the last two photographs to the wall. Over this, button A in telephone box is pressed. Harrison's voice.

HARRISON
Hello, Mrs Rodney?

STELLA
Yes?

HARRISON
It's Harrison.

STELLA
I can't hear you. Speak up.

HARRISON

It's Harrison. I hope you got home safely – the other day.

STELLA

Yes. Thank you.

HARRISON

Listen, I would like to come and see you actually – have
a word – there is something – really quite important to
talk about – how about – ?

STELLA

What do you mean? What do you mean, important?

HARRISON

Well . . . it's just quite important.

Silence on the line.

Eight o'clock on Sunday?

Silence on the line.

EXT. REGENT'S PARK OPEN-AIR THEATRE. EARLY EVENING.

A Viennese orchestra playing.

*Harrison sitting, thrusting his right fist into his left palm
spasmodically. Louie next to him, wearing an imitation camel-
hair coat. A Czech Soldier. Vacant seats between them.*

*The orchestra stops playing. Mild applause. Louie looks at a
programme sheet. She turns to Harrison.*

LOUIE

Was that number seven they've just played or number
eight?

He does not reply.

Can you tell from the programme? Would you like to
see my programme?

HARRISON

No thanks.

LOUIE

Sorry I spoke.

He turns and looks at her.

HARRISON

Have we met?

LOUIE

How do you mean, 'met'?

HARRISON

We don't know each other?

LOUIE

I've never seen you before in my life.

HARRISON

Then that settles that, doesn't it?

LOUIE

Why? Are you someone special? I'll know you from now on anyway. I never forget a face. Do you?

HARRISON

I could easily.

The bands starts to play.

INT. STELLA'S FLAT. EVENING.

Stella at the window playing with the blind cord. She looks down into Weymouth Street. Eight o'clock strikes. She walks to the mantelpiece, looks in the mirror at herself, glances at photographs on the shelf of Robert and Roderick, both in uniform.

EXT. THE PARK. EVENING.

Eight o'clock striking.

154

Harrison stands and walks away. Louie stands, joins him.

LOUIE

I've had enough too.
>   (*She looks at the lawns.*)
Look at all the shadows. It really looks ghostly, doesn't it?

HARRISON

Goodnight then.

LOUIE

Yes, I'm going home.

HARRISON

Good idea.

They walk on together.

LOUIE

Are you?

HARRISON

Am I what?

LOUIE

Going home.

Harrison stops.

HARRISON

Listen. You'll end up in trouble one of these days. Tacking on like this. There are funny people about. Don't you know that?

LOUIE

I told you, I'm going home.

HARRISON

Well, which way do you live?

LOUIE

Oh, I can go any way really.

They walk into the outer circle.

HARRISON

All right. I go this way.
                    (*He points.*)
You go that way.

LOUIE

Yes, that's right.

He turns.

Wait a minute.

HARRISON

What?

LOUIE

I don't know your name.

HARRISON

No. You don't.

He turns and walks away. She stands.

INT. THE FLAT. EVENING.

Stella waiting. She hears a door bang below. Footsteps. Finally Harrison appears at the open door of her flat. He looks in, sees her.

HARRISON

Good evening.

STELLA

Good evening.

HARRISON

I found the downstairs door on the latch. That in order?

STELLA

I left it open for you.

HARRISON

I shut it. That in order too?

STELLA

Why don't you shut this one?

He comes into the room and shuts the door.

How did you get my telephone number?

HARRISON

Oh . . . I think I met a man who knew you. Look, are you sure this is a convenient time?

STELLA

It's not in the least convenient. No time would be convenient. You said you had something important to say to me. What is it?

He looks round the room, murmurs.

HARRISON

All your things are so pretty.

He suddenly switches on a lamp. She goes to the windows quickly, lowers the blackout blinds. She turns. He is looking at the photographs on the mantelpiece.

This your son?

STELLA

Yes.

He picks up the photograph of Robert.

HARRISON

Mmmnn. Yes, this is quite a good likeness.

STELLA

What do you mean?

157

(*Pause.*)

Do you know him?

HARRISON

I know *of* him. Know him by sight. We haven't actually
met.

STELLA

By sight?

HARRISON

Yes. I've seen him around ... you know ... around ...
sometimes with you, in fact. I'd seen him with you a
number of times – before you and I met.

STELLA

Oh really?

HARRISON

That's right, yes.

STELLA

Will you please tell me what you've come to say?

He lights a cigarette.

HARRISON

You should be a bit more careful who you know.

STELLA

In general?

HARRISON

In particular.

STELLA

I am. I didn't want to know you, for example.

HARRISON

Have a cigarette.

*She takes one. He lights a match. His hand is shaking. She looks
at his hand.*

158

Yes ... funny ... that doesn't happen very often. Must be being here with you, all on our own.

STELLA

What do you want?

HARRISON

Well, I'll tell you. I want you to give me a break. That's all. I want you to let me come here, be here, be in and out of here, on and off, all the time. I want to be in your life, as they say. In your life. Except ...
(*He puts the photograph of Robert face down on the shelf.*)
... less of that. In fact none of that at all. No more of that.

She stares at him and laughs.

STELLA

You're a lunatic.

HARRISON

No, no. That's simply what I want, you see. That's what I want you to think about. Seriously.

STELLA

You want me to think about it seriously.

HARRISON

Well, yes I do. Because if you don't – your friend could be in a lot of trouble. As against that, if you and I could arrange things between us, things ... might be arranged.

STELLA

Oh, for Christ's sake get to the point! What the hell are you talking about.

Silence.

HARRISON

Your friend's been playing the fool. He *is* playing the fool, I should say. Look. As you know, he's at the War

159

Office. That's probably all you do know. But I know a little more than that. I'll tell you what he does. He gives information to the enemy. The gist of the stuff he handles is getting through to the enemy. This has been . . . satisfactorily verified. He's working for the enemy.

STELLA

This is silly.

HARRISON

I've been watching him, you see. I . . . keep my eye on him. And – the way things are – I could tip the scales either way. The thing could just turn on the stuff I send up. Or don't send up. You follow? I'm holding quite a bit of stuff on him I haven't turned in yet. It doesn't *have* to go in. They don't know it exists. Perhaps you could help me decide.

(*Pause.*)

What I'm saying is this – what finally happens to him rather depends on me. Or when I say it rather depends on me I mean it rather depends on you. Do you see?

STELLA

Yes. I see.

HARRISON

Oh, you do? Good.

STELLA

Perfectly. I'm to sleep with you in order that a man be left free to go on selling his country.

HARRISON

That's putting it a bit crudely.

STELLA

Anyway, none of this matters because we're not talking about the same man. You *are* crazy. When did you think this up?

HARRISON

You don't believe me?

She laughs shortly.

STELLA

No.

HARRISON

Why not?

STELLA

If this story were true – if you are what you say you are – would you tell *me*, of all people, knowing I'd go straight to Robert with the whole thing? What else would you expect?

HARRISON

Well, I'd expect someone like you to be more intelligent. If you warn him and we know you warn him, he's no more use to us and we pull him in. You see? That's the end of him. So I wouldn't warn him if I were you.

STELLA

What do you mean – 'we know you warn him'? How would you know? I wouldn't tell you.

HARRISON

It would stick out a mile. If you warn him, he'll change his timetable. He'll alter his course, he'll throw a smokescreen. We'd know he'd been tipped the wink and we'd pull him in.

STELLA

But if I warned him of that? What if I told him *not* to change his ... course in any way?

HARRISON

That would take a lot of nerve and some tiptop acting. How much of an actor is he? That's the question.

STELLA

Actor? What do you mean? He's never acted with me.

HARRISON

Ah. No. No, I suppose not.

STELLA

No.

HARRISON

Well ... yes ... if a man were able to act being in love, he'd be enough of an actor to get away with anything. Wouldn't he?

(*Pause.*)

Anyway, coming back to where we were ... My only point is ... if you warned him you'd sink him.

STELLA

Give me another cigarette.

He does so and lights it. His hand is still shaking.

Your hand is still shaking.

(*She smokes.*)

So you're a counter-spy, are you? A key man. And you're on the track of a man working for the enemy. And your employers trust you. Don't they? What would your employers say, I wonder, if they knew what you were up to? If they knew that by becoming your mistress I can buy out a man who you say is a traitor to his country? What view would they take of that? Why shouldn't I report you? You would be sorry, you say, if I sank Robert. How would it be if I sank you?

HARRISON

You could. Absolutely. You could sink me. But it all comes back to the same old thing. If you sink me you sink him.

Stella turns and picks Robert's photograph up so that it faces the room.

> STELLA
> (*savagely*)
> How dare you touch this photograph! How dare you!

They stare at each other.

The telephone rings. She picks it up.

> Hello? ... Roderick! ... Where are you? ... Wonderful
> ... Yes, of course ... Have you eaten? There's nothing
> ... Oh, right ... Yes, as soon as you can.
> (*She puts the phone down.*)
> That was my son. He's on leave. He's on his way round
> here.

> HARRISON
> That's nice for you. Look, there's no hurry about all of
> this. Take a bit of time to think it over.

> STELLA
> You seriously expect me ... ?

> HARRISON
> Oh, you might as well think it over. And – if it suited
> you – I might drop in from time to time. Who knows? I
> might grow on you.

Harrison goes to the door and leaves the flat.

EXT. WEYMOUTH STREET. NIGHT.

*Roderick walks down the street with kitbag. He turns the corner.
A figure under a lamp-post lights a cigarette. Harrison.*

INT. THE FLAT. NIGHT.

Roderick dumping kit inside the door. He kisses Stella.

RODERICK

Can I have a bath?

STELLA

Yes, go on, while I make coffee.

RODERICK

Any cake?

STELLA

Biscuits. Are you starving?

RODERICK

No, no. Fred knew of a pub that had pork pies.

INT. THE FLAT. NIGHT.

Roderick comes out of the bathroom wearing a dressing-gown.

RODERICK

Robert won't mind if I wear his dressing-gown, will he?

Stella comes out of the kitchen with coffee.

STELLA

Of course not.

RODERICK
(*muttering*)

I think I've got a corn.

STELLA

I wish there was something for you to eat. There are only three biscuits.

Roderick sits on the sofa.

Roderick – is that a corn?

RODERICK

I think so.

STELLA

Does it hurt?

RODERICK

Absolutely excruciating.

She half rises.

STELLA

I've got a plaster –

He stops her.

RODERICK

No, really. I want to ask you something. In Ireland – at the house – my house – there's a river –

STELLA

Yes.

RODERICK

Is there a boat?

STELLA

A boat?

RODERICK

Don't you know?

STELLA

I haven't been there for twenty years! But I remember the river.

RODERICK

I can picture it. I can see it – in my mind's eye. When we go, I'll row you down the river. Shall I?

STELLA

If there's a boat.

RODERICK

Oh, there must be.

Roderick suddenly glances at the cigarette ends in an ashtray.

Someone been here?

STELLA

What?

RODERICK

Someone's been here.

STELLA

Yes. A man called Harrison.

RODERICK

Who's he?

STELLA

No one. A bore.

He suddenly sneezes.

Oh dear.

He sneezes again.

RODERICK

Handkerchief.

He puts his hand into the pocket of the gown, brings out a piece of folded notepaper. He looks at it.

STELLA

Here's a handkerchief.

RODERICK

Thanks.

STELLA

Put it back.

RODERICK

What?

STELLA

Put that piece of paper back. Into the pocket. It's not yours. Just ... put it back.

RODERICK

Oh. Well, why don't you take it? It might fall out again.

STELLA

It didn't *fall* out this time.

RODERICK

But it might next time and ... you know ...

STELLA

You know what?

RODERICK

Well, it might be important. Top Secret or something. Isn't what Robert's doing important?

She takes the paper from him, makes to tear it up.

Hey! It isn't yours either.

She stops.

Shall we have a peep? See what it says? Just for fun.

STELLA

No.

RODERICK

Why not?

STELLA
(*smiling*)

It might be a letter from another woman.

RODERICK

Oh, I wouldn't think so.
(*Silence.*)
Look, don't you think it would be best if I just put it

back into the pocket? After all, as you said, it's Robert's
... thing ... and it's his pocket.

Stella unfolds the paper and reads.

STELLA

Nothing.

She tears it across.

INT. TRAIN COMPARTMENT. DAY.

Stella looking out of the window. She turns quickly, smiles.

Robert sitting opposite her. He smiles.

STELLA

What did you tell them?

ROBERT

I told them you were someone working in a government
office and that you liked country hikes.

STELLA

Country hikes! But look at these shoes.

ROBERT

I like them.

STELLA

Well, they're hardly shoes for a hike.

Robert laughs.

ROBERT

They're fine. Really. Anyway, it hardly matters.

STELLA

You mean we don't *have* to go for a hike.

ROBERT

No, no. We're free. Quite free.
                    (*He takes her hand.*)

They're harmless. Honestly. Anyway, I'll protect you if
mother tries to bite you.

STELLA

Will you?

EXT. COUNTRY ROAD. DAY.

*A taxi stops. Robert and Stella get out. Robert pays. The taxi
drives away.*

Notice: CAUTION: CONCEALED DRIVE.

*They walk up the drive towards Holme Dene. Evergreens. Lawns
leading to the house. Robert walks with a limp. Ernestine
suddenly appears around a bush, laughing heartily.*

ROBERT

Hello, Ernie!

Ernestine laughs. She is in WVS uniform.

ERNESTINE

What did you do with the taxi?

ROBERT

We walked from the road.

ERNESTINE

Oh, of course – you've come down to walk, haven't you?

ROBERT

Ernestine – Mrs Rodney.

They shake hands. Ernestine roars with laughter.

ERNESTINE

Muttikins is in the lounge – waiting for the sound of the
taxi!

(*To Stella.*)

We were only saying this morning that it took being shot
in the leg to make Robert walk! See you both at tea.

She goes down the drive. They walk towards the house.

STELLA

What was she laughing at?

ROBERT

Oh ... just laughing. Muttikins is my mother. That's
what we call her.

INT. THE HOUSE: LOUNGE. DAY.

*Mrs Kelway with knitting. Robert and Stella come in. She
stands. Robert bends to her. They kiss.*

MRS KELWAY

Robert ...

ROBERT

Muttikins ... This is Mrs Rodney.

Mrs Kelway frowns.

MRS KELWAY

Mrs Rodney?

She looks at Stella. Stella puts out her hand.

STELLA

How do you do?

They shake hands. Mrs Kelway turns to Robert.

MRS KELWAY

But what became of the taxi?

ROBERT

We walked up the drive.

MRS KELWAY

Ernestine was listening for it. Did she miss you?

ROBERT

No, we ran into her – a little *détraquée.*

MRS KELWAY

It is Saturday afternoon.

Mrs Kelway sits. Robert sits. After a moment Stella sits.

If I hadn't seen you walking up the drive I should have wondered if you hadn't missed the train.

ROBERT

Mrs Rodney likes to walk in the country.

STELLA

It's so nice to be out of London.

MRS KELWAY

I've hardly been up to London since the war began. I've always understood that we're asked not to travel without a good reason. I'm quite content to sit here and knit.
> (*She knits.*)

My grandson is in the army. Ernestine's boy.

STELLA

So is my son.

Mrs Kelway continues to knit.

ROBERT

Roderick.

Mrs Kelway looks up at him.

MRS KELWAY

What do you mean by 'Roderick'?

ROBERT

Roderick is Mrs Rodney's son.

MRS KELWAY

Oh.

Silence.

ROBERT
(*to Stella*)

A breath of air?

MRS KELWAY

Tea will be coming in.

ROBERT

A stroll before tea.

EXT. THE GARDEN. DAY.

Robert and Stella stroll across the lawn. She looks at him. He looks at her. She smiles. He laughs.

INT. THE HOUSE: LOUNGE. DAY.

Mrs Kelway, Robert, Stella, Peter (aged nine) and Anne (aged seven) sitting at a mahogany table. Mrs Kelway is pouring and passing tea. Silence.

Stella turns and looks out of the window to see Ernestine running towards the house. She rushes into the room.

ERNESTINE

Oh dear, I'm late! Is the bread cut yet? No! Just in time!

She sits, saws at the loaf and passes slices round the table on the flat of the knife.

ROBERT

Mrs Rodney and I forgot to bring our own butter.

STELLA

I don't often eat tea ... actually.

ERNESTINE

Well, I suppose I could lend you some of my butter. But really I don't think it would stand up in court.

Robert splits open a bun and spreads damson jam on it.

PETER

Look at all that jam!

ANNE

Do you always do that? I mean, do you always use so
much jam in London?

ROBERT

Sure.
                    (*He winks.*)
I get it on the black market.

ANNE

You might end up in prison.

ROBERT

Well, you'll have to come and visit me in my cell, won't
you?

ANNE

I don't want to!

ERNESTINE

We shall be having tears in a minute.

MRS KELWAY

If it's not too much trouble, Granny would like some
bread.

ERNESTINE

Oh Muttikins! Didn't I give you any?

STELLA
(*to Peter*)
What do those letters on your armlet stand for?

PETER

It's top secret.

ERNESTINE

Did I see you wearing your armlet *outside* the gate?

PETER

We kept under cover.

ERNESTINE

Under cover or not, this is a serious war. You have to
obey orders. Now, ask Mrs Rodney if she would like
some more tea. If she says 'yes' pass her cup and don't
drop the spoon.

PETER

Would you – ?

MRS KELWAY

Mrs Rodney doesn't care for afternoon tea.

Stella looks at her.

STELLA

Oh, I . . . do drink quite a lot of tea in the office.

MRS KELWAY

We now drink tea only once a day. Otherwise we might
not have enough for guests.
(*She sips.*)
If it weren't for the children I should be tempted to do
without tea altogether – I mean drum it out of the
house. Mind you, it can become extraordinarily cold
here.
(*To Stella.*)
The fuel shortage. And so one does benefit from a hot
beverage.
(*She looks at Ernestine.*)
My daughter doesn't feel the cold. She moves about so
much she seldom takes her hat off. Robert tells me that
in London you wouldn't notice the war. That's far from
the case here, I can assure you. But I'm glad Robert is
enjoying a period of calm. He went through so much.
So much. More than we care to speak of.

ERNESTINE

Mum's the word here. Isn't that so, children?

Robert slices a piece of cake and offers it to Stella.

ROBERT

Cake?

STELLA

No thanks.

ANNE

Why not? Do you think it will make you fat?

ERNESTINE

Mrs Rodney is free not to eat cake if she doesn't want
to. That's the difference between England and
Germany.

PETER

The Nazis would force her to eat cake.

Ernestine laughs loudly.

ROBERT
(*to Stella*)

Come and see the house.

Ernestine laughs even more loudly.

ERNESTINE

Isn't it time for your walk?

ROBERT

House first.

ERNESTINE

But there's nothing to see in the house! Honestly! What
a waste of a fine afternoon.

ROBERT

Mrs Rodney is interested in interior decoration.

MRS KELWAY
(*to Stella*)
I'm afraid we have nothing of that sort here.

ROBERT
Then I shall show her my photographs.

ERNESTINE
Won't Mrs Rodney think you're very vain?

PETER
Can we come too?

ROBERT
No. Go outside and I'll see you from the window.

ERNESTINE
The house is up for sale anyway. It's too big.

Robert and Stella walk to the door.

MRS KELWAY
You should warn Mrs Rodney that the better rooms are
all shut up. Because of the war.

INT. THE HOUSE: STAIRCASE. DAY.

Robert and Stella ascending.

ROBERT
Don't think you're making a bad impression. I assure
you you're making no impression at all.

They proceed up the attic stairs to his room.

INT. ROBERT'S ROOM. DAY.

Robert and Stella come into the room.

*A 'varsity' chair padded. A swivel lamp. Glass cases of coins,
birds' eggs, fossils, butterflies. Trophies in a pyramid over the
chimney-piece. On two walls in* passe-partout *or in frames sixty*

or seventy photographs, all featuring Robert at various ages.

Stella looks at the photographs and laughs.

STELLA

Good gracious! Did you – hang all these up?

ROBERT

No. But, as you see, I haven't taken them down. My mother and Ernie put them there.

STELLA

They really must be very fond of you.

ROBERT

No, it's not that. They expect me to be very fond of myself.

STELLA

But ... are you? I don't think you are.
        (*She examines the photographs.*)
Is this Susannah?

ROBERT

Yes.

STELLA

I don't see anything wrong with her.

Robert is silent.

And this? Is this your father?

ROBERT

Yes.

She looks about the room.

STELLA

Very odd. The room feels ... empty.

ROBERT

Yes. It is. Each time I come into it I'm hit in the face by

the feeling that I don't exist. That I never have existed. So it's extraordinary coming in here with you. Gives me a kind of vertigo. I can't explain it.

She points to the photographs.

STELLA

But there – there is your existence.

ROBERT

That's not my existence. That's my criminal record. A senseless criminal record. Don't you think? I know it by heart. A naked baby. Smirking over that tournament cup. In shorts on top of a rock with Thompson. An usher at Amabelle's wedding. Picnicking with Susannah. Larking about with Ernie's labrador. Playing cricket with Dad. God! Can you think of a better way of driving a man mad than nailing that pack of his own lies all round the room where he has to sleep?

STELLA

Then why don't you take them down?

ROBERT

They would hate that.

She opens a drawer in a chest of drawers and lifts folded tissue paper.

STELLA

Ah. Socks. Beautifully preserved.
        (*She sits on the window seat.*)
What was your father like?

ROBERT

He was like Ernie's labrador. Ernie's labrador died half-way through Munich week. He was very sensitive. So was my father. In all but one sense he was impotent. He let himself be buckled into his marriage like Ernie's labrador let himself be buckled into his collar. My father's death was a great relief. To me, that is. And probably to him.

Sound of children from below. Stella looks out of the window.

EXT. THE GARDEN. DAY.

The children march into view performing military exercises. Robert calls down.

> ROBERT
> Don't hold your breath for too long!

Anne opens her mouth, exhales and collapses on the lawn.

Peter calls up to the window.

> PETER
> Nobody can find the half-ounce weight off the weighing machine!

> ANNE
> Granny wanted to weigh the parcel for you to post in London!

> PETER
> You'll have to have it weighed *in* London!

> ANNE
> She can't weigh it because she can't find the weight!

INT. ROBERT'S ROOM. DAY.

Ernestine bursts into the room.

> ERNESTINE
> Yes, here you are!

> ROBERT
> Yes, indeed. Why?

ERNESTINE

I thought you had gone on your walk, until I heard the
children shouting. Thank goodness I caught you.
Muttikins has a parcel for you to post in London. For
Christopher.

ROBERT

What's the matter with the post office here?

ERNESTINE

Nothing. But it's closed on Sunday and in London
they're open.

ROBERT

Are they?

ERNESTINE

Well, some are.

STELLA

I'd love to post the parcel.

They look at her.

ROBERT

But it can wait until we're actually . . . leaving, can't it?

ERNESTINE

Ah well, you see, (a) there's almost always a rush at the
last moment and (b) I may have to dash off myself soon.
But the point is – there's been a complication. Nobody
can find the little half-ounce weight off the weighing
machine. Literally nobody. Muttikins is far from sure
that she may not have understamped the parcel. So the
plan is this – she will leave three pennies with the parcel,
just in case, on the oak chest in front of the stairs. If you
find the parcel is *not*, repeat *not*, understamped you can
give her back the pennies the next time you're here. Is
that clear? Shall I get the children to remind you?

ROBERT

No. It's clear.

ERNESTINE
(*to Stella*)

How do you like our gallery?

STELLA

It's quite a . . .

ERNESTINE

Robert has always photographed well. Crooked again!
(*She dashes to straighten some photos.*)
Did Robert tell you that this is our sister Amabelle, the
children's mother, caught in India for the duration? And
this is our father – oh he used to radiate such energy and
fun – in some ways Robert takes after him. And that,
poor fellow, was my dog.

STELLA

Yes, so Robert said.

ERNESTINE

He had such faith in human nature. I often think that if
Hitler could have looked into that dog's eyes, the story
might have been very different. Hark! There goes the
telephone! Someone's after me!

She dashes out.

Robert and Stella look at each other.

EXT. LONDON STREET. NIGHT.

*Stella walking through deserted streets with parcel. Occasional
figures in doorways. Lovers 'blotted' together.*

*She crosses Langham Place into Weymouth Street. She walks
towards her house, falters, stops, peers into the dark.*

A match is struck, sheltered, thrown away.

She walks on, goes up the steps.

STELLA

Been waiting long?

HARRISON

I thought you'd be back about now.

She opens the front door. He slips up the steps.

I'd rather like a word, if I may?

She looks at him, goes in. He follows.

INT. HALL. NIGHT.

The door closes. Darkness.

She climbs the stairs. A torch follows her, lights her path. When they reach the door to her flat, the beam plays on her fingers as she unlocks the door.

They go in.

INT. THE FLAT. NIGHT.

She draws the blackout blinds, pulls the curtains, switches on lamps and the electric fire. She turns.

Harrison is sitting.

HARRISON

Nice to be here again. You know, I really feel at home.

STELLA

In that case, I shall change my shoes.

She goes into the bedroom.

He sits, lights a cigarette.

She returns, wearing mules.

I've been in the country, as I expect you know.

HARRISON

Making the most of the last of the fine weather?

STELLA

What do you mean by that?

HARRISON

Were you making the most of the last of the fine weather?

She leans back, puts her feet up on a stool, sighs.

You seem more relaxed tonight.

STELLA

I'm extremely tired.

HARRISON

Must have been quite a day. How did it go?

STELLA

How did what go?

HARRISON

Look, you don't have to talk, if you don't want to. I'll be quite happy just sitting here.

STELLA

Why? Is this your evening off?

HARRISON

I don't quite –

STELLA

In this business or pleasure?

Harrison leans forward, begins to push his fist into the palm of his hand.

Why don't you tell me what else I've been doing?

HARRISON

Well, one thing I know you've been doing, Stella – you've been thinking things over.

STELLA

Have I?

HARRISON

Yes. You've thought things over. Today you did exactly what I should have done. You went to look at the first place where rot could start. The home hearth. I wonder what you found? I wouldn't dream of asking you, of course.

Pause.

STELLA

I haven't ... said anything ... to him about ...

HARRISON

Oh, I know that. He hasn't changed his habits, you see. He's doing the same things. The only change is you. You're not as natural on the telephone at nights as you used to be. Anyone would think you thought his line was being tapped.

She looks at him.

STELLA

So that's what you do in the evenings.

Pause.

HARRISON

And how have you got on with your other check-up – on me?

STELLA

I haven't got very far.

HARRISON

The thing is, not all that many people know who I am.
      (*He suddenly looks at the parcel.*)
What's this?

STELLA

It's a parcel – for posting. I should have taken it to a post office. I was too tired.

HARRISON

Would you like me to post it for you?

STELLA

Would you? Oh ... thank you. That would be one thing ... less ...

HARRISON

Leave it to me.

She lies back. He gazes at her.

The first time I saw you ... you were lying quite like this ... on the grass in Regent's Park. Your eyes were closed. Then you opened your eyes and you looked up at the sky. You didn't know I was watching every move you made.

STELLA

And was that when you ... ?

HARRISON

Yes. That's when. And then it got worse. And then I met you at the funeral and it was even worse. And now it's hell.

STELLA

Hell?

HARRISON

Yes. It's hell!

(*He punches his fist.*)

We're getting nowhere!

STELLA

You mean I'm wasting your time? What a joke. You come round and waste my time by telling me I'm

wasting yours. What the hell do you expect from me?
Sympathy?

Pause.

HARRISON

You know, I feel that we're getting to know each other.
We're not so unlike – underneath.

STELLA

You're right. We're horribly alike. You've succeeded in
making a spy of me.

*He stands abruptly, goes to the window, opens the curtains and
goes through them. The curtains swing into place behind him.*

*She hears the blind go up. A breath of wind. Silence. She stands,
goes to the curtains, through the curtains, holds the curtain aside,
looks for him. Light flashes on the pane.*

HARRISON

Mind. Either come through or go back.

*She drops the curtain. They stand together in the alcove in the
dark.*

STELLA

What are you doing?

HARRISON

It's raining.
　　　　(*He puts his hand out of the window.*)
It's not going to stop.

STELLA

Have you . . . far to go?

HARRISON

It depends where I go.

STELLA

Where do you live?

HARRISON

Oh . . . there are always two or three places where I can
turn in.

STELLA

Where do you keep your razor?

HARRISON

I've got more than one razor.
(*Silence.*)
Ah, that air's good. I needed a breath of air.

STELLA

Breathe it . . . for as long as you like.

HARRISON

Stay with me. You breathe too.

They stand.

I can feel you breathing.

They are still.

Abruptly, she goes back through the curtains. He follows.

STELLA

I'm tired.

HARRISON

Leave your parcel to me. I'll deal with it.

STELLA

Listen. If I wanted to find you – how would I find you?

HARRISON

Don't worry about finding me. I'll be in touch.

He goes.

EXT. REGENT'S PARK. DAY.

Robert and Stella walking fast.

ROBERT

I'm sorry, I just don't see why you have to go at all.

STELLA

It's for a few days. That's all.

ROBERT

I don't want you to go away at all! Ever! Anywhere!
Without me. Don't you understand?

STELLA

You don't think I want to go? I don't. In fact I dread it.
But it's simply business for Roderick. It's not a matter
of feeling.

ROBERT

Isn't dread a feeling?

STELLA

Someone's got to go. He can't – I must. Someone's got
to look at the place, the roof . . . all that. Oh really,
Robert, I've been through more than enough convincing
the Passport Office – do I have to go through it all over
again with you?

ROBERT

The Passport Office is not in love with you.

STELLA

Weeks ago, you agreed I would have to go.

ROBERT

Did I? Yes, I suppose I did.

STELLA

Has anything changed since then?

They stop by a tree.

ROBERT

Changed? No. Nothing's changed.

(*He takes her face in his hands and kisses her.*)
But what will you do while you're away? Will you keep
loving me?

STELLA

I'll keep loving you.

INT. HARRISON'S ROOM.

*Photographs of Stella on the wall. One lamp. Cigarette smoke.
The camera focuses on a photograph of Robert kissing Stella in the
park.*

EXT. COUNTRY ROAD. DAY.

Roderick walking towards Wistaria Lodge.

EXT. WISTARIA LODGE. DAY.

Roderick at the door. It opens. Mrs Tringsby.

RODERICK

Good afternoon.

MRS TRINGSBY

I am Mrs Tringsby. You are not ... Mr Rodney, are
you?

RODERICK

Yes, I am.

MRS TRINGSBY

Oh dear. I had expected you to be rather older and not
quite so early. However, do by all means come into the
drawing room.

INT. THE HALL. DAY.

The door closes.

RODERICK

Is my cousin in there?

MRS TRINGSBY

No, oh dear no. She likes to be cosy in her room. She
knows she is going to have a treat of some kind today
but you may find she has forgotten what.

RODERICK

Then I can go up?

MRS TRINGSBY

I *should* like one word with you first, if you don't mind.

They go into the drawing room.

INT. DRAWING ROOM. DAY.

MRS TRINGSBY

We are not making difficulties – but please remember
what happened last time.

RODERICK

Last time?

MRS TRINGSBY

Last time she had a visitor. It was such a dreadful shock
to us all.

RODERICK

Yes, I know. I'm sorry. In fact I'm sure Cousin Francis
would want me to apologize.

MRS TRINGSBY

He should never have come!

RODERICK

Does Cousin Nettie know he's dead?

MRS TRINGSBY

This dear room will never quite feel the same to me again.

RODERICK

Oh, that sort of thing doesn't happen twice. And the Army could tell you I'm as sound as a bell.

MRS TRINGSBY

Yes, that's another thing – I mean, your coming down here in uniform. We're so careful here not to have dreadful thoughts. You won't on any account talk to Mrs Morris about the war, will you? Just a light chat. And never, of course, mention the past.

RODERICK

I want to talk about the future. Is this the way?

INT. STAIRS. DAY.

They go up to the first landing. She whispers.

MRS TRINGSBY

She may not know who you are.

RODERICK

I relied on you to tell her.

MRS TRINGSBY

Oh, I told her – but . . .
> (*She knocks on a door.*)

Here we are!
> (*She opens the door and goes in.*)

Hello! Here I am!

NETTIE
> (*out of shot*)

I was expecting Victor Rodney's son. Has he not come?

MRS TRINGSBY

He's standing outside the door, my dear.

NETTIE

Well, why doesn't he come in?

Roderick goes in.

INT. NETTIE'S ROOM. DAY.

Nettie sitting with needlework, her back to the window.

RODERICK

Cousin Nettie.

MRS TRINGSBY

I shall be just downstairs.
(*She points to a bell.*)
Just downstairs.

NETTIE

Thank you, Mrs Tringsby.

Mrs Tringsby goes. Nettie continues with her needlework. He watches her.

I expect you would never have the patience to do this?

RODERICK

No, I expect not.

NETTIE

But you must *have* patience – to have come such a long journey. It's such a long way to here.

RODERICK

Oh, not so very long – not from where I came from.

NETTIE

I thought it was too far for anybody to come.

He sits.

So you remembered me. Even though you have never met me? Are you called Victor too?

RODERICK

No. Roderick.

NETTIE

Then I shall call you Roderick. I'm so glad you're not
called Victor.

RODERICK

I shall call my son, whenever I have one, Francis.

NETTIE

Oh, he would be so pleased. What a pity he's dead.

RODERICK

It's because he's dead that I've come. I hope my coming
doesn't upset you?

NETTIE

I hope I shan't upset you. I believe I am very odd. And
you must not tell me I'm not – or I shall begin to
wonder.

RODERICK

Do you know Cousin Francis left Mount Morris to me?

NETTIE

Mount Morris, poor unfortunate house, poor thing! So
there it is, after all this time, and here I am!

RODERICK

I wanted to ask –

NETTIE

No, you must not ask me, no! I cannot come back. I
told him again and again, and I told them – now I am
telling you. Everywhere is better without me. I cannot
come back.

(*Silence.*)

Oh, I wish you could have seen him when he was a
young man. Head and shoulders above all the rest of
them. And there could have been a different story.
There could. But there wasn't and in the end he had to
go out looking for a son.

The Maid comes in with tray.

MAID

There, dear.

NETTIE

Thank you, Hilda.

MAID

Sandwiches for the gentleman.

She goes.

NETTIE

Will you have a sandwich?

Roderick takes one.

RODERICK

Cousin Nettie, I have decided that I want to live at
Mount Morris. I'm not asking you to come back. All
I'm saying is, I shall consider the house as much yours
as mine.

NETTIE

Day after day at Mount Morris was sinking further
down a well. It became too much for me – but how
could I say so? I could not help seeing what was the
matter – what he had wanted me to be was his wife. I
tried this, that and the other, till the result was that I fell
into such a terrible melancholy that I only had to think
of anything for it to go wrong. Nature hated us. Once
the fields noticed me with him, the harvests began to
fail. So I took to going nowhere but up and down stairs,
till I met my own ghost.

EXT. MOUNT MORRIS, IRELAND. EVENING.

*The house is large. Two girls standing on the steps. A pony and
trap comes down the drive and stops. Donovan helps Stella from*

194

the trap. The two girls take Stella's cases. They all go in to the house.

INT. MOUNT MORRIS: LIBRARY. EVENING.

A large dark picture. White cards stuck around the inside frame.

Stella walks forward and peers at the cards. She reads: Locks and Hinges, my method of oiling . . . Live mice caught in traps to be drowned not dropped in kitchen fire . . . In case of blocked gutters . . . in case of parachutists . . . in case of my death . . .

Stella turns away. A fire blazing in a distant marble fireplace. She looks out of the window.

Donovan comes into the room with an oil lamp. He turns the wick high. The globe wells up with yellow light. Mary Donovan (aged nineteen) enters with another lamp. The two globes are reflected in the window panes.

DONOVAN
This has been a bare sort of time for us, ma'am, with neither master – and it's a poor welcome for you, I fear, but indeed you're welcome.

STELLA
Thank you.

DONOVAN
We killed a little chicken for your supper.

STELLA
Oh, how nice.

DONOVAN
Will you see your room?
>   (*To Mary.*)
Are there candles?

MARY
There are two candles above.

EXT. MOUNT MORRIS. NIGHT.

River flowing.

Moonlight reflected in rows of windows.

Stella's figure tiny in an upper window.

INT. MOUNT MORRIS: STELLA'S BEDROOM. MORNING.

*She draws the curtains swiftly, looks out. A brilliant morning.
Swans on the river.*

INT. MOUNT MORRIS: HALL. MORNING.

Stella and Donovan meeting.

>   DONOVAN
> They'll be here from the surveyors in about half an
> hour, ma'am.

>   STELLA
> Oh, right. Donovan, is there a boat? My son wants to
> know if there is a boat.

>   DONOVAN
> Ah, well now, there was a boat until the master sank
> her. He had the boys out one morning loading rock into
> her until she went down.

>   STELLA
> But why did he do that?

>   DONOVAN
> Mr Robertson's advice. I think he thought the Germans
> might be landing here and that they'd fancy the use of a
> boat.

>   STELLA
> Mr Robertson?

DONOVAN

Some name of that sort. He came from over. Whether he was a Mister or a Captain we never made out.

STELLA

What did he look like?

DONOVAN

He had a narrow sort of look about him, added to which he had a sort of discord between his two eyes.

INT. MOUNT MORRIS: LIBRARY. NIGHT.

Stella lifting a photograph from a magazine stuck in a frame from a corner of the room: a liner going down in a blaze with all the lights on. Title: NEARER MY GOD TO GHEE: THE *TITANIC:* 1912.

INT. MOUNT MORRIS: BEDROOM. NIGHT.

Stella lying in bed, eyes open. Half a candle burning. It goes out.

EXT. MOUNT MORRIS: WOODS. DAY.

Stella walking along path through woods. She stops. On the path is the body of a big bird, dead. She stares at it.

INT. MOUNT MORRIS: LIBRARY. EVENING.

Stella trying to open drawers in the library. They are locked.

INT. MOUNT MORRIS: DRAWING ROOM. NIGHT.

She moves about the room, catching her reflection in mirrors and window panes. She stops by a piano and strikes a chord.

INT. MOUNT MORRIS: BEDROOM. NIGHT.

A candle guttering. It goes out.

EXT. MOUNT MORRIS: RIVER. DAY.

Morning. Stella standing by the flowing river, looking into it. A call. She looks up. Donovan is standing on a parapet. His daughter, Hannah (aged twenty), stands next to him. She is beautiful. He shapes both his hands into a megaphone.

DONOVAN

Montgomery's through!

Stella makes a gesture of not hearing. Donovan calls again.

Montgomery's through! Victory!

Stella walks quickly to the house. She begins to walk up a slope towards the parapet.

STELLA

Montgomery?

DONOVAN

A terrible victory! Victory in a day!

She stumbles up the slope. He reaches for her hand, grips it.

Come up with you, ma'am.

He pulls her up to him.

The day's famous.

HANNAH

It's a beautiful day, in any event.

Stella looks at her. Hannah stands quietly in the sunshine 'indifferent as a wand'.

INT. EUSTON STATION: PLATFORM. NIGHT.

Train arriving. Doors burst open.

Stella gets off the train, walks along the platform. Through surging crowds she sees Robert, stock still under a light, looking.

She goes on. The crowd. She looks for Robert. He is gone.

Suddenly he is at her side, kissing her, taking her case.

> ROBERT

What a needle in a bundle of hay. Let's get out of this.

He steers her towards the arches.

> STELLA

Why this way?

> ROBERT

I have a car. With a driver.

> STELLA

Oh. Wonderful.

> ROBERT

One snag. Ernestine's in it.

> STELLA

Oh no! Why?

> ROBERT

She's up for the day. We're just dropping her off at a friend. That's all. Five minutes. Do you love me?

> STELLA

Why?

> ROBERT

Then nothing matters.

EXT. EUSTON STATION: FORECOURT. NIGHT.

Robert shines torch on number plates. It is raining. He bangs on a window. A driver jumps out, opens door, they get in.

INT. CAR. NIGHT.

The car is capacious. Jump seats in the back. A glass partition.

ERNESTINE

Mrs Rodney! You must be dead.

STELLA

Not quite.

ERNESTINE

How was the Emerald Isle? Plenty of eggs and bacon?

STELLA

It was rather strange that they had no blackout.

ERNESTINE

Do they actually *know* there's a war on?

ROBERT

Yes. Because they know they're not in it.

The car moves off.

Robert sits facing the women. He tucks a rug over Stella's knees.

Here.

Ernestine laughs.

ERNESTINE

So the age of chivalry is not yet dead! Robert, the driver does know we're going to Earls Court, I take it?

ROBERT

Of course.

ERNESTINE

You told him?

ROBERT

I told him.

ERNESTINE

I didn't hear you tell him. You seemed so fussed at Euston Station. However . . .

Stella lies back and closes her eyes.

Ernestine snaps her handbag open and searches about in it.

Oh God!

Stella opens her eyes.

STELLA

Have you lost something?

ERNESTINE

I hope to heaven I haven't! I thought you were asleep.

ROBERT

So did I. What were you doing? Thinking?

STELLA

No ... just ...

ERNESTINE

It must be somewhere! I'm sure I put it in my handbag
this morning. If I didn't I should be shot! Ah! Got it!
Scoundrel! Thank heaven for that!

ROBERT

Thinking what?

ERNESTINE

What?

ROBERT

I was asking Stella what she was thinking.

STELLA

I'm so glad you found it.

ERNESTINE

Why should she tell you? I really don't know why she's
not allowed to think in peace. Ask no questions and
you'll be told no lies. Where are we? Has anybody any
idea? Hey! It's Earls Court! Driver!

> ROBERT

He knows.

EXT. EARLS COURT. NIGHT.

Ernestine gets out of the car. Robert kisses her, gets back in. The car drives off.

INT. CAR. NIGHT.

Robert sitting next to Stella.

> STELLA
> (*quickly*)

What do you think she lost?

> ROBERT

Mmmnn?

> STELLA

And then found? In her handbag?

> ROBERT

I haven't the foggiest idea.

> STELLA

Whatever it was what a relief she found it. You've never told me –

> ROBERT

What?

> STELLA

You've never told me what she was like when she was young –

He kisses her. She is tense. He withdraws, regards her. As the car moves through the traffic (all cars with dimmed lights) it is only the occasional traffic light that illumines their faces.

I'm sorry. I can't . . . just be alone with you all at once.

It was a shock seeing you at Euston – it's a shock – I'm just thrown – I'll be all right – Let me ...

Pause.

ROBERT

I know you've been all by yourself in that house, but all the same ... I feel jealous, as though somehow you've been with some sort of enemy of mine – or rival. So far the best thing has been touching your coat. I know where I am with your coat. It's just the same.

STELLA

You have no enemy anywhere in me!

ROBERT

Why should you have to say that?

STELLA

My darling, who could like to feel less welcome than her own coat?

ROBERT

But I want to welcome you. Totally. You haven't let me.

STELLA

Can you give me a cigarette?

He gives her a cigarette, lights a match, the match goes out. He strikes another one, lights her cigarette.

The car enters a dark section of the street. Her voice:

Two months ago, nearly two months ago, somebody came to me with a story about you. They said you were passing information to the enemy.

Silence.

ROBERT

I what?

STELLA

They said you were passing information to the enemy. I didn't . . . I didn't know what to think.

Silence.

ROBERT

What an extraordinary woman you are.

STELLA

Why? What would an ordinary woman . . . have thought? What would an ordinary woman have done?

ROBERT

Well, I don't know really. What did you do?

STELLA

Nothing. It's not true, is it?

ROBERT

Two months ago . . . two *months*? There's certainly nothing like thinking a thing over. Or did it happen to simply slip your mind until tonight? Why didn't you just come and ask me then? What would have been wrong with that? Or was that too simple?

Traffic lights on their faces.

That's what beats me.

                    (*Pause.*)

Who *was* this?

STELLA

A man called Harrison.

ROBERT

A man called Harrison.

STELLA

It isn't true, is it?

ROBERT

It can't be true that you're asking me the question.
What do you want me to say? There's nothing *to* say!
The whole thing's so completely unreal to me I can't
believe it isn't as unreal to you. It must be.

STELLA

Yes, it is. But –

ROBERT

What you're asking me isn't the point – it's immaterial,
crazy, out of a thriller. Am I passing information to the
enemy? No, of course not! How could I be, why should
I? What do you take me for? What *do* you take me for?
What do I take you for? How well you've acted with me
for the last two months. How could you – ? I ask you
again. Why didn't you come to me two months ago and
tell me then?

STELLA

He said it would be dangerous to you to tell you.

ROBERT

What he says, then, cuts a good deal of ice with you?
(*Pause.*)
In fact you acted on the assumption that it was true.

STELLA

I didn't act! I didn't know what to do. I loved you.

ROBERT

How strange that word sounds.

STELLA

Oh my darling – for God's sake – this is breaking my
heart –

ROBERT

Is it? Am I? Or are you just saying so? How do you
expect me to know what's true? You may have had

another lover all this time for all I know. I'm not sure I wouldn't have preferred that. This is so ... So you've been watching me for two months? You're two months gone with this. And I didn't see it. I must be going blind.

STELLA

I ... loved you ...

ROBERT

No. It's the appearance of love you keep up so beautifully.

STELLA
(*closing her eyes*)

No. No.

Silence. She suddenly laughs.

Well, I suppose I owe you an apology.

ROBERT

What? Oh ... yes ... I suppose you do.

STELLA

I'm ... shocked too, you know. Until I heard my own words and heard you hear them, I really had no idea how horrible ... forgive me.

The car goes on.

Robert?

ROBERT

Yes. I'm listening to you.

STELLA

Say something.

ROBERT

You don't seem to have shown any great patriotic fervour.

                              STELLA

No.

She opens the window and breathes deeply.

                              ROBERT

What is it?

                              STELLA

I think I'm weak with hunger.

                              ROBERT

Yes, that's what it probably is. We'll get a sandwich
somewhere.

                              STELLA

Will we? Do you want to?

                              ROBERT

Oh yes. I've had quite a day too as days go. I need a
drink. We're both a bit light-headed. A drink will sober
us down.

INT. HOTEL LOUNGE. NIGHT.

*Robert and Stella at a table with drinks and sandwiches. In the
background continual movement of foreign officers.*

                              ROBERT

Must have been strange ... Ireland?

                              STELLA

Yes. It was the light as much as anything else.

                              ROBERT

Mmn.

                              STELLA

Dublin was a blaze of light – as the ship came in. It was
dazzling ... frightening. And at the house – there were
oil lamps in the window – you know – naked windows.
It was strange, yes.

They drink.

One night I took a lamp and went into the drawing room. I walked up and down it and I imagined Roderick's wife in it one day. Why not, after all? Roderick's wife . . . but there was a picture of the *Titanic* hanging crooked in a corner –

ROBERT

Stella –

STELLA

Yes?

ROBERT

Talking of that, why shouldn't we marry?

STELLA

Talking of the *Titanic*?

ROBERT

No, talking of Roderick. If anyone is to marry, why not us?

STELLA

You and me?

ROBERT

Yes. Why not?

She looks at him.

STELLA

We've got in the way of not marrying, I suppose.

ROBERT

Yes, but why not?

She does not answer.

Why not? You know it's really quite simple. The reason that I want to marry you is that I want to marry you. I made up my mind when you were in Ireland. The fact is I can't bear you out of my sight.

STELLA

But I hardly ever am.

ROBERT

I'm not so sure as I used to be about that.

STELLA

You think I run into trouble?

ROBERT

I think you do a bit, yes.

STELLA

You think I need looking after?

ROBERT

Your friend what's-his-name must have thought so.

STELLA

Why do you call him what's-his-name? His name is Harrison. It's an easy name to remember.

ROBERT

Harrison. But what if I need looking after too? Do you think that perhaps you and I have never quite been our ages?

STELLA

I thought it had all been perfect.

ROBERT

Yes, it all seemed perfect. But there must have been a catch in it somewhere. We must have been about due to take this knock.

They stare at each other.

There's only one solution. Marry me. It's not such a new idea. It's not such a wild idea.

STELLA

You've made it sound wild. You're contradicting
yourself. First you say you made up your mind when I
was in Ireland – then you say you feel forced to ask me
because of what I said in the car – because it suddenly
seems necessary for you to keep me under your eye –
also – and I understand all of this – that I owe some . . .
balm to your offended honour. Well, that's how you
make it sound – that the very least I can do is marry
you, to prove to you I'm convinced anything more I
might possibly hear about you can't be true. So any
reasons I may have of my *own* – to hesitate – go by the
board. Don't you see?

ROBERT

Look, I was clear enough. Let's get this straight. The
fact that I want to marry you has nothing to do with
what you said in the car. If Ernie hadn't been sitting
waiting I'd have asked you the moment I saw you on the
platform. I'm not saying that what happened later didn't
have an effect on me. Of course it did – it made me
more certain it was time we married. The idea of
anyone who likes coming along and frightening you is
appalling. Yes, I was hurt too – how could I hide that?
How could I not be? But – more to the point – for a
moment the whole of our love seemed futile if I couldn't
keep you . . . from that fantastic thing.

STELLA

Yes, it was fantastic.

ROBERT

But you were frightened.

STELLA

Yes.

ROBERT

Yes. For me – but also of me – a little?

STELLA

It was simply . . .

ROBERT

Do you love me?

STELLA

We're keeping the waiter waiting.

Robert looks down and sees a bill on the plate on the table.

Not just anybody can frighten me, you know. I wish you'd find out who Harrison is.

ROBERT

Is he anybody?

INT. THE FLAT. DAY.

Stella lifting the phone.

STELLA

Hello?

ROBERT
(*VO*)

Darling, it's me. I'm sorry, dammit, I can't make tonight. I have to go down to Holme Dene. A family convocation. Red alert. My mother has had an offer for the house. Thrown them completely. I have to go. What will you do?

STELLA

Oh – I'll have a quiet night.

ROBERT

I'll ring you tomorrow.

The phone cuts off. She turns. Harrison is in the room.

EXT. REGENT STREET. NIGHT.

Harrison walking with Stella. They wear raincoats. He takes her elbow as they cross into a side street.

HARRISON
Here we are. This is it. Down these steps. Careful.

They go down into a basement. A dim sign on the door. CAFÉ OPEN. *They go in.*

INT. BASEMENT CAFÉ. NIGHT.

They enter the café. It is a bar/grill. People seated along the counter. There are also tables.

Harrison takes Stella to a table for two.

HARRISON
(*handing menu*)

Here you are.

STELLA
I'm thirsty. I'd love some lager.

HARRISON
Yes, absolutely.
> (*He waves to a Waitress.*)

Two lagers please.
> (*To Stella.*)

And what about food? See anything you like? Cold cuts and salad? Fish? Wait, I'll tell you what. Let's see if they can do something . . . different. After all, this is an occasion – for me anyway.

He goes to the bar and talks to the Manageress. The Waitress brings the lagers to the table. Stella sips. Harrison returns, sits, winks.

Just the job. Mission accomplished.

STELLA

What is it?

HARRISON

A secret.

STELLA

I'm not very hungry.

HARRISON

Well ... no worry ... it's just very nice for me ... to be
your escort ... Cheers.

STELLA

Cheers.

They drink.

HARRISON

Mind you, I still have to scold you, I'm afraid.

STELLA

Oh? Why?

HARRISON

You've done what I told you not to do.

STELLA

What's that?

HARRISON

You've been naughty.

STELLA

Really?

HARRISON

Yes, really. Also ... rash. One of these days you'll be
getting some of us into trouble. Don't look blank – you
know very well what you've done.

She drinks.

You tipped him off. Didn't you? Come on. Admit it.

She looks at him.

I mean if I've got it wrong, you can always tell me to go to hell. Why don't you tell me to go to hell?

STELLA

Perhaps you're growing on me.

Harrison drinks.

HARRISON

You know, you're not as bright as I thought.

STELLA

Oh?

HARRISON

No. When I told you, at the very beginning, that I should know if you tipped him off, you really should have believed me. You see, I not only know that you have, but I can tell you when. I can tell you the very day, or rather the very night.

Waitress to table.

WAITRESS

Two lobster salad.

HARRISON

Lovely.

The Waitress puts the plates down on the table and goes.

This was my secret. My innocent secret.

STELLA

There's no such thing as an innocent secret.

HARRISON

Isn't there? But you like lobster, I hope?

STELLA

Oh, yes. I like it very much.

HARRISON

I'm glad. Looks fresh, doesn't it?

STELLA

It does ... look fresh.

They begin to eat.

What makes you think you can tell me the day or the night?

HARRISON

Because, from the morning after, he altered his course. Behaved in fact exactly, and to the letter, the way I told you he would behave the moment he knew there was someone on his tracks. That's what I said he'd do and that's what he's done. So I know you told him.

STELLA

When?

HARRISON

The night you got back from Ireland.

STELLA

Well ...

She takes out her powder compact, begins to powder her nose, looks in the mirror.

Well ...

Louie comes into the café. She sits at the bar, suddenly sees Harrison, stares at him, half smiles. Stella sees her in the mirror.

Someone has recognized you.

HARRISON

What?

215

STELLA

A friend of yours.

HARRISON

Don't be silly.

STELLA

At the bar.

Harrison looks round. Louie smiles at him. He turns back to the table.

A dog wanders among the tables, leash trailing.

HARRISON

What you've done is this – you've put us all on the spot.
You see? Thanks to you, our friend has pretty well
dished himself. The only case for leaving him loose was
the chance he would lead us on to something bigger.
Now that's out. So the case for leaving him loose falls
down. That's what it's up to me to report.

STELLA

So will you?

HARRISON

I've got myself to think of too, you know. And the
country.

STELLA

So far, who besides you knows this?

He looks at her.

HARRISON

Only I know. It still has to go up –

STELLA

And you wouldn't be telling me this if it had ... *gone*
up? Is that right?

The dog nuzzles Stella's leg. Harrison kicks at it.

HARRISON

Scram!

STELLA

It's not doing any harm.

HARRISON

It's bothering you.

STELLA

It won't bite. I wish it would. What were we saying?

HARRISON

You know what we were saying.

STELLA

I know what you were about to say, yes. That at last,
now, it really is up to me. That I either buy out Robert
for a bit longer ... or –

*Harrison claps his hand down on hers sharply. Louie is at the
table.*

LOUIE

Excuse me. I'm just after my dog. Come along, come
on Spot, bad boy. Bothering people!
    (*She looks at Harrison.*)
Hello. I haven't seen you in the park for ages.

Harrison picks up the leash and hands it to her.

HARRISON

I'm never there.

LOUIE

Well, you must have been there once. I saw you there.
Fancy seeing you here!
    (*To Stella.*)
Excuse me interrupting, it's on account of Spot. Bad
boy.

STELLA

You're not interrupting. Why do you call your dog
Spot? He hasn't got any.

LOUIE

He's my friend's dog actually. I was going to meet her in
this café. But I think I've come to the wrong place, I
mean the wrong café –

HARRISON

Well, you'd better buzz off home. And take your dog.

LOUIE

He's taken quite a fancy to you, hasn't he? They always
say a dog knows ...

STELLA

Why don't you sit down?

Louie glances at Harrison.

LOUIE

Oh, I –

STELLA

For a minute.

Louie brings a chair from the next table and sits.

LOUIE

I don't think I should, really. For one thing, you were
talking.

STELLA

Oh, we were only deciding something.

Louie looks round the café.

LOUIE

My friend's not here. I wish I knew where we were.

STELLA

I've no idea where we are!
(*To Harrison.*)
Where are we?
(*To Louie.*)
Do tell me your name. I'm Mrs Rodney.

LOUIE

I'm Mrs Lewis.

STELLA

Are you?

LOUIE

Yes. I've got a husband in India – well, somewhere like that.
(*She looks at Harrison.*)
To think of you remembering me . . .

STELLA

You're not old friends then?

LOUIE

Oh, no. We just fell into conversation at a band concert
in the park. Didn't we? Weeks ago.

Harrison ignores her.

HARRISON
(*to Stella, viciously*)
Are you off your head? Do you think we've got all night?

STELLA

Yes, I thought we had.

Louie looks at them.

LOUIE
(*violently*)
How can you talk to her like that? How can you go out
with him? Why does he talk to you like that? People to
be friendly, that's what the war's for, isn't it?

STELLA

I'm sorry.
(*She picks up Louie's gloves from the floor and gives them to her.*)
You mustn't mind him. You mustn't blame him. It's
been my fault. He's in trouble too. This evening was to
have been a celebration, the first of many more
evenings. It may still be the first of many more evenings,
but what will they be worth? I don't know.

Louie stands.

LOUIE

Well, I'll be off. Goodnight.

STELLA

Say goodnight to him.

LOUIE

I don't know his name.

STELLA

Harrison. You must congratulate me before you go. I've
good news, I think.

LOUIE

You have?

STELLA

Yes. A friend is out of danger.

*Harrison's hand moves abruptly to his eye. The table jolts. He
rubs his eye, puts his cigarette out in the ashtray.*

HARRISON

Why don't you two both go along together?

Stella stares at him.

Didn't you hear what I said? You two had better both be
getting along.

STELLA

But ...

HARRISON

What?

STELLA

But ... we don't know where we are ...

HARRISON

Turn right, first left and you're in Regent Street.

STELLA

I don't understand. What has been decided? I thought
we ... What have you decided? What are you going to
do?

HARRISON

Pay the bill.

INT. HOLME DENE: LOUNGE. NIGHT.

*Mrs Kelway and Ernestine sitting. Robert standing, pacing about,
sometimes coming to rest on the hearth rug. He paces, stops.*

ROBERT

Let's sum up: (a) we don't know if we want to sell (b) if
we do, how much more than the offer do we hope to
get? (c) again, if we do sell, where are you both to go?

MRS KELWAY

I am afraid it is not so simple as that.

ERNESTINE

Muttikins feels there must be something behind the
offer.

ROBERT

What's behind the offer is that someone wants to buy
the house.

ERNESTINE

Who can want to buy a house they haven't seen?

ROBERT

How do you know they haven't seen it?

ERNESTINE

Well, no one has been to the door!

ROBERT

You can see the house from a little way down the drive.

MRS KELWAY

We do not care for people coming down the drive.

ERNESTINE

Why can't they come to the door and openly ring the bell? Creeping and spying about . . .

MRS KELWAY

No one is going to rush us. We did not ask these people to buy the house.

ROBERT

But we left 'For Sale' on the agent's books for years.

MRS KELWAY

Nevertheless, this is our home.

ROBERT

In that case – we turn 'em down.

MRS KELWAY

But it *is* too large.

ROBERT

In that case – we jack 'em up.

MRS KELWAY

I am afraid it is not so simple as that.

Pause.

ERNESTINE

You talk, Robert, as though this was just a business transaction.

MRS KELWAY

It always has been too large. And too expensive. Your father made a mistake. One of many.

ROBERT

Could you actually be happy in something smaller?

MRS KELWAY

It is not a question of happiness. It is a question of the future. That is for you and Ernestine. I have had my life and I hope I have done my best. But you must not expect me to be with you for long.

ERNESTINE

Muttikins! Don't say such dreadful things!

MRS KELWAY

You talk as though you expected not to die yourself. We shall –

The telephone rings in the hall.

Robert starts violently, stops walking.

Ernestine jumps up and goes into the hall.

ERNESTINE

It'll be for me!

Robert remains still as Ernestine's voice is heard.

Yes, yes! Of course! Nine thirty. But can we all get in ... Oh, yes I'm all for it ... yes, yes – all hands on deck!

She returns.

Oh, it has been a day! One thing after another.

MRS KELWAY

Ernestine has not been able to take her hat off.

ERNESTINE

Well, ought we to sell or not?

ROBERT

Do we want to?

ERNESTINE

One can't always be thinking of what one wants.

MRS KELWAY

I have never thought of what I wanted. Don't forget that this house is to be left to you both jointly. If you do not care for that you had better say so.

ERNESTINE

Of course we care! How can I ever forget this is my home?

ROBERT

How can I?

Mrs Kelway looks at Robert.

MRS KELWAY

And so, what is your advice?

Pause.

ROBERT

Sell.

Ernestine laughs.

MRS KELWAY

Robert does not remember anything about his life.

Robert regards her coldly.

ROBERT

There you are quite wrong ... Muttikins.

She looks at him and then at Ernestine.

MRS KELWAY

He talks like a man.

Silence.

A sound from the hall.

ROBERT

Who's there?

He goes to the door. Anne comes down the stairs and into the room.

ANNE

Me, Uncle Robert.

ERNESTINE

Anne!

ANNE

Oh, Auntie Ernie, please.

ERNESTINE

Both of you ought to be sound asleep.

ANNE

Peter is.

ERNESTINE

Granny doesn't like people creeping about in the middle of the night.

ANNE

I know, but –

ERNESTINE

Don't say 'I know' to Granny.

Robert scoops Anne up and sits her on the arm of an armchair, in which he sits.

Robert, you encourage her.

ROBERT
No, she encourages me.
(*He rocks Anne to and fro by her belt.*)
But I think you might have cooked up something
cleverer? Why couldn't you be walking in your sleep?

ANNE
Because I'm awake. Can you stay here tonight?

ROBERT
No. Got anything to tell me?

ANNE
I was top at mental arithmetic.

ERNESTINE
You can tell Uncle Robert all about that next time –

ROBERT
No, really, Ernie.

ERNESTINE
Well then, a moment. Only a moment, mind.

ANNE
(*to Robert*)
How many moments are there? How long, compared to
a minute, is a moment?

ROBERT
That depends on –

Telephone.

Robert jumps. Anne falls off the chair.

MRS KELWAY
The telephone is never for anybody but Ernestine. What
is the matter, Robert? Are you expecting a call?

ERNESTINE

If it's for you, do answer it.

MRS KELWAY

Knocking the child off the chair ... Oh, need we have all that ringing? Will, someone answer it?

ANNE

I will.

She runs into the hall.

ERNESTINE

Anne, no!

Robert stands up.

Oh, I'll answer it.

MRS KELWAY

Is it for Robert?

ERNESTINE

Does anyone know you're here?

ROBERT

If it's for me, say I'm on my way back to London, will you?

ANNE

But you're here.

The telephone stops.

ERNESTINE

There – you see! If it should turn out to be important, I shall always blame myself. Now, Anne – to bed.

Anne flings her arms around Robert. He stoops, presses her cheek to his.

ANNE

Are you going to London?

> ROBERT

Yes.

> ANNE

You're always going away. Always.

> ROBERT

You're giving me a crick in my back. You must grow taller.

> ANNE

Just one more.

She pulls his head down and gently butts her forehead against his.

INT. STELLA'S FLAT: BEDROOM. 2 A.M.

Light from the electric fire.

Stella is sitting in the bed. Robert is sitting at the foot of the bed. They are both naked.

Silence.

> ROBERT

And if I am? If that is what I am doing?
> (*Silence.*)
Because it has been that, all the time.

Silence.

> STELLA

Why?

> ROBERT

Oh ... we should have to try to understand each other all over again. It's too late now.

> STELLA

Too late in the night?

Pause.

ROBERT

Too late.

STELLA

Why are you against this country?

ROBERT

Country?

STELLA

Yes.

ROBERT

There are no countries. Nothing but names. What sort
of country do you think exists outside this room?
Exhausted shadows, dragging themselves to fight. How
long can they drag the fight out? We've come out on the
far side of that.

STELLA

We?

ROBERT

We ... who are ready for the next thing.

STELLA

What is it? What is the next thing?

ROBERT

The next thing ... is something ... on an altogether
different scale. It's ... sight in *action*. When I *act* I see.
        (*Pause.*)
Do you think I'm a traitor? All that language is dead
currency. It means nothing. What it once meant is gone.
        (*Pause.*)
Are you against me?

STELLA

You're the one who's against. But not this country, you
say? Then what are you against?

ROBERT

The racket.

STELLA

What racket?

ROBERT

Freedom. Freedom to be what? Muddled, mediocre, damned. Look at your free people. Mice let loose in the middle of the Sahara. It's insupportable. Tell a man he's free – you know what that does to him? It sends him scuttling back into the womb. Look at it. Look at your mass of 'free' suckers - look at your 'democracy' – kidded along from the cradle to the grave. Do you think there's a single man of *mind* who doesn't know *he* only begins where his 'freedom' stops? Freedom is just a slave's yammer. One in a thousand may have what it takes to be free – if so, he has what it takes to be something better. And he knows it. Who would want to be free when he could be strong? We must be strong. There must be law.

STELLA

But you break the law.

ROBERT

No. Not the real law, not the true law.

He stands, walks silently to the window, pulls the curtains. Moonlight. His silhouette at the window. He stands still.

STELLA

Come back.

He turns, goes back to the bed, sits, not touching.

ROBERT

Do you feel I've been apart from you in this? I haven't. There's been you and me in everything I've done.

STELLA

Why didn't you ... talk to me?

ROBERT

I couldn't involve you. How could I! And how was I to
tell you? How?

STELLA

You could have ... just let me know.

ROBERT

Sometimes I thought I had. There were times it seemed
impossible you didn't know. I found myself waiting for
you to speak. When you didn't I thought you had
decided silence was better – and I thought, yes, silence
is better. But I didn't know that you didn't know – until
you asked me.

She suddenly sobs.

STELLA

Oh, why did you? What made you have to? Such ideas
to have ... Why?

ROBERT

I didn't choose them. They marked me out. They're not
mine. I'm theirs. Haven't I a right to my own side?
        (*He leans towards her and takes her hand.*)
It is enough to have been in action once on the wrong
side. You don't know the disgust – of Dunkirk. An army
of freedom queuing up to be taken off by pleasure boats.
That was the end of *that* war. What was left? The scum
– the Dunkirk wounded.

STELLA

I never knew you before then ... before you were
wounded.

ROBERT

I was born wounded. My father's son. Dunkirk was

waiting there in us. What a race! A class without a
middle. A race without a country. Never earthed in.
Thousands and thousands of us – breeding and
breeding – breeding what?

Pause.

STELLA

Were you never frightened – to do what you were doing?

ROBERT

The opposite. It undid fear. It bred my father out of me.
It gave me a new heredity. I was living. I was under
orders.

STELLA

So you're with the enemy.

ROBERT

They're facing us with what has got to be the
conclusion. They may not last. But it will.

STELLA

It's not just that they're the enemy – but that they're
horrible, unthinkable, grotesque.

ROBERT

In birth anything is grotesque. But they've started
something. You may not like it but it's the beginning of
a new world.

STELLA

Roderick may be killed.
                    (*Silence.*)
Roderick may be killed.

He does not speak.

I have *not* been in what you've done. The more I
understand it the more I hate it. I hate it.

232

She stands, puts on gown, goes to door, goes out of bedroom, closes door.

INT. SITTING ROOM. NIGHT.

Darkness. She switches on a lamp. She walks to the mantelpiece. She looks at Robert's photograph. She turns the photograph to the wall.

She trembles, holds on to the shelf, tries to call 'Robert' but has no voice.

The bedroom door opens. Robert in dressing-gown.

ROBERT

Yes?

She looks at him.

You called me?

They fall into each other's arms. He holds her to him.

The photograph of Robert falls off the mantelshelf on to the floor.

STELLA

I should never have let you come here. This will be the first place they –

ROBERT

Last night at Holme Dene I was in terror of never seeing you again. I knew I was in danger but I'd never pictured arrest before. I suddenly did. What a place to be taken in! Theirs to be the last faces I saw! My mother had been waiting for this. She wished it! It would be she who had got me into this trap, so that I should never see you again. It never suited her that I should be a man.
> (*He lights a cigarette, sits on the sofa.*)
I wonder how they got on to me? I wonder what I did – what I didn't think of? I was so careful. It had become second nature.

233

She sits.

STELLA

If I had slept with Harrison, could he have . . . saved you?

ROBERT

What, did he say so? Naturally he would. You didn't try?

STELLA

I thought I would, last night. But he sent me home.

ROBERT

You left it pretty late.

STELLA

I left it late, yes.

ROBERT

He sounds crazy. What a chance to take. What was to stop you turning him in? It would have been the end of him.

STELLA

It would have been the end of you too.
(*She takes a cigarette. He lights it.*)
What are you then? A revolutionary? No, a counter-revolutionary? What are you exactly? You know, for somebody doing something so definite, you talk so vaguely. Wildness and images. It's as though you haven't formulated . . . everything in your mind.

ROBERT

I've never talked about it before.

STELLA

Not even to your . . . friends?

ROBERT

You think we meet to swap ideas?

Pause.

STELLA

Something's missing. You are out for the enemy to win because you think they have something. What?

ROBERT

They have something. This war's just so much bloody quibbling about a thing that's pre-decided. Either side's winning would stop the war – only their side's winning would stop the quibbling. I want order. I want shape. I want discipline. I want the cackle cut. What have I still not said?

They sit.

STELLA

I wish we could sleep.

ROBERT

I must dress.

STELLA

Going? But there might be someone outside the door?

ROBERT

Yes. There has been a step.

STELLA

When? I didn't hear. And if it had been his step I should have heard it. I should have known it before I heard it.

She goes towards the window.

ROBERT

Don't touch the curtain!

She stops.

STELLA

I want to. I want to say:
'Yes, he's here – we're here together, he's with me, I love him!

235

Robert goes into the bedroom and begins to dress. They speak through the open door.

I could let you out the back.

ROBERT

If there's somebody at the front there'll be someone at the back.

STELLA

That could depend on whether the somebody at the front is Harrison or not.

ROBERT

Why?

STELLA

He's in love. He could be watching the house for his own reasons. People torment themselves.

ROBERT

He's still what he is.

STELLA

You were made to come here.

Robert comes out of the bedroom, dressed, goes to her.

ROBERT

I had to hold you in my arms ... once more. And I had to tell you. I came here to tell you but I had to hold you in my arms first. I had to love you first and then tell you. I wonder ... would we ever have spoken if we hadn't known this was goodbye?

STELLA
(*dully*)

This is goodbye.

ROBERT

Isn't there a way out on to the roof?

STELLA

Yes, yes ... the skylight ... you know it ... but there
could be somebody there ... there could be somebody
on the roof.

ROBERT

There's one great thing about a roof. There's one sure
way off it.

They stand.

STELLA

It's steep. I wish you hadn't got your stiff knee.

ROBERT

I wish I hadn't got my stiff knee. We've never danced
... have we?
(*Silence.*)
I'll go by the roof. Come on.

He goes to the door. She follows.

INT. LANDING. NIGHT.

*The ladder to the skylight down. Robert goes up it, pushes the
skylight. It opens. He secures it. He comes down the ladder, kisses
her.*

ROBERT

Take care of yourself.
(*He goes up the ladder, stops.*)
Now, turn off the light, get back into the flat and shut
the door.

The light goes out.

STELLA'S VOICE

Goodnight.

EXT. FRONT OF THE HOUSE. NIGHT.

A figure standing.

EXT. BACK OF THE HOUSE. NIGHT.

A figure standing.

A moving figure on the roof.

EXT. FRONT OF THE HOUSE. NIGHT.

Figure on the roof.

EXT. BACK OF THE HOUSE. NIGHT.

Roof empty. A man running. A thud.

CLICK OF A CAMERA.

Photograph of Robert, spreadeagled in basement, still.

EXT. LONDON STREET. NIGHT.

Fifteen months later. An air raid taking place. Bombs. Gunfire. Searchlights, etc.

Harrison standing in street looking up at block of flats in Victoria. He enters.

INT. LOBBY. NIGHT.

Harrison goes towards the lift, gets in. The lift doors close.

INT. FLAT DOOR. NIGHT.

Harrison rings the bell.

Stella opens the door, holding cat.

They look at each other.

HARRISON

Is this convenient?

STELLA

Where have you been?

He does not reply.

Come in.

INT. THE FLAT. NIGHT.

She closes the door.

STELLA

I was just sitting – listening to the guns.

He takes off his coat.

HARRISON

Yes, it has been quite a time since we met. I see you've
got a cat.

STELLA

No, it belongs to next door. They're not there. It's
nervous.

HARRISON

It's a dirty night. Animals don't care for this sort of
thing.

They sit.

STELLA

How did you know where to find me?

HARRISON

Oh, I heard you'd moved ...

Pause.

STELLA

What have you been doing?

HARRISON

Well, I've been out of the country most of the time.

STELLA

You didn't lose your job then?

HARRISON

What, over that affair, you mean? No, no, no, no. I
didn't lose my job.

Gunfire. The room shakes.

*She stands, moves round the room, looking for the cat. His eyes
follow her. She finds the cat, picks it up. She strokes it, her hand
trembling.*

STELLA

It's so long since we had anything like this. I can't get
used to it.

HARRISON

You shouldn't be up here – with all this heavy stuff. You
should be in a shelter. You should be down in a shelter.

Stella shrugs.

STELLA

Oh . . .

HARRISON

You're not sorry I came, anyway? Bit of company?

STELLA

I wish you'd come before. A long time ago. There was a
time I had so much to say to you. I went on talking to you
– in my mind. So I clearly didn't think you were dead.
Because you don't talk to the dead, you just listen to what
they said, over and over again, and try to piece it together.
(*Silence.*)
I missed you. Your dropping out left me with absolutely
nothing. Why did you do it?

240

HARRISON

I was switched. That was the long and the short of it. I was switched.

STELLA

But when? What happened? After all, you killed Robert.

HARRISON

Now, how do you make that out?

STELLA

Oh, you killed him.
(*Silence.*)
Why did you send me away that night? That night in the café?

Pause.

HARRISON

It wasn't going to work out.

Bombs. Flares in the sky. The room shakes.

STELLA

But if you hadn't gone away – if you hadn't disappeared – who knows?
(*Pause.*)
But now we can say goodbye, can't we? We're not what we were. We're no longer two of three. We're apart.

HARRISON

Goodbye?

STELLA

Yes, we had to meet again to say goodbye. Don't you understand ... Harrison?

HARRISON

That's the first time you've ever called me anything.

STELLA

I don't know your Christian name.

HARRISON

You wouldn't care for it.

STELLA

Why? What is it?

HARRISON

Robert.

Pause.

STELLA

Listen. I think it's over. Don't you? I think the raid's over.

Harrison listens, looks at her.

HARRISON

I'll stay till the All Clear.

They sit in silence.

After a time the All Clear sounds.

They do not move.

The Comfort of Strangers

The Comfort of Strangers was made in 1990. The cast included:

ROBERT Christopher Walken
COLIN Rupert Everett
MARY Natasha Richardson
CAROLINE Helen Mirren

Director of Photography Dante Spinotti, AIC
Production Designer Gianni Quaranta
Editor Bill Pankow
Music Angelo Badalamenti
Wardrobe Giorgio Armani
Costume Designer Mariolina Bono
Producer Angelo Rizzoli
Director Paul Schrader

INT. ROBERT'S APARTMENT. VENICE. EVENING.

A long gallery. At the end of the gallery sliding glass doors give on to a terrace. Light from chandeliers is reflected in the glass.

Dark oil paintings. Dark mahogany cabinets, carved and polished, cushioned in velvet. Two grandfather clocks in a recess, ticking.

Stuffed birds and glass domes, vases, brass and cut-glass objects. A large polished dining-table.

The camera pans to a man's hand carefully setting a needle on to a record. The record starts. It is Gigli, singing an aria. The camera pans away, across a Nikon camera with a zoom lens and strips of developed film on a shelf.

The camera moves towards the glass doors. A painting: a landscape with leafless trees towering over a dark lake; on the shores shadowy figures dancing. A sideboard, a brass knob on every drawer in the shape of a woman's head.

On the top of the sideboard a tray of silver-backed men's hair and clothes brushes, a decorated china shaving bowl, several cut-throat razors arranged in a fan, a row of pipes in an ebony rack, a riding crop, a fly-swat, a gold tinder-box, a watch on a chain, a pair of opera glasses. Sporting prints on the wall.

The night sky through the glass doors. On the terrace an impression of flowering plants, creepers, trees in tubs, statuary.

Gigli's voice fades down.

ROBERT
(*VO*)

My father was a very big man. All his life he wore a
black moustache. When it turned grey he used a little
brush to keep it black, such as ladies use for their eyes.
Mascara.

Pause.

Everyone was afraid of him. My mother, my four sisters.
At the dining-table you could not speak unless spoken
to first by my father.

Pause.

But he loved me. I was his favourite.

*Caroline comes through a door into the gallery. She limps. She
opens the glass doors and goes out on to the terrace. The camera
reaches the glass doors and goes through on to the terrace, losing
her. Sounds of concertinas and singing from below.*

EXT. LAGOON. VENICE. DAY.

A vaporetto passing.

EXT. WATERFRONT. DAY.

Boats jiggling up and down in the wash of the vaporetto.

EXT. HOTEL ROOM: BALCONY. DAY.

*Colin standing on the balcony. He is leaning with one hand on the
balcony wall, looking out on to the lagoon.*

Mary's voice from inside the room.

MARY
(*VO*)
Yes, I want to call England –

A VIEWFINDER.

Colin's figure framed in the viewfinder.

BALCONY.

*Colin's arm and back leaning against wall. Lagoon in
background.*

                    MARY
                    (*VO*)
    No, no, not London – it's not London.

CLOSE SHOT.

Vaporetto.

A zoom lens moving.

EXT. HOTEL ROOM: BALCONY. DAY.

Colin standing. Sound of a zoom lens.

Colin turns, sits, picks up a loosely bound typescript, reads.

*The camera looks past him, through the open windows, to see
Mary holding the telephone.*

                    MARY
    It's in Sussex. Hastings in Sussex . . . You know the
    code, you got it for me yesterday . . . well, someone did
    . . . yes – 458261 . . . Hastings, Sussex . . .
                    (*She puts the phone down.*)
    God!

                    COLIN
    I can't read this damn book! Honestly. It's unreadable.
                    (*Pages slip from his fingers on to the floor.*)
    They can't even bind the bloody thing properly.
                    (*He slams the rest of the typescript on to the table.*)
    Why don't we go out?

MARY

I'm trying to get through to the children! Can't you hear?

The phone rings. Mary picks it up.

Hello? Yes? Mother! Hello! Yes – lovely – Yes, absolutely – How are they? – Yes, lovely – are they? – Darling – it's Mummy – How are you?

Colin closes his eyes.

INT. CARPACCIO SCUOLA DI SAN GIORGIO.

Dark interior. Carpaccio paintings. Silence. Colin and Mary stand looking at a painting (Visione de sant'Agostino).

The camera moves through an arch to see them in long shot. Sound of a scraping shoe on stone. The camera retreats.

COLIN AND MARY WITH PAINTING.

Scrape of shoe.

Colin looks over his shoulder.

There is no one else in the chapel.

MARY

Incredible, isn't it?

EXT. SCUOLA. CANAL. DAY.

They emerge into the light and walk.

MARY

I think the St Augustine is incredible, particularly, it's so . . . I don't know . . .

COLIN

Yes, you thought that last time.

MARY

What do you mean?

COLIN

Well, you said it was incredible last time – the last time
we were in Venice.

MARY

Did I?

COLIN

Yes.

MARY

Well, so what?

COLIN

Nothing. I'm just –

MARY

I mean what's the *point*? What's the point of saying that?
Why did you say that?

COLIN
(*laughing*)
I didn't mean it as an insult!

MARY

Christ.

COLIN

I'm simply making an observation –

MARY

What observation?

COLIN

I'm simply pointing out that you haven't changed your
mind. You feel the same now as you did then.

FROZEN LONG SHOT. COLIN AND MARY BY SIDE OF CANAL.

EXT. CANAL. DAY.

He takes her hand.

> COLIN
>
> Anyway I agree with you. I think it's incredible too.

INT. HOTEL BATHROOM. DAY.

Colin in the bathroom shaving. He cuts himself.

> COLIN
>
> Shit!

Mary looks in.

> MARY
>
> What is it?

He dabs himself.

> COLIN
>
> Look. I think it was a pimple.

> MARY
>
> Tch. Tch. The girls won't love you any more.

> COLIN
>
> I think I need to eat more salt or something.

> MARY
>
> You don't need salt, you need sex.

> COLIN
>
> Can I have it with salt?

> MARY
>
> Why not?

The phone rings.

> COLIN
>
> Oh, God! Don't they know I'm trying to shave?

She picks up the phone.

MARY

Yes? Oh, hold on.

(*Calls.*)

It's Simon.

Colin sighs, goes into the room. Mary comes into the bathroom and begins to brush her hair.

Colin into phone.

COLIN

Yes? . . . Oh, come on, give me a break – I'm only halfway through the damn thing – it's unreadable anyway – this is supposed to be my holiday – all right, all right, I'll finish it – when's the deadline?

INT. HOTEL BEDROOM. NIGHT.

Colin and Mary in bed. She is asleep. His eyes are open. He looks at her, gets out of the bed, gets into the other bed and lies still.

EXT. VENICE WATERFRONT. DAY.

Colin and Mary at a stall, looking at T-shirts. Colin selects two.

COLIN

OK. This for Cathy. And this for Jack.

MARY

Lovely.

COLIN

What do you think?

MARY

They'll be thrilled.

Colin pays for the T-shirts.

COLIN

Now I'm going to do a little drawing of Cathy for Cathy
. . . and a little drawing of Jack for Jack.

He does two pencil drawings on the two bags.

What do you think?

MARY

Fantastic. You're a genius.

*They walk away through tourists and pigeons. She stops, focuses
her camera, takes a snap of Colin.*

Smile.

*He smiles. She takes another snap. Two women stop and look at
Colin. Mary turns to them, offering camera.*

Would you take one of us?

WOMAN
(*Swedish*)

Of course. Very much so.

Mary takes Colin's arm. They stand.

*The click of another camera off-screen. A man in a white suit
passes.*

The Woman takes the photograph.

EXT. ROBERT'S TERRACE. NIGHT.

Moonlight. The shrubs. Statuary.

*Camera moves to find the back of Caroline's head. A man's hand
in a white-coated sleeve comes into the shot. It begins to massage
her neck.*

ROBERT
(*VO*)

My youngest sisters, Alice and Lisa, came to me in the

garden and said, 'Robert, Robert, come to the kitchen quickly. Eva and Maria have a treat for you.'

EXT. VENICE SQUARE. NIGHT

The camera moves into the square. Colin and Mary voices over:

> MARY
>
> Cathy's been selected for the football team, did I tell you?

> COLIN
>
> What football team?

> MARY
>
> The school football team! What else?

> COLIN
>
> Oh.

> MARY
>
> Do you think it's dangerous – I mean to play with all those boys? I mean – she's a girl.

> COLIN
>
> I know she is.

> MARY
>
> I think it's dangerous

The camera finds Colin and Mary at a table with wine. Men at another table look at them with interest, exchanging remarks in low voices. It is not clear whether they are focusing on Mary or Colin.

> Tell me something. Tell me the truth. Do you like children?

> COLIN
>
> What children?

MARY

My children.

COLIN

Yes. I like your children.

MARY

No. What I meant was, do you actually like children?

COLIN

You mean all children?

MARY

Children. Do you actually like children?

COLIN

You mean as such – you mean the species – as such?

MARY

What I mean is – the real truth is – you don't like children.

COLIN

You mean you think I don't like *your* children?

MARY

What about me? Do you like me?

COLIN

I like you. Do you know why?

MARY

No. Why?

COLIN

I like you because you're always asking me such challenging questions. You're always testing my intellect.

She makes a lazy motion of slapping his face. He catches her hand and kisses it.

EXT. SECOND CAFE. S. GIACOMO DELL'ORIO. LATER.

Colin and Mary at a table with wine.

MARY

Did I ever tell you the terrible thing that happened to
me when I was a little girl, the worst thing that ever
happened to me?

COLIN

You never told me.

MARY

Well, I was about seven – or eight – and I was part of a
gang of kids – boys and girls – and we were this gang
. . .

COLIN

Uh-huh?

MARY

And one day some of them said, 'One member of this
gang isn't really good enough to be a member of this
gang and does everyone agree that we should throw that
person out?' And I said, 'Yes! Yes!' I clapped –

COLIN

You clapped?

MARY

Yes. I clapped. And I said, 'Yes – throw this person
out!' And you know who that person was?

Colin stares at her.

COLIN

You.

MARY

Yes.

He stares at her.

COLIN

God. That's a terrible story.

INT. HOTEL LOBBY. NIGHT.

The Night Porter lets Colin and Mary in. They sway slightly.

COLIN

What do you say – up at dawn – Get into a speedboat.
Where shall we go?
                    (*To Porter.*)
Where can we go?

PORTER

Murano. They blow beautiful glass. Very nice.

MARY

Murano. Lovely.

COLIN
                    (*to Night Porter*)
What time's dawn?

PORTER

Dawn, signore?

COLIN

Daybreak! A speedboat at daybreak to go to Murano!

INT. ROBERT'S APARTMENT. KITCHEN. NIGHT.

*Caroline in the kitchen making tea. She fills the kettle with water
and puts it on the stove and takes the lid off a jar of lime leaves.*

There are two cups on a tray.

*In the background, through the open kitchen door, a man in a
white suit is sitting at a table.*

Over this Robert's voice:

> ROBERT
> (*VO*)

And on the table were two big bottles of lemonade, a cream cake, two packets of cooking chocolate and a big bunch of marshmallows. And Maria said, 'Look, darling, this is all for you.'

INT. MURANO. GLASS-BLOWING FACTORY.

Glass being blown fiercely.

INT. MURANO. GLASS-BLOWING FACTORY.

Glass exhibition in cabinets.

Colin and Mary perusing the objects. Colin turns suddenly. He sees through glass the distorted figure of a man in a white suit.

> MARY

Look at this, this is beautiful.

Colin turns to her, looks back through the glass. The figure has disappeared. He joins Mary.

> COLIN

What?

EXT. LAGOON. DAY.

Colin and Mary in a speedboat, going fast. They are hanging on to the rails. The speedboat approaches the Grand Canal.

Sound fades.

> ROBERT
> (*VO*)

And Maria said, 'Look, darling, this is all for you.'

INT. HOTEL BEDROOM. NIGHT.

Colin and Mary lying on their beds. He turns and looks at her.

COLIN

Are you asleep?

No response.

Colin gets off his bed, goes to her bed, stands looking down at her. She does not move. He goes to the window, opens the shutters.

Cobalt light over the lagoon. He looks out. Gondolas jogging up and down.

He goes to the bed and shakes her.

Mary. It's late. Mary.

She wakes up.

MARY

What is it?

COLIN

We haven't had any dinner.

MARY

What's the time?

COLIN

Late.

INT. HOTEL LOBBY. NIGHT.

Colin and Mary with Concierge.

CONCIERGE

No, no. Padovani will be closed.

COLIN

What about –

CONCIERGE

No, no. Is quite late. Too late. All closed. But I know a very good bar. Late-night bar. Nice sandwich, good drinks. Very nice place. Very easy to find.

COLIN

Fine. Can I take the map?

CONCIERGE

Is my only one. Sorry.

MARY

Let me look.

She peers at the map. The Concierge points to a section of it.

CONCIERGE

Here. You see? Very nice. You go straight out of here.
>   (*He makes a swivelling movement.*)
And then you . . . is right ahead.
>   (*He points to map.*)
Right there.

MARY

Uh-huh . . .

EXT. ACCADEMIA BRIDGE. A KIOSK. NIGHT.

*The kiosk is closed. Colin and Mary walk towards it. Colin peers
into it.*

COLIN

Plenty of maps in there. Christ, you'd think a bloody
hotel porter would have more than one map!

EXT. A SQUARE. NIGHT.

*A man stacking chairs outside a café. The square is empty. A dog
barking.*

EXT. A STREET. NIGHT.

*Shop with television sets. Brightly lit window. On some of the TV
sets Italian housewives are stripping silently.*

They come to an alley.

COLIN

Down here.

MARY

How do you know?

They turn into the alley.

THE ALLEY.

They walk down the alley towards another street.

COLIN

What do you think?

A STREET.

A large furniture store. In the window an enormous bed. Two dummies lie on it on their backs, their arms up. One wears pyjamas, another a nightie. They are both smiling.

MARY

She reminds me of someone.

COLIN

Look at that headboard.

The headboard spans the width of the bed. Embedded in the upholstery are a telephone, a digital clock, light switches and dimmers, a cassette recorder and radio, a small refrigerated drinks cabinet.

It's like a Boeing 747. Listen – what do you think?
Where are we? Is this right?

MARY

Yes. Definitely.

They walk on.

A wall filled with posters. Announcements, graffiti, etc. Mainly feminist.

Look at all this.

He peers.

COLIN

Gruppa Femminista di Venezia.

MARY

You know, women are really radical here. They're really aggressive. It's great.

COLIN

I wish we had a map.

MARY

They want convicted rapists castrated.

COLIN

You see that monument? I think we passed it about ten minutes ago.

MARY

Quite right too.

COLIN

What is?

MARY

To castrate rapists.

She walks on towards a long, dark, narrow alley.

COLIN

Where are you going?

MARY

This way.

He catches her up. They come to a water fountain. Mary presses it. Water comes out.

It works.

She drinks.

Tastes of fish.

They walk into the dark alley.

COLIN

I'm starving.

In the distance, in the dim light, a figure appears walking towards them, silently. It disappears into the shadows. Colin and Mary continue walking down the alley, their footsteps echoing.

MARY

I think we're on the right track.

A MAN'S VOICE

So do I.

Robert steps out of the dark into a pool of street light and stands blocking their path. He is thick-set, muscular. He wears a tight-fitting black shirt, unbuttoned almost to his waist. On a chain round his neck hangs a gold imitation razor blade. He carries a camera over his shoulder. He laughs shortly.

ROBERT

Good evening to you. You need help?

MARY

Well, we're looking for a place where we can get something to eat.

COLIN

Come on, Mary.

ROBERT

It's very late. There's absolutely nothing in that direction. But I can show you a very good place that way.

He grins and nods in the direction they have come from.

COLIN

Look. We know there's a place down this way.

ROBERT

No, no. Closed. Everything is closed. My name is
Robert. Trust me. I'll show you this place. You must
both be terribly hungry. Come. It excites me to meet
English people. I'm always eager to practise my English.
I once spoke it perfectly. Such a beautiful language.

*Mary is examining posters on a wall. They join her and follow her
gaze. She is looking at a crude stencil in red paint – a clenched fist
within the female organ. Robert gestures to the wall.*

All these – are women who cannot find a man. They
want to destroy everything that is good between men
and women. They are very ugly. Now – would you like
to eat some beautiful Venetian food?

MARY

I would absolutely love to.

Colin and Mary look at each other.

COLIN

All right. Let's go.

VARIOUS SQUARES AND ALLEYS.

*The trio walking, Robert leading the way. A man putting up
shutters outside a shop calls to Robert. Robert laughs and waves.
Two men standing in a dark doorway mutter something to Robert
as they pass. Robert cackles. They finally reach a brightly lit
doorway. A notice says BAR.*

INT. BAR.

*Robert parts the strips of a plastic curtain for Mary. They all come
down a steep flight of stairs into the bar, which is cramped and
crowded. There are no women present. A few dozen young men,*

dressed mainly in black, sit on high stools at the bar or stand around listening to a song on the jukebox. The majority are smoking or craning a neck forward and pouting to have a cigarette lit or putting out a cigarette with swift jabs. The song on the jukebox is powerful and sentimental and comes to a triumphant climax. The men seem to be moved.

Colin and Mary sit at a table. Robert comes from the bar carrying a bottle of wine, three glasses and some breadsticks in a jar. He sits.

ROBERT

There is no food. I'm sorry. The cook is sick. It's a tragedy. I could kill him. I'm very sorry. But this is a wonderful wine. Full of nourishment.

He pours wine. They bite into the breadsticks.

Cheers.

COLIN AND MARY

Cheers.

ROBERT

Now tell me – I am a man of immense curiosity – passionate curiosity. Are you married, you two?

COLIN

No.

ROBERT

But you live together? You live together in sin?

MARY

No.

ROBERT

Why not? In this day and age, no one would stop you. In this day and age, as you well know, there are no standards.

COLIN

What about you? Why don't you tell us about you?

He pours wine into his glass.

Who are you anyway?

Robert stares at Mary.

ROBERT
(*to Mary*)

But you have a child? Am I right?

MARY

How did you know?

ROBERT

I feel it.
(*He touches his heart.*)

Here.

MARY

I have two children.

She takes photographs from her handbag.

A boy and a girl.

Robert examines the photographs.

ROBERT

This is your boy and your girl?

MARY

Yes.

ROBERT

Beautiful. Beautiful.
(*To Colin.*)

Not yours?

COLIN

Not mine.

ROBERT

Beautiful children. They take after their beautiful
mother.

Mary giggles.

MARY

Thanks.

They all drink. She looks around the room.

I like this place.

ROBERT

I am truly pleased.

MARY

Your English is terribly good.

ROBERT

I grew up in London. My wife is Canadian.

COLIN

Any more breadsticks?

Robert turns to the bar. He calls in Italian.

ROBERT

More wine! More breadsticks!

MARY

Your wife is Canadian?

ROBERT

Oh, certainly.

MARY

How did you meet her?

ROBERT

Ah, that would be impossible to explain without
describing my mother and sisters. And that would only
make sense if I first described my father.

266

He pours from the second bottle. A song ends. Low conversations begin around the room.

Robert stares into his glass. He suddenly looks old, lined. He murmurs:

> In order to explain how I met my wife I would have to describe my father.

He looks at them both intently.

> Do you want me to do that? Would you really like me to do that?

They look at him.

> Shall I do that? What do you say?

COLIN
Why not?

Robert stares at Colin and then speaks.

ROBERT
My father was a very big man. All his life he wore a black moustache. When it turned grey he used a little brush to keep it black, such as ladies use for their eyes. Mascara.

During Robert's speech, various images are seen from Colin's or Mary's P.O.V.

a) Men combing their hair at the bar.

b) A woman, brought in by a man, sits alone at a table, ignored.

c) Men's bodies pass close by their table on their way to the urinal.

d) A man holding a chapstick at his lips.

e) A woman enters with a man, looks about, goes out, followed by the man.

f) Glasses piling up on the bar, cigarettes piling up in ashtrays.

g) Rubbish being thrown into plastic bags and dragged out.

h) The bar emptying. Distant voices of men in the street.

Robert's voice never stops. He chain-smokes throughout.

> Everybody was afraid of him. My mother, my four
> sisters. At the dining-table you could not speak unless
> spoken to first by my father.
> But he loved me. I was his favourite.
> He was a diplomat all his life. We spent years in
> London. Knightsbridge.
> Every morning he got out of bed at six o'clock and went
> to the bathroom to shave. No one was allowed out of
> bed until he had finished.
> My eldest sisters were fourteen and fifteen. I was ten.
> One weekend the house was empty for the whole
> afternoon.
> My sisters whispered together. Their names were Eva
> and Maria. Then they called me and they led me into
> my parents' bedroom. They told me to sit on the bed
> and be quiet. They went to my mother's dressing-table.
> They painted their fingernails, they put creams and
> powder on their faces, they used lipstick, they pulled
> hairs from their eyebrows and brushed mascara on their
> lashes.
> They took off their white socks and put on my mother's
> silk stockings and panties. They sauntered about the
> room, looking over their shoulders into mirrors. They
> were beautiful women. They laughed and kissed each
> other. They stroked each other. They giggled with each
> other. I was enchanted. They fed my enchantment.
> It was a beautiful day. The sun began to set. They
> washed themselves, they put everything away, in its
> place, leaving no clue. They whispered to me that it was
> our secret, that we would keep it in our hearts for ever
> and never reveal it.

Mary puts her hand out to find Colin's hand. He does not take it. Her hand remains on his knee.

But that night at dinner I felt my father staring at me, staring deep into me. He chewed, swallowed. He put his knife and fork down, he looked at me. My heart started to beat, to thump, to beat, to thump. My father said, 'Tell me, Robert, what have you been doing this afternoon?' He knew. I knew he knew. He was God. He was testing me. And so I told him. I told him all that my sisters had done. I told him everything. My mother was silent. My sisters' faces were white. No one spoke. My father said, 'Thank you, Robert', and finished his dinner.
After dinner my sisters and I were called to my father's study. They were beaten with a leather belt, without mercy. I watched this.

Colin takes Mary's hand.

A month later they took their revenge. We children were again alone in the house. My youngest sisters, Alice and Lisa, came to me in the garden and said, 'Robert, Robert, come to the kitchen quickly. Eva and Maria have a treat for you.' I was suspicious but I went. I was so innocent. On the kitchen table were two big bottles of lemonade, a cream cake, two packets of cooking chocolate and a big box of marshmallows. And Maria said, 'Look, darling, this is all for you.' 'Why?' I asked. 'We want you to be kinder to us in future,' she said. 'When you have eaten all this you will remember how nice we are to you – and then you will be nice to us.' This seemed reasonable. 'But first,' Eva said, 'you must drink some medicine. This is very rich food and this medicine will protect your stomach and help you to enjoy it.' I was too greedy to question this. I drank the medicine – only slightly disgusting – and then I ate the

chocolate and the cake and the marshmallows and
drank a bottle of lemonade. And they applauded and
said that only a *man* could drink a second bottle of
lemonade, it would be beyond my capabilities, and I
said, 'Give it to me,' and I drank the second bottle and I
finished the chocolates and the marshmallows and the
cake and they said, 'Bravo, bravo!' And then the kitchen
began to spin round me and I badly needed to go to the
lavatory and then suddenly Eva and Maria held me
down and tied my hands together with a long piece of
rope behind my back and Alice and Lisa were jumping
up and down singing, 'Bravo, Robert!' And Eva and
Maria dragged me across the corridor and hallway and
into my father's study. They took the key from the
inside, slammed the door and locked it. 'Bye, bye,
Robert,' they called through the keyhole. 'Now you are
big Papa in his study.'

I was locked in my revered, my feared father's study,
where he received the diplomatic corps of London, the
élite of the world. And I puked and pissed and shat all
over my father's carpets and walls.

Mary clutches Colin's hand.

My father found me there. He said, 'Robert, have you
been eating chocolate?' Then he nearly killed me. And
then he didn't speak to me for six months.

I have never forgiven my sisters.

My only solace was my mother. I grew so thirsty . . . at
night. She brought me a glass of water every night and
laid her hand upon my brow. She was so tender. When
my father was away I slept in her bed. She was so warm,
so tender.

But one afternoon the wife of the Canadian Ambassador
was invited to tea. She brought her daughter, Caroline.
When my mother showed her mother our garden – we
were left alone, the children. Suddenly Eva said, 'Miss

Caroline, do you sleep with your mother?' Caroline
said, 'No. Do you?' And Eva said, '*He* does.' And all my
sisters giggled and Caroline looked at me and smiled
and said, 'I think that's really awfully sweet.'

He smiles.

And she became my wife. Not at that moment of
course. We were both only eleven years old at the time.

He roars with laughter.

EXT. SOTTOPORTICO DELLA MALAVASIA. NIGHT.

Colin and Mary wandering up a dark alley.

COLIN
Where are we? Do you know?

MARY
God, I must sit down. I've got such a –
            (*She clutches her head.*)
Oh, I've got such a headache.

COLIN
What can I –

MARY
Press the back of my neck. That's right. Just there.

COLIN
There.

MARY
Yes.

COLIN
Is that . . .?

They stand, Colin massaging her neck.

MARY

I don't feel –

She lurches away, goes to the gutter, is sick.

Colin stands.

She comes back.

I'm all right. Let's sit over there. I can't walk any more.

They sit on the steps of a dark house.

Hold me. –

He does.

What a terrible man.

(*She yawns.*)

Who was he?

She closes her eyes.

He holds her.

EXT. SOTTOPORTICO. JUST BEFORE DAWN.

Colin and Mary sitting.

She is leaning on him. He is leaning against the wall. They are asleep.

A cellophane wrapper blows.

A dog passes by.

Mary murmurs.

MARY

We're on our holiday.

EXT. SOTTOPORTICO. DAYLIGHT.

The two figures asleep against the wall. Children's voices, laughter. A high-pitched bell.

They open their eyes.

Small children in bright-blue smocks approaching. Colin stands, holds his head. The children converge about him.

A little girl tosses a tennis ball against his stomach and catches it on the bounce. Squeals of glee. The children pass on.

EXT. CAMPIELLO DE PIOVANO. MORNING.

The street empty. Mary is scratching her ankle.

> MARY
>
> I've been bitten.

Colin bends, looks, lifts her up.

> COLIN
>
> Try not to scratch.

> MARY
>
> I'm so thirsty.

She leans on his shoulder.

> You're going to have to look after *me* today.

> COLIN
>
> Did you look after me yesterday?

He kisses her ear, holds her.

> MARY
>
> I'm so thirsty.

> COLIN
>
> I can see the waterfront. There'll be a café.

They begin to walk towards the waterfront.

EXT. ST MARK'S SQUARE. MORNING.

It is breakfast time. Hundreds of tourists are sitting at the café tables eating.

Colin and Mary stand in the shade of an arch and look across the square. Every table seems to be taken.

They wander into the square and finally see an elderly couple at the edge of a café writhing in their seats waving a bill. They stand by the table. A waiter comes. The couple pay the bill and stand. Colin and Mary sit down. The waiter clears the table. Colin begins to speak. The waiter goes without taking an order.

Colin stands, goes to a group of waiters standing in the shade.

COLIN

We're over there. We'd like something to drink.

WAITER

Yes, yes. I will tell your waiter.

Colin walks back to the table and sits. At another table sits a family. A baby stands on the table supported by its father, swaying among the ashtrays and empty cups. It wears a white sunhat, a green and white striped matelot vest, bulging pants frilled with white lace and pink ribbon, yellow ankle socks and scarlet leather shoes. A dummy is in its mouth, its eyes are wild. It is doing a mad dance.

Colin waves to a waiter, who passes by with a tray of empty bottles.

Mary speaks through thick, dry lips.

MARY

I wonder how the children are.

COLIN

You spoke to them – when was it?

MARY

Was it yesterday?

COLIN

How were they then?

274

He waves to another waiter.

MARY

It's like a prison here.

An orchestra starts to play, very close.

Let's go home.

COLIN

Our flight is paid for and it doesn't leave for five days.

MARY

We could get a train.

COLIN

Why do you want to go home?

Colin waves to a Waiter. The Waiter comes towards him.

I can't believe it! He's coming!

MARY

We should have brought the children with us. It would have made all the difference. To me anyway.

WAITER

Signore?

COLIN

A jug of water – with ice –

WAITER

Water?

COLIN

And coffee –

WAITER

Croissants? Eggs?

COLIN

No, no. Just a jug of water.

The Waiter turns and goes. They sit, slumped.

MARY

Let's go to the hotel. Get water there.

COLIN

All right.

MARY

Oh, he's probably bringing the coffee anyway.

They sit.

I don't know why we came here. Why did we come?
We've been here before. Why did we come again?

He is silent.

Actually, I remember why we came. We thought we'd
find out what to do. Didn't we? What to do about you
and me. Well . . . have you found out?

He is silent.

I haven't. I just want to go home. To my own bed. And
my kids.

Pause.

Or maybe you have. Maybe you've decided what you
want – what you want to do.

Pause.

Have you?

COLIN

No.

*They suddenly tense. In their eye-line is a man in a white suit, his
back to them. A camera in his hand. He turns and walks in their
direction.*

We should have gone to the hotel.

276

Robert walks along the edge of the tables.

He's missed us.

Robert turns, looks in their direction, opens his arms wide in delight. He comes to the table.

ROBERT

My friends!

He shakes Colin's hand, kisses Mary's hand. He sits.

And how are you both this morning?

MARY

Terrible. We slept in the street.

ROBERT

The street?

MARY

After we left you. We were just too tired to . . .

COLIN

We didn't have a map –

ROBERT

I am horrified. It is entirely my fault. I kept you late with wine, my stupid stories –

COLIN
(to Mary)

Stop scratching.
(*To Robert.*)
No, no, it's not a question –

ROBERT

It is my fault and it is my responsibility to correct it. You must come to my house –

COLIN

No – we have a hotel –

277

ROBERT

My house is a thousand times more comfortable,
peaceful, serene –

Mary stands.

COLIN

Wait a minute.

Robert stands.

ROBERT

We'll take a taxi.

*Robert takes Mary's arm and walks with her across the square.
Colin follows.*

EXT. ST MARK'S WATERFRONT. DAY.

*They walk through the crowds on to the waterfront. Robert hails a
taxi. They climb in.*

EXT. WATERFRONT BELOW ROBERT'S APARTMENT. DAY.

*The taxi arriving. Robert helps Mary out. Colin jumps off. They
walk towards the house.*

INT. ROBERT'S APARTMENT. BEDROOM. DAY.

*The shutters half open. Light. Colin and Mary lie on two beds,
naked, asleep.*

The click of a camera.

A soft sigh is heard, off-screen.

A door closes quietly.

INT. ROBERT'S APARTMENT. BEDROOM. LATE AFTERNOON.

*Through the half-open shutters, the setting sun. Orange bars
against the wall. They fade, blur, brighten, fade.*

Mary's eyes open. She watches this. Colin remains asleep.

Dry leaves rustle in the warm draught.

She stands, pours water from a jug, sips.

She looks down at Colin, gazes at his body.

She goes to the window, opens shutters. Footsteps, sound of television, rattle of cutlery, dogs, voices. She closes the shutters, lies on the marble floor, starts to perform yoga exercises.

Colin suddenly wakes, sits up, looks at her on the floor.

COLIN

Where are we?

MARY

Robert . . . brought us here.

COLIN

Robert. Where is he?

MARY

I don't know.

He stands.

COLIN

What's the time?

MARY

Evening.

COLIN

Did you sleep?

MARY

Oh, yes. Wonderful.

COLIN

What about your bite?

279

MARY

It's gone.

He looks around the room.

COLIN

Where are your clothes?

She looks at him.

Have you seen them? Where are they?

He walks to the bathroom, looks in, comes out.

They're not in there.

He opens a wardrobe. Looks in.

Nor in here.

MARY

No.

COLIN

Well, don't you think we ought to find them?

MARY

I feel good.

COLIN

I must find out what's going on. But I can't walk about stark bloody naked.

MARY

Look. There's a dressing-gown on the back of that door.

COLIN

Oh, right.

He takes the gown and goes into the bathroom.

She lies still.

The toilet flushes.

(VO)

I can't wear this!

He comes out of the bathroom wearing the gown. She stares at him.

MARY

Oh yes you can. You look lovely. You look like a god. I think I'll have to take you to bed.

She goes to him, feels his body beneath the gown.

COLIN

This isn't a dressing-gown. It's a nightie.

He points to an embroidered cluster of flowers.

MARY

You've no idea how good you feel in it.

He begins to take it off.

COLIN

I can't walk around in a stranger's house dressed like this.

MARY

Not with an erection.

He gives the nightdress to her.

COLIN

Put it on. Find out what he's done with our clothes.

She slips it on, looks at herself in the mirror.

MARY

How do I look?

INT. ROBERT'S APARTMENT. GALLERY. EVENING.

Mary walking along the long gallery in the nightdress.

She looks through the glass door on to the terrace and sees a small pale face watching her from the shadows, disembodied, oval. It moves and disappears.

The reflected room shakes as the glass doors open. A woman comes in.

> CAROLINE

Hello. I'm Caroline. Robert's wife.

> MARY

Hello.

They shake hands.

> CAROLINE

Come outside. It's nice.

EXT. TERRACE. EVENING.

Stars. The lagoon.

Caroline lowers herself into a canvas chair. A little gasp of pain. She looks up at the sky.

> CAROLINE

It is beautiful. I spend as much time as possible out here.

> MARY

I'm Mary . . . Kenway.

> CAROLINE

Yes, I know.

Mary sits. She fingers the sleeve of the nightdress.

> MARY

Is this yours?

> CAROLINE

Yes. I made it. I sometimes sit out here doing embroidery. I like embroidery.

MARY

It's lovely.

Mary looks at a plate of biscuits on a small table.

CAROLINE

Would you like a biscuit? Take one.

MARY

Thanks.

CAROLINE

Are you hungry? You must be. Robert wants you to stay
to dinner. He'll be back for dinner. He's gone to his bar.
A new manager starts there tonight.

MARY

His bar?

CAROLINE

You were there last night . . . weren't you?

MARY

He didn't say it was *his* bar.

CAROLINE

It's a kind of hobby, I guess. But you know more about
it than I do. I've never been there.

She stands, moves awkwardly to the edge of the terrace.

MARY

Have you done something to your back?

CAROLINE

It helps to move. Sometimes I just stand up . . . and
move about . . .

She stands looking over the edge of the terrace.

Are you fond of your friend?

MARY

Colin?

CAROLINE

I hope you don't mind. There's something I must tell
you. While you were asleep I came in and looked at you
both. I sat on the chest for about half an hour. I just sat
there and looked at you . . . both.

MARY

Oh . . .

CAROLINE

Colin is very beautiful, isn't he? Robert said he was. You
are too, of course. You both have such wonderful skin.
Are you in love?

MARY

Well, I . . . I do love him, I suppose – but not quite like
when we first met . . . But I trust him, really. He's my
closest friend. But . . . what do you mean by 'in love'?

CAROLINE

I mean that you'd do absolutely anything for the other
person . . . and you'd let them do absolutely anything to
you.

MARY

Anything's a big word.

CAROLINE

If you're in love with somebody, you'd be prepared –

*The glass doors open. Colin comes out to the terrace, a towel
around his waist.*

MARY

This is Colin. This is Caroline, Robert's wife.

CAROLINE

Hello. Are you having a nice time?

COLIN

Uuhh . . .

CAROLINE

On your holiday?

COLIN

Oh . . . yes . . . except we keep getting lost.

CAROLINE

Pull up a chair.

Colin draws a canvas chair nearer to them and sits, carefully adjusting his towel.

Oh my God! Your clothes!
> (*She laughs.*)

I forgot! I washed and dried them. I clean forgot. I must tell you where they are.
> (*She turns to Mary.*)

But before I do I think you should tell him what I told you . . . don't you?

MARY

What?

CAROLINE

What I did while you were both asleep.

MARY

Oh.
> (*To Colin*)

Caroline came in and looked at us while we were asleep.

COLIN

Oh . . . did she?

CAROLINE
> (*to Colin*)

You were so peaceful. Like a baby.

MARY

Babies can be very ratty in their sleep.

CAROLINE

But not him. I'm sure he always sleeps sweetly.

COLIN

But I'm not a baby.

Caroline laughs.

CAROLINE

I didn't say you were. I just said you slept like a baby.
Now listen, Robert is very keen for you to stop and have
dinner with us. He told me not to let you have your
clothes until you agreed.
> (*She giggles.*)

You must be starving anyway.

COLIN

I am.

CAROLINE

So you will?

MARY

Well . . .

Caroline grasps her arm.

CAROLINE

Please! If you don't he'll blame me.

COLIN

Let's stay.

CAROLINE

Oh good!

COLIN

And now can I have my clothes?

Caroline giggles.

286

CAROLINE

They're locked in your bathroom cupboard. Here's the key.

He takes it, holding his towel to him.

COLIN

I'll just . . .

He goes into the gallery. Caroline looks after him. She turns to Mary.

CAROLINE

Isn't it sweet, when men are shy? It's so sweet.

She smiles at Mary.

Tell me what you do. Do you work?

MARY

Well, I mainly do voice-overs these days, you know . . . commercials. I *was* with a women's group until about six months ago –

CAROLINE

What do you mean? What do you mean by a women's group?

MARY

A theatre group.

CAROLINE

You're an actress! What a beautiful thing that must be.

Mary laughs.

MARY

Well, sometimes . . . Anyway, the group broke up –

CAROLINE

Women? All women?

MARY

Well, some of us wanted to bring in men – from time to time. The others wanted to keep it pure. That's what broke us up.

CAROLINE

But how can you do a play with only women? I mean what could *happen*?

MARY

Happen?
(*She laughs.*)
Well, you could have a play about two women who've only just met sitting on a balcony talking.

CAROLINE

But they'd probably be waiting for a man. And then he'd come. And then something would happen.

Caroline giggles. She clasps her back.

It hurts when I laugh.

MARY

Can I do . . .

CAROLINE

Yes. Touch me there. My neck.

Mary does so.

Press it. A little harder.

Mary does so and then stops.

Thank you.

MARY
(*uneasily*)

We did an all-woman *Hamlet* once.

CAROLINE

Hamlet? I've never read it. I haven't seen a play since I was at school. Isn't it the one with the ghost?

Lights go on in the gallery behind them. Footsteps.

And someone locked up in a convent?

Footsteps stop, start. A chair scrapes. Sound of glass. Robert comes out on to the terrace.

ROBERT

Hello!

Caroline limps across the terrace into the apartment. Robert does not look at her. He crosses to Mary, smiling. He is wearing black.

Have you slept well?

MARY

Wonderfully. Thank you so much. What a beautiful apartment.

ROBERT

It belonged to my grandfather.

He takes Mary's elbow and leads her to the edge of the terrace. He points across the lagoon.

You see that island? That is Cemetery Island. My grandfather and my father are both buried there. You're staying for dinner, I trust?

MARY

I'll get dressed.

He leads her into the apartment.

INT. THE GALLERY.

ROBERT

A glass of champagne first!

A bottle and four glasses are set on the table.

Robert opens the bottle. Colin comes into the gallery, dressed and shampooed. His shirt and jeans have been cleaned and ironed. They cling to his body. Robert stares at him as he walks slowly towards them

You look like an angel.
> (*Calls*)

Caroline!
> (*To Colin*)

How are you feeling?

COLIN
Better.

Robert pours the champagne. Caroline appears. She takes her place at Robert's side facing the guests. They lift their glasses.

CAROLINE
To Colin and Mary.

They drink. Mary laughs shortly. She drinks. Caroline turns and goes into the kitchen.

MARY
I'll dress.

She goes. Colin drinks. Robert fills his glass. He takes Colin's elbow and steers him gently down the gallery to a carved mahogany bookcase.

ROBERT
You see these books? They are the favourite literature of my father and my grandfather. All first editions.

He steers Colin to a sideboard. On top of the sideboard, hairbrushes, clothes brushes, pipes, razors, etc., a pair of opera glasses.

These are things my father used every day. Small things.

They look at them in silence.

COLIN
He used opera glasses every day?

Robert stares at him.

ROBERT
No. He used opera glasses at the opera. They belonged
to my grandfather.

They move to the champagne. Robert empties the bottle.

COLIN
Your father is very important to you.

ROBERT
My father and his father understood themselves clearly.
They were men and they were proud of their sex.
Women understood them too. Now women treat men
like children, because they can't take them seriously.
But men like my father and my grandfather women took
very seriously. There was no uncertainty, no confusion.

COLIN
So this is a museum dedicated to the good old days.

*Colin bends to put his glass down. As he straightens Robert hits
him in the stomach with his fist, a relaxed, easy blow which sends
Colin jack-knifing to the floor. He lies on the floor writhing,
fighting for air. Robert takes the empty glasses to the tray. He
comes back, helps Colin to his feet, makes him bend at the waist
and straighten several times. Colin breaks away, walks about the
room, taking deep breaths, dabbing his eyes.*

*Robert lights a cigarette and walks to the kitchen door. He turns
and looks back. Colin glares blearily at him.*

Robert winks.

INT. APARTMENT. NIGHT.

The dinner table. Robert in a pale-cream suit. Mary in her clean dress. Caroline in another dress. They are eating steak and drinking red wine. Colin sits slightly removed from the others, eating slowly.

> ROBERT
>
> So how is England? Lovely dear old England? Hampshire! Wiltshire! Cumberland! Yorkshire! Harrods! Such a beautiful country. Such beautiful traditions.

> MARY
>
> It's not quite so beautiful now. Is it, Colin?

Colin does not respond.

> Colin? Are you feeling all right?

> COLIN
> (*quietly*)
>
> Sure.

> ROBERT
>
> In what way? In what way not beautiful?

> MARY
>
> Oh, I don't know – freedom . . . you know . . .

> ROBERT
>
> Freedom? What kind of freedom? Freedom to do what?

> MARY
>
> Freedom to be free!

> ROBERT
>
> You want to be free?
> (*He laughs.*)
> Free to do what?

MARY

You don't believe in it?

ROBERT

Sure I believe in it. But sometimes a few rules – you know – they're not a bad thing. First and foremost society has to be protected from perverts. Everybody knows that. My philosophical position is simple – put them all up against a wall and shoot them. What society needs to do is purify itself. The English government is going in the right direction. In Italy we could learn a lot of lessons from the English government.

COLIN

Well, I'm an Englishman and I disagree violently with what you've just said. I think it's shit!

ROBERT

I respect you as an Englishman, but not if you're a communist poof. You're not a poof, are you? That's the right word, no? Or is it 'fruit'? Talking about fruit – it's time for coffee.

They all stand.

COLIN

We must go.

CAROLINE

But coffee –

COLIN

No. We must go. Now.

MARY

Yes, it's been a long day.

Mary suddenly sees a bookcase upon which a number of photographs stand. She walks to it and peers. Robert joins her.

ROBERT

I'm a keen amateur photographer.

Mary focuses on a large photograph, which is grainy and indistinct. It is taken from some distance and seems to have been enlarged many times. It is of a man standing on a balcony of a hotel, leaning with one hand on the wall.

She picks it up and looks at it. Robert looks at her looking at it for a few seconds and then takes it from her.

Caroline whispers to Colin.

CAROLINE

Please come back. Please. It's important. I can't get out.

COLIN

Come on, Mary.

She turns from the bookcase.

MARY

Well, thank you both so much for your hospitality – and for such a lovely dinner.

ROBERT

It has meant a great deal to us.

EXT. STREET. NIGHT.

Colin and Mary walking hand in hand.

INT. HOTEL ROOM. BALCONY. NIGHT.

Colin and Mary sitting in the moonlight.

COLIN

You know – when I came on to the balcony tonight and saw you in that nightdress – I thought you looked so beautiful, my heart . . . jumped.

                              MARY
      But I told you how *you* looked in that nightdress, didn't
      I?

They sit in silence. After a while, they stand and go into the room.

A heavy green curtain is drawn across the window.

Moon on the balcony. A moan from within the room.

EXT. HOTEL ROOM. BALCONY WINDOW. DAY

Shutters closed.

Sun striking the shutters.

A long sigh from within the room.

                              COLIN
                              (*VO*)
      Jesus!

INT. HOTEL BEDROOM. DAY/NIGHT.

The room is suffused with green light, neither night nor day.

A knock on the door.

A maid peeps in.

                              MAID
      Permesso?

                              COLIN
                              (*VO*)
      Please!

                              MAID
      We must clean the room.

                              COLIN
                              (*VO*)
      We're on our bloody holiday, for Christ's sake!

The maid withdraws.

> MARY
> (*VO, whispering*)
>
> Come here, come here.

INT. HOTEL BEDROOM. DAY/NIGHT.

The mattress has been taken from one of the beds, propped against the door.

Clothes and glasses on the floor.

Colin and Mary lie partially clothed half on, half off the bent mattress.

> COLIN
>
> What's it like? I often wonder what it's like.

> MARY
>
> What's what like?

> COLIN
>
> To be a girl. How does it feel? What does it feel like?

Mary looks at him and smiles.

> MARY
>
> Like this.

She places her tongue in his ear and moves it about.

INT. HOTEL CORRIDOR. DAY/NIGHT.

Food stacked on trolley outside the room, half eaten.

INT. HOTEL BEDROOM. NIGHT.

Colin and Mary asleep, lying across each other on the bed. Green glow.

MARY
(*VO, softly*)

I'm crazy about you.

Their eyes suddenly open. They turn, twist, look at each other.
They kiss.

COLIN

I'm crazy about you.

INT. HOTEL CORRIDOR. DAY/NIGHT.

Sheets and towels stacked alongside the trolley.

INT. HOTEL BEDROOM. DAY/NIGHT.

Mary, naked, looking through the green curtains on to the lagoon.

Colin seen dimly in background in the room. He lies on the bed.

COLIN

Close the shutters.

She closes them.

Come here.

She goes to him.

EXT. LA COLOMBA RESTAURANT. NIGHT.

Colin and Mary eating pasta.

COLIN

Listen. Why the hell did they do that to you? Those
kids. Why did they hound you out of the gang? I can't
understand it.

MARY

They didn't like me.

COLIN

They were just jealous of you. That's what it was. They were jealous of your beauty.

He takes her hand. She giggles.

I am myself. You know that, don't you? I'm jealous of your beauty. I mean it belongs to me. Jealous in that sense. No one else can touch your beauty. It's all mine.

MARY

Is it?

COLIN

All mine.

He nuzzles her hand.

Well-dressed Venetians are at another table. One woman, sumptuous, vivid, bejewelled, eyes Colin and Mary, murmurs to the others.

The others look across, smile. The woman speaks in a low voice. Another woman laughs.

MARY

You know what they're doing?

COLIN

No, what?

MARY

They're talking about us.

COLIN

About you.

MARY

No. You.

COLIN

Or perhaps us?

They laugh.

    Hey, listen, this actually reminds me – I wanted to ask
you –

MARY

What?

COLIN

Well, you know all this thing about thighs and bottoms?

MARY

What thing?

COLIN

Well – you know – people look at other people's thighs
and bottoms and they say, 'Christ, what thighs, what
bottoms – or what an arse – or an ass, what an *ass* – or
tits of course – what . . . tits . . . or what boobs . . . or
what a can,' if you see what I mean. I mean – what I
mean is – I mean my first point is – that only the word
thighs is constant. Get me? You've got all these other
words for all the other words. But there's no other word
for thighs. Isn't it amazing?

MARY

You don't need another word. Thighs is a perfectly
good word. What's your question?

COLIN

I'm really very glad that you've asked me what my
question is. It's this. When people look at you and . . .
you know . . . talk about your thighs or your bottom or
both, etc. . . . well, are you sensing them in the same
way that they're sensing them? I mean, to what extent
are you sensing their sense of you – or when I say you –
I mean your thighs and your bottom – in other words –
listen – to put it in a nutshell – when people talk about
your thighs and bottom – what sense of your thighs and
your bottom do you, at such a time, have?

MARY

People are not talking about my thighs and bottom.

COLIN

How can you – how can you *know* that?

MARY

Because the whole damn restaurant is talking about your thighs and bottom.

COLIN

Mine? I don't believe it.

He looks round at the other tables.

Really?

The woman at the other table catches his eye. Colin turns back to Mary.

Incredible.

They giggle.

INT. HOTEL BEDROOM. NIGHT.

Mary at dressing-table putting cream on her face.

Colin stretched out in an armchair reading a newspaper.

MARY
(*casually*)

Oh, I forgot to tell you . . .

COLIN
(*vaguely*)

What?

MARY

I had rather a good idea . . .

COLIN

Uh-huh?

MARY

Mmnn. I'm going to hire a surgeon – a very handsome
surgeon – to cut off your arms and your legs –

COLIN

Oh yes?

MARY

Yes. And then you'll be quite helpless, you see. I'll keep
you in a room in my house . . . and use you just for sex,
whenever I feel like it.

COLIN

Uh-huh . . .

MARY

That's right. And sometimes I'll lend you to my
girlfriends . . . and they can do what they like with
you . . .

COLIN

Oh, right.

*Mary stands, slips into bed, picks up a book, starts to read. Colin
continues to read the newspaper. Silence.*

It's funny you should say that . . . because I've sort of
come to a decision . . . and I haven't told you yet . . .

MARY

A decision?

COLIN

Yes, I've come to this decision . . .

MARY
(*turning a page*)

What is it?

COLIN

Well, it's this – I'm going to invent a machine . . . you

see . . . made of steel. It's powered by electricity. It has
pistons and controls –

MARY

Oh, really?

COLIN

That's right. It has straps and dials. It makes a low hum
. . . like this . . .

He hums.

MARY

Like that?

COLIN

Yes. And you'll be strapped in . . . you see . . . quite
securely . . . tight . . . and the machine will fuck you –
not just for hours and weeks but for years and years and
years. For ever.

MARY

For ever?

COLIN

That's right.

He walks over to the bed, sits on it.

What do you think?

INT. HOTEL BEDROOM. DAWN.

Colin and Mary are asleep.

*Mary suddenly gasps and shouts out and sits up. She clasps her
knees, trembling.*

Colin wakes. He holds her. She recoils from his touch.

COLIN

You're having a nightmare.

He touches her again. She wrenches free, gets out of bed.

A door opens. Footsteps in the corridor.

She stands still. Colin gets out of bed.

Mary?

She looks at the bed, walks to the window. Goes out. He follows.

EXT. HOTEL BALCONY. DAWN.

COLIN

What was it? You've had a terrible dream. What –

She puts her finger to her lips.

She indicates to Colin that he stand in a precise position on the balcony. She turns him to face out to the lagoon, lifts his hand so that it rests on the balcony wall. She studies him.

MARY

You're beautiful.

COLIN

Are you awake?

She stumbles into his arms, kissing him wildly.

MARY

I'm so frightened.

She begins to shake violently.

COLIN

What is it? What is it?

MARY

Touch me.

He pulls her back inside the room.

INT. HOTEL BEDROOM. DAWN.

He sits her down on the bed and holds her shoulders hard.

> COLIN
>
> Are you awake? Mary?

She gradually becomes still.

> You had a nightmare. Do you remember it?

She lies back on the bed. He lies by her, takes her hand. He yawns.

> Can you tell me?

> MARY
>
> That photograph on Robert's bookcase was of you.

> COLIN
>
> What photograph?

> MARY
>
> I looked at a photograph in Robert's apartment. It was on his bookcase. It was of you.

> COLIN
>
> Of me?

> MARY
>
> It must have been taken from out there – along the waterfront – or from a boat . . . You were standing on this balcony.

> COLIN
>
> I didn't see any photograph –

> MARY
>
> No, you didn't see it.

They lie still.

> Don't fall asleep. Keep awake.

COLIN

I'm awake.

Mary whimpers.

MARY

You're in his photograph.

Silence.

Colin?

He is still, breathing quietly.

She suddenly leans over him and looks down at him.

She kisses him.

EXT. LIDO BEACH. DAY.

Large crowds on the beach.

Solitary men and women, bodies oiled.

Transistors.

Babies.

Babble of children playing.

Colin and Mary walking through this, looking for a place to rest.

They settle finally near two teenage girls. A small knot of young men close by are turning cartwheels, etc.

Colin and Mary sit.

MARY

Turn on your front.

He lies on his stomach. She sits astride him, rubs oil on his back.

The young men start to throw a ball hard at each other. The ball hits one of the girls. She cries out. All the young men immediately drop to their haunches and introduce themselves to the girls.

COLIN
(*murmuring*)
Something happened at Robert's flat. I didn't tell you.

MARY
I can't hear you. What?

COLIN
Something happened at Robert's flat. I didn't tell you.
When you had gone to change – to dress – remember?
He was talking to me . . . about his father and so on and
then he suddenly hit me in the stomach – very hard. He
. . . totally winded me.

MARY
He hit you?

COLIN
Yes.

MARY
But why?

Pause.

You didn't say anything – why didn't you say anything?

COLIN
I don't know. I don't know why he hit me. And I don't
know why I didn't say anything. And I don't know why
he took a photograph of me on the hotel balcony either.

She rolls off his back and lies still. She stands.

MARY
I'm going to swim.

She walks towards the water.

EXT. LIDO BEACH. AFTERNOON.

*Colin and Mary walking along the beach. A beach vendor
approaches.*

COLIN

I want to buy you something.

She smiles.

MARY

Why?

COLIN

Choose something.

MARY

No, you. You choose.

He looks at a selection of scarves, selects one.

COLIN

This.

MARY

Lovely.

COLIN

Try it.

She puts it round her neck.

MARY

OK?

COLIN

Lovely.

The sun goes behind a cloud.

INT. ROBERT'S APARTMENT. DAY

The glass doors on to the balcony. Silence.

The sun comes out.

The Gigli record begins.

EXT. LIDO BEACH. AFTERNOON.

Colin and Mary walking along the water's edge. The beach is emptying. The sun is low over the water. She stops and looks out to sea. He touches her arm.

> COLIN
>
> Listen. I've been thinking –

She looks at him.

> Why don't we do it?

> MARY
>
> Do what?

> COLIN
>
> Get together. Live together . . . you know . . . with the children . . .

She stands, looking at him.

> I mean it. I love you.

She looks at him.

> I love you.

She smiles.

> I mean it.

> MARY
>
> Yes, but . . . we don't have to . . . commit ourselves to all that . . . just now. I mean . . . it's such a lovely day.

> COLIN
>
> Don't you want to? I thought you wanted to.

MARY

I've just had such a wonderful swim, that's all. It was so
beautiful – I can't describe it. I could have gone on for
ever. I can't get back to . . . things like this . . . just like
that.

Colin laughs.

COLIN

Things like this?

MARY

I was so happy swimming.

Pause.

COLIN

I thought you wanted it.

MARY

Oh, we'll see. Shall we?

INT. ROBERT'S APARTMENT. DAY.

*The gallery. Gigli singing. Robert's hand picks up an object from
the windowsill. He draws the blinds.*

Sun glinting through the chinks.

MARY
(*VO*)

It goes round the other side of the island first.

EXT. QUAYSIDE. LIDO. VAPORETTO OFFICE.

*The vaporetto is approaching. Colin and Mary are studying the
schedule in the ticket office.*

MARY

It goes round the other side of the island first. Then it
cuts through by the harbour round to our side.

INT. ROBERT'S APARTMENT. BEDROOM.

Hands folding a white suit on a bed. An empty suitcase.

Gigli.

EXT. VAPORETTO/GIARDINI. DAY.

Colin and Mary sitting on adjacent benches, not speaking.

The vaporetto slows to its landing by the hospital. Groups of old people waiting. The boat stops, the old people get on. The boat moves off.

In background, Gigli singing, faintly.

INT. ROBERT'S APARTMENT.

Hands wrapping a riding crop, a fly swat, a watch on a chain, a pair of opera glasses.

> COLIN
> (*VO*)
> We could get off at the next stop and walk through if you like . . .

EXT. VAPORETTO MOVING.

Mary turns to him.

> MARY
> What?

> COLIN
> We could get off at the next stop and walk through if you like. It's probably quicker than going right round the harbour.

> MARY
> Possibly . . . yes.

The vaporetto approaches the landing.

She kisses him lightly on the lips.

The vaporetto stops, the barrier is lifted. Colin and Mary stand quickly, walk off the boat on to the landing stage.

The pilot calls sharply to the crew, who lift the rope clear.

From inside the boat sudden laughter.

Gigli singing faintly.

EXT. QUAYSIDE. DAY.

Rope being drawn back on to the ferry. The ferry draws away from the quayside.

Colin and Mary walk in silence along the quayside. Gigli is singing faintly.

They look up.

On a balcony hung with flowers, a small figure in white waving.

Soft throb of the departing vaporetto.

Caroline's distant voice calling.

Mary stops.

> MARY
> Do you want to go up there?

> COLIN
> Well, she's seen us. We can't be rude.

They hail a gondola. They do not hold hands or look at each other.

INT. APARTMENT HOUSE. STAIRWELL.

Colin and Mary come into the stairwell. She hesitates. He goes up a few steps, turns, looks down at her. He leans against the wall – as in the photograph. She stares at him. Robert appears looking down from a top landing.

ROBERT

Hello!

COLIN

Hello.

They walk up. Caroline is standing in the doorway of the apartment. Robert descends.

ROBERT

How delightful. How delightful to see you.

He claps Colin on the back. Kisses Mary's cheek.

MARY

The boat brought us round this side from the beach, so we thought we'd say hello.

ROBERT

We were expecting you sooner.

They reach the door. Caroline offers her cheek to Colin and to Mary.

CAROLINE

How lovely.

ROBERT

You got my message?

COLIN

No. What?

ROBERT

I left a message at your hotel today. We're going away, you see. We didn't want to miss you.

COLIN

No, we didn't get it.

ROBERT

But you came anyway! How wonderful.

MARY

Going away?

CAROLINE

To Canada. To see my family. So we wanted to say
goodbye, to have a farewell drink – so it's wonderful you
came. It really is.

ROBERT
(*to Caroline*)
Look, take Mary and give her some refreshment.
(*To Colin*)
I have to go to my bar. I have business to finish. Very
quick. Will you come with me?

Caroline draws Mary in through the door.

CAROLINE

Have you been swimming?

COLIN
(*to Mary*)
I'll just –

ROBERT

Walk with me. Keep me company.
(*To Mary*)
We won't be long.

MARY

Colin –

Robert closes the door.

INT. APARTMENT.

*Mary looks about her. The apartment is transformed. Furniture,
pictures, rugs, etc., have all gone. There is a makeshift table
sitting on three boxes. A number of suitcases stand by the door.
Her sandals echo loudly.*

MARY

Are you moving?

CAROLINE

We're selling up. We *are* taking a holiday but when we come back we'll buy a ground-floor apartment. That's what I need. Would you like some herb tea?

EXT. STREET. DAY.

Robert and Colin walking. Robert waves to some men outside a bar, looks at Colin.

INT. APARTMENT. KITCHEN.

Caroline reaches for the kettle. She winces.

MARY

Can I do anything?

CAROLINE

It's been like this a long time now.

She puts the kettle on the gas stove, turns on the gas.

EXT. VENICE SQUARE.

Robert stops at a café. He is holding Colin's elbow. He speaks to some men. They laugh.

A hand pinches Colin's buttock. He turns. Robert pulls him on. Laughter follows him.

COLIN

Someone just pinched me.

ROBERT

Venetians are very friendly people.

INT. APARTMENT. KITCHEN.

Caroline pouring tea into two cups. She stirs.

> **CAROLINE**
> Robert said he told you about his childhood. He
> exaggerates a lot, you know. He turns his past into
> stories to tell at the bar.

> **MARY**
> No sugar for me.

> **CAROLINE**
> Just stirring in the lemon to make it taste. Shall we take
> it on to the terrace?

They move to the door.

> **MARY**
> What happened to your back?

INT. ROBERT'S BAR.

Robert behind the bar examining documents with the manager.

*Colin sitting with a mineral water at a table. Robert glances at
him.*

One customer and then another glance at Colin.

Colin prises open pistachio nuts, sips his drink, tilts the chair back.

The bar very quiet. Robert murmuring to the manager.

Colin goes to the jukebox, looks at the lights, puts a coin in.

EXT. TERRACE. EARLY EVENING.

Caroline and Mary sitting sipping tea.

> **CAROLINE**
> I've never told anyone this. Never.
> But I want to tell you.

Soon after we were married Robert started to hurt me
when we made love. Not a lot, enough to make me cry
out. I tried to stop him but he went on doing it. After a
time I found I liked it. Not the pain itself – but
somehow – the fact of being helpless before it, of being
reduced to nothing by it – and also being punished,
therefore being guilty. I felt it was right that I should be
punished. And I thrilled to it.
It took us over totally. It grew and grew. It seemed
never-ending.
But there was an end to it. We both knew what it was.
We knew what it had to be. We knew it. We wanted it.

INT. BAR.

Music from the jukebox bursts out.

Robert comes and sits with Colin with his documents.

ROBERT
Did you understand what I was telling people as we
walked here?

COLIN
No.

ROBERT
I was telling them you are my lover. And that Caroline
is jealous because she likes you too.

The music stops.

COLIN
Why? Why were you telling them that?

Robert laughs and mimics Colin.

ROBERT
Why? Why?

He touches Colin's hand.

We knew you would come back.

COLIN

Why did you take the photo of me – the one you showed
Mary?

ROBERT

Aah. She's very quick. I thought I hadn't given her
enough time . . . to recognize it.

COLIN

What was the point?

*A man turns the jukebox on. Robert winks at Colin and indicates
the manager at the bar.*

ROBERT

I'm selling the bar – to him.

He smiles.

EXT. TERRACE.

Caroline and Mary sitting.

CAROLINE

My back happened – suddenly – one night. It was very
bad indeed. Then there was an incompetent surgeon
. . . you know. So I'm like this. I've never told anyone
the truth – except you.

She takes Mary's hand.

He's terribly strong, you see. When he pulled my head
backwards I blacked out with the pain – but I remember
thinking: It's going to happen now. I can't go back on it
now. It's going to happen – now. This is it. This is the
end.

Mary yawns.

I'm boring you.

MARY

No, not at all. It's the long swim, I think, the sun . . .

CAROLINE

Do you and Colin do . . . strange things?

MARY

Oh, no. I don't think so.

CAROLINE

I'm sure Colin does. I'm certain he does.

She stands.

There's something I want to show you.

Mary stands, sways, nearly falls.

MARY

Oops.

Caroline holds her.

Bit dizzy.

CAROLINE

I must show you something.

EXT. FONDAMENTA NOVA. EVENING.

Robert and Colin walking.

ROBERT

You see that barber shop? My grandfather and my father used that barber shop. And I use that barber shop.

Robert waves to a waiter standing outside a café.

COLIN

I want to know why you took that photo? What does it mean?

ROBERT

That waiter was once a fisherman. But pollution has
ruined the fish. So fishermen become waiters.
(*Points.*)
That is Cemetery Island.

Colin stops.

Robert walks on.

*Colin turns, looks out to the Cemetery Island and then down a
long side street, light at the end.*

Robert stops, half turns, stands still, waiting.

INT. APARTMENT. BEDROOM.

The bedroom is in semi-darkness. Caroline and Mary enter.

CAROLINE

You haven't been in our bedroom, have you?

Mary sits heavily on the end of the bed.

MARY

My legs ache.

Caroline turns on a lamp.

*Mary suddenly sees the wall. She stares at a wide baize-covered
board, upon which are dozens of photographs of Colin.*

Caroline sits with her.

CAROLINE

God, he's so beautiful. Robert saw you both by chance,
the day you first arrived.

*She points to a photograph of Colin standing by a suitcase, street
map in hand, talking.*

Caroline holds Mary.

That was the first picture I saw of him. I'll never forget it. Robert came back so excited. Then every day he brought more and more photographs home. We became so close, incredibly close. Colin brought us together. It was my idea to put him here on the wall – so that we could see him – all the time, as we fucked.

Mary rubs her legs. Caroline points to a photograph of Colin naked, prone on a bed.

I took that one myself. Isn't it brilliant?

Mary tries to speak.

MARY

Why?
> (*She struggles with the word.*)

Why?

CAROLINE

Then Robert brought you home. It was as if God was in on our dream. I knew that fantasy was passing into reality. Have you ever experienced that? It's like stepping into a mirror.

Mary attempts to say the word 'Colin'.

Wake up, what's the matter with you? Robert and Colin are back. Do you know where we are now? Shall I tell you?

She takes Mary's head in her hands and whispers into her ear.

We're on the other side of the mirror.

INT. APARTMENT. GALLERY. EVENING.

Robert opening champagne. Colin standing with glasses.

Caroline and Mary come in. Mary is stumbling, one hand on Caroline's shoulder.

COLIN

Mary, what is it?

The cork pops.

ROBERT

Glasses.

Colin holds out the glasses. Robert pours.

Caroline seats Mary. Colin goes to her.

COLIN

Mary, what is it? What's the matter?

ROBERT

Cheers.

CAROLINE

It's a mild touch of sunstroke. That's all.

Colin takes Mary's hand.

COLIN

She's not hot.
                    (*To Mary*)
What is it? Is it sunstroke?

Mary tries to speak.

Tell me. Try to tell me.

She manages a strangled hard 'C'.

Are you saying my name?

She pants. She holds his hand tightly. She manages to say:

MARY

G . . . G . . . Go . . .

ROBERT

Cold. She's cold.

> CAROLINE

We shouldn't crowd her.

> COLIN

She needs a doctor.

He moves away.

Where's your telephone?

> CAROLINE

It's been disconnected.

> COLIN

Disconnected?

> CAROLINE

We're going away.

> COLIN

Well, you must know a doctor! Go and fetch a doctor! She's very ill.

Robert and Caroline link hands and walk towards him.

> ROBERT

No need to shout.

> CAROLINE

She'll be fine.

Colin retreats, knocks the champagne bottle over. It falls and spills.

> ROBERT

What a waste.

Colin's back is against the glass door.

Robert puts an arm against the window, boxing Colin in.

Caroline strokes his cheek.

CAROLINE

Mary understands. You understand too, don't you? You understand. You do understand. Don't you?

She pulls his shirt out from his jeans and strokes his stomach.

From outside voices and sounds drift up; gondoliers.

Colin springs forward, banging Caroline's face with his forearm. He runs towards Mary.

Robert moves quickly, bends, grasps Colin's ankle, tips him on to the floor. He picks him up by an arm and a leg, drags him to the wall, stands him up and slams him against the wall, holding him with one hand at his throat.

Silence.

You've cut my lip.

She collects the blood from her lip and daubs Colin's mouth with it.

COLIN

What have you done to Mary? Look. I'll do anything you want – but get a doctor for her. Do you hear? I'll do what you want. What do you want?

ROBERT

Want? I'll show you what we want.

Caroline kisses Colin. He wrenches away and spits in her face.

CAROLINE

Silly boy.

She starts to undo Colin's jeans. She caresses him. Robert is still holding him by the throat. With his other hand he takes a razor from his pocket and flicks it open.

ROBERT

I'll show you.

MARY'S P.O.V.

An unfocused mating dance with three figures.

Sudden flash of razor blade.

Blood.

Robert and Caroline kissing.

COLIN AGAINST THE WALL.

Colin begins to slide slowly down the wall to the floor. His eyes are glazed. His body twitches.

> COLIN
> (*emptily*)

Mary?

MARY STARING.

Over her face, excited incoherent whispers, gasps, moans, whimpers, giggles.

These sounds fade away to silence.

The screen darkens. Mary's eyes in nightlight. Sound of distant dogs.

Slowly the light grows and changes on Mary's face. It becomes morning. Growing sounds of distant radios and motorboats.

Sunlight.

APARTMENT. MORNING.

Mary sitting still in her chair.

Colin's body slumped by the wall, shrunken.

An open razor. A large bloodstain on the floor.

The luggage by the door has gone.

MARY STARING.

A POLICEMAN'S VOICE-OVER.

> POLICEMAN
> (*VO*)
> What did you want from these people?

Pause.

> I ask you again. What did you want from these people?

INT. POLICE STATION. DAY.

Mary sitting with two Policemen. Mary speaks vacantly, without emotion.

> MARY
> Nothing. They were friends.

> POLICEMAN
> Friends?

> MARY
> We had dinner there.

> POLICEMAN
> Why did you go back with your boyfriend to these people?

Pause.

> What did you want from them?

She stares at him.

> Did your boyfriend like the woman?

> MARY
> I liked her . . . I don't think he . . .

> POLICEMAN
> Did your boyfriend like the man?

MARY

No. No, he didn't.

POLICEMAN

And you? You liked the man? Did you like the man?

She stares at him.

MARY

No.

POLICEMAN

So why did you go to dinner? And why did you go back?
For more dinner?

She stares at him.

SECOND POLICEMAN

Why did you come to Venice? What were you looking
for?

MARY

Nothing. We . . .

SECOND POLICEMAN

Were you looking for some fun?

MARY

We were going to get married.

Silence.

The First Policeman stamps a document and gives it to her.

INT. POLICE STATION. MORTUARY.

Colin's body on a bench. A Policeman and Mary.

POLICEMAN

Is this the body of Colin Mayhew?

MARY

Yes.

POLICEMAN

Sign here.

She signs a document.

MARY

They've combed his hair the wrong way.

POLICEMAN

Sorry?

MARY

It doesn't go that way.

She starts to comb Colin's hair with her fingers.

It goes this way.

INT. POLICE STATION. CORRIDOR.

Mary and Policeman walking down the corridor.

They pass doors with circular windows looking into the rooms.

In one room Caroline is sitting quite still, looking out of a window.

In the next room Robert is sitting at a table with two detectives.

Mary walks on.

The camera stops at the window of Robert's room and slowly goes in.

INT. INTERVIEW ROOM.

The Detectivs and Robert.

DETECTIVE

We don't get it. You plan everything in advance – you prepare everything – you sell your bar – you sell the apartment – you buy the drug – and so on and so on – but then on the other hand you leave your razor with your own fingerprints – you book tickets under your

own name and you travel on your own passport – we
don't get it.

ROBERT

Listen. I'll tell you what it is.
                    (*He smiles.*)
Let me tell you something.

He looks at them both.

My father was a very big man. All his life he wore a
black moustache. When it turned grey he used a little
brush to keep it black, such as ladies use for their eyes.
Mascara.

He sits, staring at the detectives.

The Trial

The Trial was made by BBC Films and Europanda Entertainment B.V. The cast included:

JOSEF K Kyle MacLachlan
THE PRIEST Anthony Hopkins
DR HULD Jason Robards
FRÄULEIN BÜRSTNER Juliet Stevenson
LENI Polly Walker
TITORELLI Alfred Molina
BLOCK Michael Kitchen
K'S UNCLE Robert Lang
WASHERWOMAN Catherine Neilson
FRANZ David Thewlis
WILLEM Tony Haygarth
INSPECTOR Douglas Hodge
EXAMINING MAGISTRATE Trevor Peacock
COURT USHER Patrick Godfrey
THE FLOGGER Don Henderson

Directed by David Jones
Producer Louis Marks
Screenplay Harold Pinter
Music Composed and Conducted by Carl Davis
Associate Producer Carolyn Montagu
Costume Designer Anushia Nieradzik
Film Editor John Stothart
Production Designer Don Taylor
Director of Photography Phil Meheux, BSC
Executive Producers Kobi Jaeger, Reniero Compostella,
Mark Shivas

Filmed on location and at Barrandov Film Studios, Prague, Czechoslovakia, March–May 1992.

Author's Note

This screenplay was shot in its entirety. During the editing of the film, however, a number of scenes were cut. These cuts were made with my approval.

HP

INT. JOSEF K'S BEDROOM. MORNING.

K is in bed, asleep. Low murmurs from another room. Men's voices. K's eyes open. He lies, listening. He looks up and out of the window.

WINDOW ACROSS THE STREET. K'S P.O.V. DAY.

An old woman, holding the curtain, looking across the street into his window.

INT. K'S BEDROOM. DAY.

K sits up and looks at the door into the other room. He picks up a bell and rings it. The voices stop abruptly.

The door opens. A man (Franz, the first warder) comes in.

> JOSEF K

Who are you?

> FRANZ

You rang?

> JOSEF K

I'm waiting for Anna to bring me my breakfast.

The man looks back into the other room and speaks to someone.

> FRANZ

He says he's waiting for Anna to bring him his breakfast.

A guffaw from within. The man turns back to K.

It's not possible.

K gets out of bed. He is wearing a nightshirt. He puts on a pair of trousers.

JOSEF K

I'm going to find out what Frau Grubach has to say
about this.

FRANZ

Listen. I think you'd better stay here.

K pushes past him and goes into the other room.

INT. K'S SITTING ROOM. DAY.

*A second man (Willem, the second warder) is sitting by the
window reading a book. He looks up.*

WILLEM

You should have stayed in your room. Didn't he tell
you?

JOSEF K

Who are you? What do you want?

He looks from one to the other. They study him in silence.

*Through the window K sees across the street the old lady at her
window, holding the curtain, looking into the room.*

Where's Frau Grubach?

He moves towards the door. Willem stands up.

WILLEM

You can't go out. You're under arrest.

JOSEF K

Am I? Why?

WILLEM

We're not authorized to tell you. Go to your room and
wait. Eh, wait a minute, let's have a look at this. That's a
very nice nightshirt you're wearing.
          (*To Franz*)
Isn't it?

FRANZ

It's beautiful.

WILLEM

Listen. We're going to take care of this nightshirt for you. You don't mind that, do you? We're going to look after all your underwear, in fact. But don't worry. If your case turns out all right, you'll get it all back.

FRANZ

You see, it's much better to give it to us than leave it in the depot. If you leave it in the depot it'll either be pinched or they'll sell it. In any case you'll never see it again. You'll never see your underwear again.

WILLEM

If you leave it in the depot.

JOSEF K

Excuse me.

He goes into his room.

INT. K'S BEDROOM. DAY.

K opens a drawer in his desk, looks through papers, finds his bicycle licence, which he puts aside, rummages until he finds his birth certificate. He goes back into the sitting room.

INT. K'S SITTING ROOM. DAY.

As K enters, Frau Grubach is at the door of the sitting room leading into the hall. She sees K, mutters 'Excuse me' and goes out. K looks across to the window. The two men are sitting by it eating his breakfast.

JOSEF K

That's my breakfast.

WILLEM

Bloody good.

JOSEF K

These are my identity papers. I want to see yours. And I want to see the warrant for my arrest.

WILLEM

Oh good Christ, why do you keep trying to provoke us? Let me tell you something. We're probably the closest friends you've got in the world at this moment.

FRANZ

It's a fact.

JOSEF K

Here are my identity papers.

Willem dips his bread and butter into a pot of honey.

WILLEM

What do we want with those? Do you think you'll get this trial of yours over quicker by arguing with your warders about identity papers and warrants? We're just warders, don't you understand? We can't make head or tail of a legal document. We've got nothing to do with your case, except to guard you for as long as we're told and get paid for it. But we do know one thing. We know that the authorities would never order an arrest like this without very good grounds indeed.
(*To Franz.*)
Right?

FRANZ

They don't make mistakes.

WILLEM

Oh no. They never go looking for crime, you see. They're just drawn to the guilty and then they send us

out to make the arrest – which is according to the Law.
This is the Law. So how could they make a mistake?

JOSEF K

I don't know this Law.

WILLEM

Well, that's so much the worse for you, isn't it?

FRANZ
(*to Willem*)
Did you hear that? He admits he doesn't know the Law
and at the same time he claims he's innocent.

WILLEM

You can't talk to some people.

K walks away from them to the window. He looks out.

WINDOW ACROSS THE STREET. DAY.

*The old woman is now standing with an even older man. She is
clinging to him. They are both staring into the window of the
sitting room.*

INT. K'S SITTING ROOM. DAY.

K turns back to the men.

JOSEF K

Take me to your Inspector.

WILLEM

When he tells us to, not before. Listen. Why don't you go
to your room and sit there quietly? You're going to need
all your strength, I can tell you that. But look, if you want
to give us a little money we're perfectly happy to bring
you some breakfast from the café down the street.

*K stands still. He looks at the men. He looks at the door leading
to the hall. He looks back at the men.*

337

He turns, goes back into his bedroom.

INT. K'S BEDROOM. DAY.

K takes off his nightshirt and quickly slips into a shirt. While doing this, he peers out of his window at the window across the street.

WINDOW ACROSS THE STREET. DAY.

There is no one at the window.

INT. K'S BEDROOM. DAY.

K tucks the shirt into his trousers. He picks up a green apple and bites into it. He puts the apple down carefully on the plate. He goes to a cupboard, takes out a bottle of brandy, pours a nip, drinks it, pours another, drinks it.

A shout from the next room.

WILLEM

The Inspector wants you!

JOSEF K
(*shouting back*)

At last!

He goes into the sitting room.

INT. K'S SITTING ROOM. DAY.

The two men stare at K, rush at him, push him back into his room.

INT. K'S BEDROOM. DAY.

WILLEM

What do you think you're doing? Going to appear before the Inspector in your shirt? He'd have you flogged and us as well!

338

JOSEF K

Leave me alone! Stop pushing me.

WILLEM

Put on a jacket! Come on!

JOSEF K

Ridiculous!

He takes a jacket out of his wardrobe.

FRANZ

Not that!

WILLEM

It has to be black.

JOSEF K

But it's not the official trial yet, is it?

WILLEM

It has to be black.

JOSEF K.

Well, in that case I'll put on a black tie too.

They watch K closely as he ties his black tie.

WILLEM
(*to Franz*)

Go and tell the Inspector he's getting dressed.

Franz goes out.

K puts on his jacket, combs his hair, regards himself in the mirror. He turns.

He and Willem go back into the sitting room.

INT. K'S SITTING ROOM. DAY.

Willem leads K through the sitting room into Fräulein Bürstner's room.

INT. FRÄULEIN BÜRSTNER'S ROOM. DAY.

Fräulein Bürstner's bedside table is in the middle of the room. The Inspector is using it as a desk. He sits with his legs crossed.

In a corner of the room three young men are standing looking at an arrangement of snapshots on a mat hung up on a wall. The two warders sit on a chest.

A white blouse is hanging on the catch of the open window.

Through the window, across the street, the old woman and the man are staring into the room. Behind them stands a tall man, his shirt open at the chest, squeezing a reddish pointed beard.

                    INSPECTOR
Josef K?

                    JOSEF K
Yes?

                    INSPECTOR
I suppose you're a bit surprised at what's happened this morning?

                    JOSEF K
I certainly am.

The Inspector casually rearranges objects on the bedside table.

I certainly am surprised, but not very surprised.

                    INSPECTOR
You're not very surprised?

                    JOSEF K
I mean – Can I sit down?

                    INSPECTOR
It's not usual.

                    JOSEF K
I mean of course I'm surprised. But after all, the world

is the world, one gets used to surprises, one doesn't take them too seriously, especially the kind of thing that's going on here today.

INSPECTOR

Oh? Why's that?

JOSEF K

I'm not going as far as to say that I look on the whole thing as a joke –

INSPECTOR

Quite right.

JOSEF K

But it's hardly to be taken seriously, is it? I mean I know I'm being charged – but with what and on what grounds and who is making the accusation? That is what I would like to know. This is a legally constituted state, the rule of law is fully established. Who are you? What is your authority? I demand clear answers to these questions.

The Inspector throws a matchbox on to the table.

INSPECTOR

You've really got it all wrong. We know nothing about your case. I don't even know whether you've been charged. You've just been arrested. That's all we know. But don't worry about us. Worry about yourself. Worry about what might happen to you. And don't talk so much.

K stares at him. He then walks up and down the room.

JOSEF K

I must phone a lawyer.

INSPECTOR

Phone who you like.

JOSEF K

I need a lawyer.

INSPECTOR

I don't see the point, quite frankly.

JOSEF K

You don't see the point of my calling a lawyer when I'm supposed to be under arrest? What the hell are you talking about?

INSPECTOR

No – all I meant was . . . I just don't see the point of calling a lawyer.

Pause.

JOSEF K

Well I won't then.

INSPECTOR

No no, do, if you feel like it. There's a phone in the hall. I saw it.

JOSEF K

No I won't. I don't want to.

K goes to the window. The three people are still at the window opposite.

K opens the window, shouts across the street.

Get away from that window!

The two old people hide behind the tall man.

(*To the Inspector.*)
Look. Why don't we bring this matter to a close? Why don't we shake hands all round and call it a day? I don't see –

342

(*standing*)

Can't do that. Can't call it a day, I'm afraid.

He walks towards K.

Can't bring it to a close . . . just yet. But on the other hand I'm not saying you should give up hope. You're only under arrest, that's all. Well, we're off. You can go to work. You can go to your bank.

JOSEF K

Go to the bank? How can I go to the bank if I'm under arrest?

INSPECTOR

There's nothing to stop you going to the bank.

JOSEF K

Then this arrest isn't serious, as I said?

INSPECTOR

That's not for me to say. It's just an arrest. It's not for me to say how serious it is. That's for others. You don't have to go to the bank, of course. Do what you like. But I did arrange for these three colleagues of yours to be at your disposal to make your arrival at the bank as inconspicuous as possible.

K studies the three young men for the first time. They bow in turn.

RABENSTEINER

Rabensteiner.

KULLICH

Kullich.

KAMINER

Kaminer.

JOSEF K

Good morning. I didn't recognize you. What are you all doing here?

Kaminer giggles.

EXT. GRUBACH'S HOUSE. DAY.

K and the three young men come out of the house. Kaminer runs to the corner to look for a taxi.

The tall man with the red beard comes out of the house opposite. He stops when he sees K and flattens himself against the wall. K glares at him.

Kaminer runs up with the taxi. They all get in.

INSIDE THE TAXI. DAY.

Rabensteiner looking out of the right window. Kullich looking out of the left. Kaminer sitting with a fixed grin.

K closes his eyes.

EXT. BANK. DAY.

The taxi draws to a halt outside a large bank. K and the others get out and go into the bank.

INT. BANK. STAIRS AND MAIN HALL. DAY.

Rabensteiner, Kullich and Kaminer follow K up the stairs and across the main mall. K stops, turns, glares at them. They stop still. K goes on towards the stairs at the rear of the hall.

He is greeted by various colleagues. He responds cheerfully.

INT. BANK. UPPER FLOOR. DAY.

As K reaches the landing, the Deputy Manager comes towards him, looking at his watch briefly. He greets K warmly, shakes his hand and puts his arm around K's shoulder.

> DEPUTY MANAGER
> Just the man. We've had a very encouraging letter from . . .

They walk away.

INT. BANK: K'S OFFICE. DAY.

K walking into his office. His Assistant at the filing cabinet.

> K'S ASSISTANT
> Happy birthday, sir.

> JOSEF K
> Thank you. Thank you very much.

K sits at his desk.

> K'S ASSISTANT
> There are some presents for you, sir, from the staff.

> JOSEF K
> Oh, really? How nice of them.

He looks at some wrapped packages on his desk, but does not open them. He opens a file and studies it.

INT. GRUBACH'S HOUSE. HER KITCHEN. NIGHT.

Frau Grubach with a cake.

> FRAU GRUBACH
> A little birthday cake. For my best and favourite lodger. I made it this afternoon.

> JOSEF K
> Very kind. But you shouldn't have done it. I've given you enough work today as it is.

FRAU GRUBACH

What work?

JOSEF K

I mean the men who were here this morning.

FRAU GRUBACH

They didn't give me any work.

She cuts the cake and offers him a piece.

There. Many happy returns of the day.

JOSEF K
(*taking cake*)

Well, it won't happen again.

FRAU GRUBACH

No, it can't happen again. Shall I join you? Shall I take a piece of cake?

JOSEF K

Yes of course, of course.

They both eat.

FRAU GRUBACH

You mustn't take it to heart. Admitted you're under arrest, but it's not as if you're a thief or anything like that, is it?

JOSEF K
(*smiling*)

I'm not a thief, no. No no, I quite agree with you. I don't think it matters in the least. I was just taken by surprise, that's all. It could never have happened to me in the bank, for example. I have my wits about me there. I'm absolutely on top of things. But this morning I was simply half asleep. Still, it's all over now. There's nothing more to say about it. I just wanted your

opinion, that's all. I'm glad we agree. Now, let's shake
hands on it and have done with it.

He extends his hand.

FRAU GRUBACH
Don't take it so hard, please, Herr K.

JOSEF K
I didn't know I was taking it hard.

FRAU GRUBACH
Have some more cake. You haven't said whether it's
nice cake. Do you like the cake?

JOSEF K
It's extremely nice cake. Tell me. Is Fräulein Bürstner
at home?

FRAU GRUBACH
No, she went to the theatre.

JOSEF K
I wanted to apologize to her for making use of her room
today.

FRAU GRUBACH
But that isn't necessary. She knows nothing about it and
it's all been tidied up anyway.

JOSEF K
Show me. Let me see.

She leads him to the door of Fräulein Bürstner's room. They go in.

INT. FRÄULEIN BÜRSTNER'S ROOM. NIGHT.

Moon in the room. High pillows on the bed.

FRAU GRUBACH
You see, you'd never know anyone had been in here at
all, would you?

JOSEF K

She's often out late, isn't she?

FRAU GRUBACH

She's young.

JOSEF K

Mmnn.

FRAU GRUBACH

I don't want to say anything against her. But it's true that I've seen her twice this month in out-of-the-way streets and each time with a different man. I shall really have to speak to her about it.

JOSEF K

You've totally misunderstood me. I didn't mean anything like that. I warn you not to say anything to Fräulein Bürstner. I know her well. There's not a grain of truth in what you're implying. I warn you to say nothing to her.

He stares at her.

Oh say what you like to her! Good night.

He moves to the door. She blocks his way.

FRAU GRUBACH

Oh Herr K, I just meant that it was in the interests of all the lodgers that I keep the house clean. That's all I meant.

JOSEF K

Clean! If you want to keep the house clean, you'll have to start by throwing me out!

INT. K'S SITTING ROOM AND HALL. NIGHT.

K at the window looking down into the street.

He walks up and down the room. He opens his door a little, lies on the couch, lights a cigar, lies looking out into the hall.

He stubs out his cigar, closes his eyes.

He suddenly opens them.

Fräulein Bürstner, wearing a silk shawl over her dress, comes in the front door and goes towards her room. K goes to the crack in the door and whispers.

JOSEF K

Fräulein Bürstner.

She looks round.

FRÄULEIN BÜRSTNER

Yes?

JOSEF K

It's me.

He steps into the hall.

INT. GRUBACH'S HALL. NIGHT.

FRÄULEIN BÜRSTNER

Herr K! Good evening.

She holds out her hand. He takes it.

JOSEF K

I've been waiting to have a word with you.

FRÄULEIN BÜRSTNER

A word?

JOSEF K

Yes.

FRÄULEIN BÜRSTNER

Does it have to be now?

JOSEF K

I've been waiting for you since nine o'clock.

FRÄULEIN BÜRSTNER

It's just that I'm so tired I could drop. Well – if it must
be now – come into my room for a minute. We can't
talk here. There are people asleep.

They go into her room.

INT. FRÄULEIN BÜRSTNER'S ROOM. NIGHT.

She puts a light on.

FRÄULEIN BÜRSTNER

Please sit down.

He does.

What is it?

JOSEF K

This morning your room was disarranged a little. It was
disarranged by other people but it was partly my fault. I
wanted to apologize to you.

Fräulein Bürstner looks about the room.

FRÄULEIN BÜRSTNER

My room?

JOSEF K

That's right, yes. How it came about is not worth
talking about.

FRÄULEIN BÜRSTNER

But surely that's the really interesting part? Isn't it?

JOSEF K

No. No it isn't.

FRÄULEIN BÜRSTNER
Well, I'm not going to . . . pry . . . so I can't see . . .

She walks about the room.

Nothing's been disturbed as far as I –

She stops at the wall of photographs.

Oh, no! Look. All my photos have been muddled up. What's been happening? Who did this?

K goes to her.

JOSEF K
Not me. It wasn't me. I swear to youI didn't touch your photographs. The fact is the Commission of Enquiry brought along three bank clerks – one of them – I'll get him sacked as soon as possible – must have interfered with your photographs.

FRÄULEIN BÜRSTNER
A Commission of Enquiry?

JOSEF K
Yes. To see me.

FRÄULEIN BÜRSTNER
No? I don't believe it!

She laughs.

JOSEF K
Why? Do you believe I'm innocent?

FRÄULEIN BÜRSTNER
Innocent? Innocent of what? Anyway I hardly know you. What I really meant was that you've got to be a pretty big criminal, haven't you, for them to set up a Commission of Enquiry. Isn't that right?

JOSEF K

I can see you don't know much about legal matters.

FRÄULEIN BÜRSTNER

No I don't. But guess what? I'm joining a law firm next
month. I've always been attracted by the law.

JOSEF K

Really? Good. Well . . . perhaps you might be able to
help me with my case.

FRÄULEIN BÜRSTNER

Why not?

JOSEF K

You see the thing's too petty for me to drag in a lawyer,
but I might well need an adviser. Who knows?

FRÄULEIN BÜRSTNER

But if I'm to be your adviser I must know what it's all
about.

JOSEF K

I don't know what it's about. I haven't been told what
it's about.

FRÄULEIN BÜRSTNER

Is this a joke?

(*She yawns.*)

And it's so late! And I'm so tired.

JOSEF K

It wasn't actually a Commission of Enquiry at all. I only
called it that because I couldn't think of a better name
for it. There was no interrogation, you see. I was merely
placed under arrest.

She laughs.

FRÄULEIN BÜRSTNER

What was it like?

JOSEF K

Horrible.

She is sitting on the settee. Her hand is slowly, abstractedly, caressing her hip. He watches this movement.

FRÄULEIN BÜRSTNER

That's too vague.

JOSEF K

Is it? Shall I show you what it was like then?

FRÄULEIN BÜRSTNER

I'm tired.

JOSEF K

You came in so late.

FRÄULEIN BÜRSTNER

I didn't know –

JOSEF K

The Inspector was sitting in the middle of this room – at your bedside table. The two warders sat on the chest. The three clerks stood by your photographs. A white blouse was hanging on that window. It still is. Look. A white blouse. I was awake. Wide awake. But the Inspector shouts at me as if I'm asleep, as if he's waking me up. He shouts: 'Josef K!'

The sound reverberates. There are knocks on the wall. She gasps. K grasps her hand. They whisper.

Don't be afraid. I'll sort everything out. But who's in there? There's no one sleeping there.

FRÄULEIN BÜRSTNER

There is! A nephew of Frau Grubach. A captain. I

forgot about it myself. Oh why did you shout? Why did you have to shout?

JOSEF K

There's nothing to be worried about.

He takes her in his arms and kisses her.

FRÄULEIN BÜRSTNER

Oh please go away, please, go on, go on, he can hear everything.

JOSEF K

Come here.

He takes her to the far corner of the room.

He can't hear us here. What's his name?

FRÄULEIN BÜRSTNER

His name? Oh . . . Lanz . . .

JOSEF K

Lanz . . . Lanz. I don't know him.

FRÄULEIN BÜRSTNER

Please –

JOSEF K
(*taking her hand*)

Listen. There's no danger. I promise you. Frau Grubach adores me. I'm her favourite. I've also lent her a substantial sum of money. Now listen. Listen to me. I'll agree to any explanation you suggest of how we came to be together in your room, provided it's plausible. If you want it spread around that I assaulted you then we'll tell Frau Grubach precisely that and she'll believe it, she believes everything I say.

Fräulein Bürstner is staring at the ground.

Why shouldn't she believe I assaulted you?

FRÄULEIN BÜRSTNER
The knocking frightened me, that's all. I take full
responsibility for anything that happens in my room.
Now please go. Please go

JOSEF K
But you're not angry with me?

FRÄULEIN BÜRSTNER
No no, I'm never angry with anyone.

She leads him to the door, slips out into the hall. She whispers.

Come here. Look.

INT. GRUBACH'S HALL. NIGHT.

K joins her. She points to a light under a door.

FRÄULEIN BÜRSTNER
He's listening.

K kisses her on the mouth, all over her face, her neck.

Good night.

*He kisses her hand. She walks back to her room and closes the
door. He stands.*

INT. BANK: K'S OFFICE. MORNING.

K at his desk. K's Assistant comes in the door.

K'S ASSISTANT
The telephone for you, Herr K.

K stands and goes out of the room.

INT. BANK: ANTE-ROOM. DAY.

The telephone stands on a table. K picks it up.

JOSEF K

Good morning. Josef K.

VOICE

Josef K?

JOSEF K

Yes.

VOICE

There will be a first hearing of your case this coming
Sunday.

JOSEF K

This Sunday?

VOICE

This coming Sunday.

JOSEF K

I see.

VOICE

We don't want to disturb your working week. So we
assume Sunday suits you? But if not, do please say so.
Hearings can be heard at night.

K says nothing.

Herr K?

JOSEF K

Yes?

VOICE

So we assume Sunday suits you?

JOSEF K

Yes, yes. Quite convenient.

VOICE

It is essential that you appear, of course. Absolutely
obligatory.

356

JOSEF K

Yes, of course.

VOICE

So the date is agreed – which is this coming Sunday.
The address is No. 48 Juliusstrasse.

JOSEF K

Juliusstrasse –?

*The line goes dead. K stands still. He replaces the receiver. The
Deputy Manager is at his elbow.*

DEPUTY MANAGER

Bad news?

JOSEF K

No, no.

*The Deputy Manager lifts the receiver and depresses the button to
call for the operator.*

DEPUTY MANAGER

Oh, Herr K, would you like to join me on my yacht on
Sunday?
                    (*Into telephone.*)
Operator – yes – I would like Vienna 24046 please.
                    (*To K.*)
A small party. The Public Prosecutor will be there. Do
you know him? We would very much like you to come.

JOSEF K

I'm sorry. I'm afraid I have another engagement on
Sunday.

DEPUTY MANAGER

Oh, what a pity.
                    (*Into telephone.*)
Hello, hello? Yes. Herr Strauss. Good morning.

The Deputy Manager talks on. K stands still, frozen. The Deputy

Manager's voice is distant, muffled. He finally puts the telephone down and looks at K curiously. K turns sharply.

> JOSEF K
> Someone just rang me up and asked me to go somewhere but they forgot to say the time.

> DEPUTY MANAGER
> Well, why don't you ring them back and ask?

> JOSEF K
> Oh, it's not that important.

K bows and walks back to his office.

EXT. TRAMWAY. SUNDAY MORNING.

K walking. A tram passes. K suddenly sees Rabensteiner and Kullich (two of the clerks) standing on the tram. They peer out at him.

EXT. CAFÉ. DAY.

K walks. He passes a café. On the terrace of the café he sees Kaminer (the third clerk). Kaminer leans over the balustrade and gazes at K. K walks on.

EXT. JULIUSSTRASSE. DAY.

A street of tenements. People at windows in shirtsleeves, some holding small children. Other windows piled high with bedding. People call to each other across the street. Laughter. Fruit vendors. A gramophone playing.

K finds No. 48. A barefooted man sitting on a case reading a newspaper. Boys playing. A girl in a dressing-gown pumping water into a can. Washing being stretched between two windows.

K goes through the gate into the yard. He looks at four flights of stairs, finally decides on one.

EXT. TENEMENT STAIRWAY. DAY.

K climbs the stairs. On the first landing children playing with marbles. A marble rolls towards his feet. Two small boys hold on to K's trousers. He walks on. He stops at a door of a flat and knocks. The door opens. A Woman with a baby in her arms. Behind her a Man in bed.

> **JOSEF K**
>
> Good morning.

> **WOMAN WITH BABY**
>
> Yes?

> **JOSEF K**
>
> I'm looking . . .

He stops, is blank.

> **WOMAN WITH BABY**
>
> Yes? What is it?

> **JOSEF K**
>
> I'm . . . I'm looking for a plumber . . .

> **WOMAN WITH BABY**
>
> A plumber?

> **JOSEF K**
>
> Called Lanz.

> **MAN IN BED**
>
> What does he want?

> **WOMAN WITH BABY**
>
> He's looking for a plumber called Lanz.

> **MAN IN BED**
>
> Shut the door.

She does.

K walks up the next flight of stairs.

EXT. TENEMENT STAIRWAY. NEXT LANDING. DAY.

K knocks on a door. There is no answer. A door two flats along opens. A man looks out.

FIRST STAIRMAN

Yes? What is it?

JOSEF K

I'm looking for a plumber called Lanz.

FIRST STAIRMAN

A plumber called Lanz?

JOSEF K

Yes.

FIRST STAIRMAN

Lanz, Lanz. You're sure his name is Lanz? No, I'll tell you what, there is a plumber upstairs, at least I think he's a plumber, I mean that's what he says he is, but I wouldn't swear his name was Lanz, I mean if I had to swear it on oath, I wouldn't swear it.

Another Man appears.

SECOND STAIRMAN

What's the trouble?

FIRST STAIRMAN

This man is looking for a man called Lanz. He says he's a plumber.

SECOND STAIRMAN

Who is?

JOSEF K

Lanz.

SECOND STAIRMAN

Ah. Lanz, yes. Yes yes, there used to be a man called Lanz on the fifth floor. That's right, I remember. He was a plumber. Definitely. But I haven't been up there for years.

JOSEF K

On the fifth floor?

SECOND STAIRMAN

I've got no reason to go up there now, you see.

JOSEF K

Thank you.

EXT. TENEMENT STAIRWAY. TOP FLOOR. DAY.

K walks to the door, knocks, turns the handle and goes in.

INT. TENEMENT. WASHERWOMAN'S FLAT. DAY.

The room is quite bare. A young Woman is washing clothes in a tub. A clock on the wall says ten o'clock.

JOSEF K

I'm looking for a plumber called Lanz.

WASHERWOMAN

Yes.
           (*She points to an inner door.*)
In there.

K goes to the door and opens it.

INT. THE COURTROOM. DAY.

The room is packed. There is a low dais at the end of the room. A small fat man sits at a table, laughing with another. Everyone is talking. K goes back into the room.

INT. TENEMENT. WASHERWOMAN'S FLAT. DAY.

K goes to the Woman at the tub.

JOSEF K

I said I was looking for a plumber, a man called Lanz.

WASHERWOMAN

Yes, that's right. In there. I told you. Go in there.
You're very late anyway.

She goes to the door. He follows.

I've got to shut the door after you. No one else is
allowed in.

She opens the door. He stares into the room.

Come on.

He goes in. She closes the door.

INT. THE COURTROOM. DAY.

*There is still a great deal of noise. Nobody looks at K. He stands.
Someone touches his hand. He looks down. It is a small Boy. K
takes the Boy's hand. The Boy leads him through the crowd to the
dais. The fat man (the Examining Magistrate) is still laughing
and whispering with another man. The Boy stands on tiptoe,
touches the Magistrate's arm. The Magistrate looks down.*

*The Boy mutters. The Magistrate looks at K. He takes out a
watch, glances at it, looks back at K.*

MAGISTRATE

You should have been here an hour and five minutes
ago.

People in the room turn to look at the dais. A murmur grows.

You should have been here an hour and five minutes
ago.

The murmur grows and then dies away. The room becomes quiet.

JOSEF K

I may be late, but at least I've come.

A burst of applause from the room.

MAGISTRATE

Yes, but I'm no longer obliged to hear you. However, I'm willing to make an exception in this case. Step up.

K gets on to the dais. The Magistrate picks up a small, dirty notebook. He looks through it.

You are a house painter.

JOSEF K

No, I am senior clerk in a large bank.

A burst of laughter from the room. People rest their hands on their knees and shake with laughter. K. joins in. The Magistrate jumps up and glares at the room.

Your question, Mr Examining Magistrate, as to whether I am a house painter – although it wasn't a question but a statement – demonstrates the kind of proceedings that are being instituted against me. You may argue that they are not legal proceedings at all, and you would be right, for they are in fact only legal proceedings if I recognize them as such. Well, for the moment I choose to recognize them, but only out of a kind of pity.

K stops. There is absolute silence in the room, a tense attention. The Magistrate remains standing.

The door opens. The Washerwoman comes in. People turn to look at her. She stands at the back wall. The Magistrate sits and picks up the notebook. K snatches the notebook from him and holds it up with two fingers, wrinkling his nose. He waves it about.

There are the Court records! Look at this miserable smelly grimy little book! Pathetic!

He drops it on the table.

> What has happened to me, ladies and gentleman, is only an isolated incident and of little importance. But it is an indication of the kind of intimidation many people are being subjected to. It is for these people I am speaking – not for myself.

VOICES

Bravo! Bravo! And bravo again!

JOSEF K

I was arrested ten days ago. Those who arrested me were at the very best degenerate, arrogant, ignorant and corrupt. Their every action declared this. They ate my breakfast, they even tried to steal my underwear. Such an arrest is exactly the same as being waylaid by a bunch of louts in a dark alley. No more, no less. The dignity of the law – what a joke! They chain-ganged three junior clerks from my bank as witnesses, in order, obviously, to damage my public reputation and undermine my position at the bank. I want to remind you that I am quite detached from this whole business and so am able to judge it calmly.

Silence.

> There is no doubt that behind all the outward manifestations of this tribunal's authority there exists a huge organization. An organization which not only employs corrupt warders, stupid inspectors, totally incompetent examining magistrates, but which also makes use of a judicial network of senior officials with a vast and indispensable retinue of servants, clerks, policeman and other auxiliaries – perhaps even hangmen – no I'm not afraid to use that word. And what is the significance of this great organization? I'll tell you. It consists of securing the arrest of innocent people

and instituting against them senseless proceedings that usually – as in my case – lead to nothing.

A scream from the back of the room.

A Man is pressing the Washerwoman into a corner. Her blouse is off. People jump up and crowd around them.

Stop that! Throw them out! Order! Order!

K glares at the Magistrate, who is sitting calmly at his table.

I'll throw them out myself.

K jumps down from the dais. He tries to get through the crowd. He is barred, prevented. People grapple with him, grab him. He fights his way through and gets to the door. The Washerwoman is on the floor, the Man on top of her.

A sudden silence. The Examining Magistrate is at the door of the room.

MAGISTRATE
It is my duty to point out to you that you have today thrown away all the advantages that a hearing can afford an arrested man.

JOSEF K
To hell with your damn hearings!

He opens the door, goes through it and slams it.

INT. BANK: THE MAIN HALL. MORNING.

K walking through the hall. Various men wish him good morning and shake his hand.

INT. BANK: ANTE-ROOM. DAY.

He walks into the ante-room. The telephone is ringing. His Assistant takes it.

K'S ASSISTANT

For you, Herr K. Paris branch.

JOSEF K

I'll call back later.

K'S ASSISTANT

But it's Monsieur Schrader himself.

JOSEF K

I'll call back later.

K walks towards his office. In background the Assistant speaks into the phone.

K'S ASSISTANT

Herr K is extremely sorry but he's unable to come to the telephone at this precise moment . . .

INT. BANK: K'S OFFICE. DAY.

K at his desk examining files. The Assistant comes in.

JOSEF K

Have there been any telephone messages for me this morning?

K'S ASSISTANT

Telephone messages?

JOSEF K

Yes.

K'S ASSISTANT

Well, Monsieur Schrader from Paris –

JOSEF K

No, no. Apart from that.

K'S ASSISTANT

I'm sorry Herr K . . . Who from?

JOSEF K

Who from? From anybody!

Pause.

K'S ASSISTANT

No, sir.

INT. GRUBACH'S HOUSE. HALL. NIGHT.

K comes through the front door into the hall. Frau Grubach comes out of her room.

FRAU GRUBACH

Herr K –

JOSEF K

Have there been any telephone messages for me?

FRAU GRUBACH

No, no, none. Herr K, I'm worried about you. Are you eating? I don't think you're eating.

JOSEF K

I asked you if anyone had left a message for me on the telephone.

FRAU GRUBACH

I'm sorry . . . what kind of message?

JOSEF K

What kind? Any kind. It doesn't matter what kind. It's a simple question. I would be grateful if you would answer it simply.

FRAU GRUBACH

But Herr K . . . the telephone hasn't rung at all today.

JOSEF K

How do you know? Weren't you out shopping this morning?

FRAU GRUBACH

Yes. Yes . . .

JOSEF K

So how can you know it hasn't rung? How can you know?

She stares at him.

I really don't know why we're having this conversation. Good night.

He goes to his room.

INT. K'S SITTING ROOM. NIGHT.

K at his desk feverishly writing a letter. He puts it in an envelope, addresses the envelope to Fräulein Bûrstner, goes out.

INT. GRUBACH'S HOUSE. THE HALL. NIGHT.

K sliding the envelope under Fräulein Bürstner's door.

EXT. JULIUSSTRASSE. SUNDAY MORNING.

K walking towards the house.

INT. TENEMENT STAIRWAY. DAY.

K climbing the stairs. A third man appears.

THIRD STAIRMAN

Oh, hello, sir. Good morning to you. Tell me, did you find the plumber Lanz?

JOSEF K

The plumber Lanz? Yes I did. Yes. I found him.

THIRD STAIRMAN

So he's still here after all these years, eh?
(*He shakes his head.*)

After all these years!

JOSEF K

JOSEF K

Good morning.

K climbs the next flight of stairs.

EXT. TENEMENT STAIRWAY: TOP FLOOR. DAY.

K knocks on the door. The woman opens it.

JOSEF K

Good morning.

INT. WASHERWOMAN'S FLAT/COURTROOM. DAY.

He walks through the room to the other door.

WASHERWOMAN

There's no session today.

JOSEF K

No session?

*She goes to the door and opens it. They look in. The room is
empty.*

JOSEF K

You're right. There's no session. Why didn't they tell
me? How can they expect me to know? What are those
books on the table?

WASHERWOMAN

They belong to the Examining Magistrate. You're not
allowed to touch them.

She closes the door.

Do you want me to give any message to the Examining
Magistrate?

JOSEF K

Do you know him?

WASHERWOMAN

Of course I know him. My husband is the Court Usher.

K looks about the room. It is fully furnished.

JOSEF K

Last Sunday there was just a washtub in here.

WASHERWOMAN

We have to clear everything out of the room on days
when the Court is in session. It's so tiring. Listen. I'm
sorry I caused a disturbance in the middle of your
speech. It wasn't my fault. That man never leaves me
alone, he's wild about me, he can't keep his hands off
me. There's nothing I can do to stop it. Even my
husband has come to accept it. If he wants to keep his
job he's got to put up with it – the man is a law student,
you see – they say he's going to be really powerful some
day. But it was a pity he disturbed your speech. I was
really enjoying it. Of course I only heard part of it. I
missed the beginning and during the last bit I was on
the floor with the law student. But I was really
impressed. I thought to myself – I only wish there was a
way I could help him.

JOSEF K

There is.

WASHERWOMAN

How?

JOSEF K

Let me examine those books in the other room.

She looks at him and opens the door. They go in.

INT. EMPTY COURTROOM. DAY.

K and the Washerwoman go to the table.

JOSEF K

God this place is filthy.

The Washerwoman picks up the books and wipes them with her apron. K takes one from her and opens it.

Obscene photographs! Ha!

He opens another.

More.

He opens another.

And more. And more.

He throws the books down.

So these are the law books that are studied here. These are the kind of men who are supposed to be judging me.

WASHERWOMAN

I'll help you. Let me help you. Come. Sit down with me.

They sit.

You've got lovely dark eyes. Haven't you? Such lovely dark eyes.

JOSEF K

I don't see how you can help me. To help me you'd have to know the senior officials well. You only know that fat lout the Examining Magistrate. He's hardly a senior official.

WASHERWOMAN

Well, he may be a minor official but I can tell you he never stops writing reports, especially about you. Last

Sunday he stayed up writing till all hours. I woke up in the middle of the night and he was looking down at me (my husband was fast asleep) and he whispered to me that he would never forget the sight of me in my nightie in bed. So you see he really fancies me – so I can influence him. And guess what he sent me yesterday? These lovely silk stockings. Look.

She lifts her skirt.

Aren't they lovely stockings? Can you believe that an Examining Magistrate would give such beautiful stockings to a woman like me? Sshh. Berthold is watching us.

K looks up. Berthold, the student, is standing in the doorway.

Listen, don't be angry with me, but I've got to go to him, he's a disgusting man, I can't bear him, just look at his bandy legs, but I've got to go to him. But I'll come back. Then I'll go with you wherever you like and you can do whatever you like with me.

She goes to the Student. He puts his arms around her, presses his body against her, whispers.

K raps on the table.

The Student kisses her mouth and throat.

K bangs on the table with his fist.

The Student feels her body.

K stands and stamps around the room.

BERTHOLD
Why don't you get out of here?

JOSEF K
Not me, sir. You.

BERTHOLD
(*to Washerwoman*)

They've given him too much leeway. He should have
been confined to his room. I've been trying to tell the
Examining Magistrate but it's like talking to a brick wall.

K goes towards them. He holds out his hand to the Woman.

JOSEF K

Come here.

BERTHOLD

Oh no.

*The Student picks the Woman up and runs to the door of the flat.
The Woman calls to K.*

WASHERWOMAN

It's no good, the Examining Magistrate has sent for me,
this little monster won't let me go –

K follows them.

JOSEF K

I'll save you.

WASHERWOMAN

No, no you mustn't! It would be the end of me. He's
just carrying out the orders of the court. Leave us alone.
Please!

JOSEF K

Yes! I'll leave you alone! I never want to see you again!

*The Student carries the Woman out of the flat, followed slowly by
K.*

EXT. TENEMENT STAIRWAY: TOP FLOOR. DAY.

*The Student carries the Woman up a narrow wooden staircase.
She waves down to K and shrugs helplessly.*

373

K suddenly notices a piece of cardboard near the stairs. On it is written in childish handwriting Court Offices Upstairs.

The Usher comes up the stairs. He looks through the open door into the flat and turns to K.

USHER
Have you seen a woman around here? My wife?

JOSEF K
You're the Court Usher.

USHER
Yes. And I know you. I recognize you. You were here last Sunday. Right? You're defendant K.

The Usher offers his hand. K takes it. They shake hands.

JOSEF K
I was speaking to your wife a short while ago. The student has taken her off to the Examining Magistrate.

USHER
You know, if I didn't depend on them so much I'd have squashed that student on the wall ages ago. Here, next to the notice. I'm always dreaming of doing it. I think of him right here, just here, a little above the floor, his arms outstretched, do you follow? His fingers spread out, his bandy legs twitching, blood all over the place, total agony, do you know what I mean? Unfortunately so far it's only a dream.

K smiles.

JOSEF K
I understand your feelings.

USHER
And now it's gone from bad to worse. Before, he only took her to his own place, but now he's taking her to the

Examining Magistrate as well. It's pretty humiliating, I can tell you. And there's bugger-all I can do about it.

JOSEF K

No, I see that.

USHER

But you could do something about it. You could give that student such a hiding, if you felt like it, that he might really think twice before he touched her up again. But only a man like you could do it.

JOSEF K

A man like me? Why?

USHER

Because you're an accused man. You've got nothing to lose.

K is silent.

Perhaps you could think about it.

K is silent.

Well, I've got to report to the Court offices. You want to come and have a look?

JOSEF K

A look?

USHER

At the offices. No one'll notice. I just thought you might be interested.

JOSEF K

Oh. Yes. Why not?

He follows the Usher up the stairs. The Usher opens the door at the top. They go in.

INT. THE COURT OFFICES. DAY.

A corridor. Two rows of long wooden benches. People sitting on the benches. As K and the Usher pass, they stand.

> **JOSEF K**
> What are they standing for?

> **USHER**
> They're all defendants.

> **JOSEF K**
> Yes, but why are they standing? Who do they think I am? It's idiotic.

K stops by a tall thin man.

> What are you doing here? Why are you waiting here?

The man does not reply.

> **USHER**
> Come on, sir. The gentleman is only asking you what you're waiting for. Answer him.

> **THIN DEFENDANT**
> I'm waiting . . .

Men collect around them.

> **USHER**
> Move out of it. Don't block the corridor.

They withdraw.

> **JOSEF K**
> I asked you what you were doing here.

> **THIN DEFENDANT**
> A month ago I offered some evidence to the Court concerning my case. I am now waiting for the Court's view of it. I am waiting for the Court's view of my evidence.

JOSEF K

You're waiting for the Court's view?

THIN DEFENDANT

That's right. Precisely. I'm waiting for the Court's view.

JOSEF K

Well, let me tell you, I am also a defendant, but you'll have to wait a very long time before I 'offer evidence' to this Court. I can assure you of that. A very long time. I wouldn't demean myself. And I am also an accused man. Do you understand me?

The man stares at him.

THIN DEFENDANT

I have offered evidence . . .

JOSEF K

What are you saying? Are you saying that you don't believe that I'm also a defendant? That I'm also an accused man?

THIN DEFENDANT

Oh yes, yes –

JOSEF K

No, tell me the truth. Are you saying you don't believe me? Are you saying you don't believe I'm an accused man? What are you saying? Speak up. Are you saying you don't believe me?

He grasps the man's shoulders and shakes him violently. The man screams. K pushes him back on to his bench. K and the Usher walk on.

USHER

They're very sensitive, some of these defendants.

In the background a group collects around the man who screamed. K and the Usher walks on.

JOSEF K

I think I'll go now.

USHER

But you haven't seen everything yet.

JOSEF K

I don't want to see everything. Actually I'm tired. I feel
tired. Which is the way out?

USHER

Well . . . just go as far as the corner – turn right – then
straight down the corridor until you reach the door.

JOSEF K

Can you show me the way? Please.

USHER

What do you mean? There's only one way. I just told
you the way. Anyway I've got to deliver a message.

JOSEF K

Come with me! Show me!

USHER

Don't shout! Stop all that shouting.

JOSEF K

Come with me. Show me. Come with me.

K suddenly staggers and falls on the Usher, who catches him.

*The Usher holds on to K, turns him round and runs him down the
corridor to the door.*

*A sudden flash of light, a draught of fresh air. The Usher's voice
– distant – then suddenly louder.*

USHER

First he wants to go and then when you tell him a
hundred times that this is the exit, he won't move.

The door is open. K falls out, sits, gasps, takes in the air. The Usher slams the door.

EXT. TENEMENT STAIRWAY. DAY.

K blinks, picks up his hat and bounds down the stairs.

INT. K'S BEDROOM. DAY.

K sitting still. A knock on the door. Frau Grubach's voice.

> FRAU GRUBACH
> Herr K?

He looks at the door.

> Herr K?

> JOSEF K
> Yes.

> FRAU GRUBACH
> Fräulein Montag would be grateful if she could have a word with you in the dining room.

K stands and looks at the door. Silence.

He opens the door. The sitting room is empty.

He goes into the hall.

INT. GRUBACH'S HALL. DAY.

The hall is empty. K goes into the dining room.

INT. GRUBACH'S DINING ROOM. DAY.

Fräulein Montag is standing by the window. K closes the door.

A long dining table is set for lunch.

> FRÄULEIN MONTAG
> I don't know whether you know me.

JOSEF K

Of course. You have a room here. You've been living here for quite a long time.

FRÄULEIN MONTAG

But we've never spoken.

JOSEF K

No.

FRÄULEIN MONTAG

Would you mind if I had a few words with you now?

K is silent.

It's on behalf of my friend, Fräulein Bürstner.

K is silent.

I shall be sharing her room with her from tomorrow, at her invitation. We are friends. She hopes you will listen to me for a minute, no more.

K is silent.

Over the last few weeks you have written a number of letters to Fräulein Bürstner asking for a talk with her. She knows what this talk would be about and is convinced that it would be in neither her interest nor yours for such a talk to take place. She thinks it would be pointless. I volunteered to let you know this as I am quite uninvolved and know nothing about the matter. That is all I have to say.

JOSEF K

I am grateful to you.

K goes to the door. As he reaches it, it opens. Captain Lanz comes in. He ignores K.

CAPTAIN LANZ

Fräulein Montag.

He goes to her, bows, kisses her hand.

FRÄULEIN MONTAG

    Captain Lanz. Good morning.

K leaves the room.

INT. GRUBACH'S HALL. DAY.

K goes to Fräulein Bürstner's room, knocks. He knocks again. He opens the door and looks in.

INT. FRÄULEIN BÜRSTNER'S ROOM. DAY.

The room is empty.

K looks about the room. There is a second bed. The wardrobes are open. Women's dresses, underwear, etc., lie all over the room. He closes the door.

INT. BRUBACH'S HALL. DAY.

In the doorway of the dining room Fräulein Montag and Captain Lanz are talking quietly.

They glance at him.

He goes to his room.

INT. BANK. K'S OFFICE AND ANTE-ROOM. EVENING.

K packing up his desk. He switches off the lights. In a far office lights are on and figures move.

INT. BANK: BACK CORRIDOR. NIGHT.

K walks down the corridor, stops.

He hears moaning.

He listens, turns to look at the lumber-room door.

Moaning.

He goes to the door and opens it.

INT. BANK: THE LUMBER ROOM. NIGHT.

A candle on a shelf. Three men are in the room: the two Warders and the Flogger.

> ### FRANZ
> Sir! We're going to be flogged! Look! We're going to be flogged because you complained about us to the Examining Magistrate!

> ### JOSEF K
> I didn't complain. I just gave him my views.

> ### WILLEM
> But sir, if you only knew how badly we were paid you wouldn't be so hard on us. I have a family to feed, Franz wants to get married –

> ### JOSEF K
> But I never asked for you to be punished. I promise you. I was only concerned with the principle of the thing.

> ### THE FLOGGER
> The punishment is well deserved.

> ### WILLEM
> Don't listen to him.

The Flogger hits him with his birch. Willem cries out.
> (*To K.*)
> This is a terrible tragedy, can't you see that? We're professionals, we've never fallen down on a job, we had every prospect of promotion, we would have become floggers like him and now look at us!

K turns to the Flogger.

JOSEF K

Can we perhaps discuss this? Is there any chance of – ?

THE FLOGGER

There's no chance.

(*To the two men.*)

Get your shirts off! Strip!

(*To K.*)

They're talking rubbish. Do you think they would ever have made him a flogger? Don't be ridiculous. Look how fat he is. Do you know how he got so fat? He eats the breakfasts of all those he arrests. He ate your breakfast too, didn't he? I'll tell you something. No man with a belly like that stands a chance of becoming a flogger. It's out of the question.

WILLEM

It's not true!

THE FLOGGER

Shut up!

He hits him with his birch. K takes out his wallet.

JOSEF K

If you let them go, we could come to an arrangement.

THE FLOGGER

You want to get me flogged as well, do you? No thanks.

JOSEF K

Listen. They're blameless. Honestly. It's the organization that's to blame. It's the high officials who are to blame.

BOTH WARDERS

That's right!

The Flogger hits them. K pushes the birch down.

JOSEF K

If you were birching one of the senior judges – believe me – I would be right behind you.

THE FLOGGER

It's my job to flog people I'm told to flog and that's what I'm going to do.

Franz falls on his knees in front of K.

FRANZ

Please. Get me off. He's older than me, he's not as sensitive as me. I'm sensitive. I'm in love with my fiancée. Please.

He weeps.

THE FLOGGER

I'm not waiting any longer.

He whips Franz's back savagely. Franz screams.

The scream is unending.

JOSEF K

Don't scream!

Franz lurches towards him. K pushes him back. Franz falls over. The Flogger follows him, hitting him.

INT. BANK: BACK CORRIDOR. NIGHT.

K looks up the corridor. Two Clerks are approaching, curiously.

K shuts the door, goes to a window in the corridor and looks down. He calls to the two men.

JOSEF K

It's all right! It's me – the senior clerk.

CLERK

Is everything all right?

JOSEF K
There was a dog howling in the yard.

They stand uncertainly.

You can get back to your work.

The Clerks walk away.

K looks at the lumber-room door. He goes to it and listens.

Absolute silence.

EXT. CITY STEPS. NIGHT.

Crowds of people climbing and descending the steps. K standing quite still at the centre of the activity.

INT. BANK: K'S OFFICE. MORNING.

K at his desk. He is dictating a letter to his Assistant. He stops in mid-sentence, falls silent. The Assistant sits, pencil poised, finally looks at him.

K'S ASSISTANT
Herr K?

JOSEF K
I need to consult my files. Will you come back in an hour?

K'S ASSISTANT
Yes, Herr K.

K sits still. Over this the sounds of hundreds of voices in the bank, filing cabinets opening, closing, echoing, etc.

INT. BANK: BACK CORRIDOR. LATE AFTERNOON.

The lumber-room door.

The corridor is silent, empty.

K appears at the top of the corridor. He walks slowly down it to the lumber-room door.

Silence.

He opens the door.

INT. BANK: LUMBER ROOM. LATE AFTERNOON.

The Flogger flogging the Warders. The Warders turn to the door.

WARDERS
Sir! Sir!

K slams the door.

INT. BANK: BACK CORRIDOR. LATE AFTERNOON.

K turns up the corridor. Three young Clerks come round the corner. K runs into them. He shouts at them.

JOSEF K
It's time you cleared out that lumber-room! We're going to be smothered in filth!

K walks fast in the direction of his office.

INT. BANK: K'S OFFICE. LATE AFTERNOON.

K comes in and sits at his desk. His Assistant follows with documents.

K'S ASSISTANT
I've been through the Amsterdam documents, Herr K. They're ready for your signature.

JOSEF K
Are they in order?

K'S ASSISTANT
Absolutely in order, sir.

JOSEF K

Good, good.

(*Looks at the page.*)

Let me see . . .

K'S ASSISTANT

Here, sir.

He signs. The Assistant gives him another page.

And here, sir, if you would be so kind.

K signs

The door bursts open. K's Uncle comes in.

K'S UNCLE

Josef?

JOSEF K

Uncle! What a –

K'S UNCLE

Is it true? Tell me. Is it true?

JOSEF K
(*to Assistant*)

Excuse me please.

K'S UNCLE

Is it true? I'm asking you.

The Assistant goes out.

JOSEF K

Sit down, Uncle.

K'S UNCLE
(*sitting*)

I'm asking you if it's true?

JOSEF K

I wish I knew what you were talking about.

K'S UNCLE

I am your guardian. Your welfare is of the utmost importance to me. You know that.

K glances absently out of the window.

K'S UNCLE

You're looking out of the window!

JOSEF K

Oh I'm sorry – what – ?

They stare at each other.

Oh, I suppose you've heard something about my trial.

K'S UNCLE

Yes, I've heard about your trial. But just that there's a case against you – not what it is. So it is true?

JOSEF K

Mmnn. Yes, it is.

K'S UNCLE

But what sort of case is it? Surely not a criminal case?

JOSEF K

Yes. A criminal case.

K'S UNCLE

And you can just sit there calmly with a criminal case hanging over your head?

JOSEF K

The calmer I am the more chance I have.

K'S UNCLE

Just tell me what it's all about! Is it something to do with the bank?

JOSEF K

No, it isn't. But, Uncle, you're talking too loudly. We'd better go out. Come on.

*They go to the door and out. K has a brief word with his
Assistant.*

INT. BANK: MAIN HALL. DUSK.

*The Deputy Manager and other officials are standing in the hall
talking. K and Uncle walk towards the main exit.*

> K'S UNCLE
> But what kind of trial is it? I just don't understand!

The officials glance at K. K takes Uncle's elbow and laughs.

INT. BANK: STAIRS. DUSK.

They go down the steps towards the street.

> JOSEF K
> Now I can speak.

> K'S UNCLE
> Speak.

> JOSEF K
> First of all, Uncle, this is not a case which will be heard
> by an ordinary court.

> K'S UNCLE
> That's bad.

> JOSEF K
> Why?

> K'S UNCLE
> It's bad.

> JOSEF K
> It's not something you should take too seriously, you
> know.

EXT. BANK. DUSK:

> **K'S UNCLE**
> Josef! You used to be intelligent! Have you gone mad?
> Do you know what it will mean if such a case goes
> against you? You'll be wiped out. Wiped out! Finished.

He hails a passing taxi.

> Jump in. Jump in.

He gives the driver an address.

INT. TAXI. NIGHT.

> **K'S UNCLE**
> We're going to Huld, the lawyer. He was at school with
> me. He's a great lawyer, a great lawyer.

> **JOSEF K**
> Oh. But does he know anything about cases . . . like
> mine?

> **K'S UNCLE**
> He knows. Yes.

EXT. DR HULD'S HOUSE. NIGHT.

The taxi stops by a dark house.

EXT. DR HULD'S FRONT DOOR. NIGHT.

Uncle rings the bell.

Black eyes appear at a peephole.

> **K'S UNCLE**
> Open up! I'm a friend of the lawyer's.

Leni opens the door. They go in.

INT. HULD'S HALL. NIGHT.

> **LENI**
>
> Dr Huld is ill.

> **K'S UNCLE**
>
> What is it? His heart?

> **LENI**
>
> I think so.

Holding a candle, she leads them to the bedroom.

INT. HULD'S BEDROOM. NIGHT.

Dr Huld is in bed. The room is full of shadows.

> **HULD**
>
> Who is it, Leni?

> **K'S UNCLE**
>
> It's your old friend Albert.

> **HULD**
>
> Ah, Albert.

He slumps back.

> **K'S UNCLE**
>
> Not too good, eh?

> **HULD**
>
> I'm weaker every day.

Leni goes to the bed, arranges his pillows, whispers to him. K watches her. She is aware of his gaze.

Uncle paces up and down.

> **K'S UNCLE**
> *(to Leni)*
>
> Please leave us alone. I have some personal business to discuss with my friend.

LENI

Dr Huld is ill. He isn't able to discuss any business.

K'S UNCLE

You damned impertinent bitch!

HULD

Leni's a good girl. She looks after me. You can say anything in front of her.

K'S UNCLE

But this isn't my business. It's somebody else's business.

HULD

Whose?

K'S UNCLE

My nephew. I brought him along with me.

Uncle brings K forward.

Josef K. Senior clerk.

Huld leans out of the bed. He takes K's hand.

HULD

Forgive me, I didn't see you. All right, Leni, you can go.

She goes. Huld sits up.

So you've come to see me on business. That's a different matter.

K'S UNCLE

You look better already.

HULD

Let me say at once that your nephew's case interests me so much that – while my heart is not good – if he wished me to act on his behalf I would be unable to resist such a challenge.

JOSEF K

I don't understand –

HULD

Have *I* misunderstood? I thought you wanted to talk to
me about your trial?

K'S UNCLE

Of course he did! That's why we're here.
(*To K.*)
What do you mean, you don't understand?

JOSEF K
(*to Huld*)

I would like to know how on earth you can possibly
know anything about me and my trial.

HULD

Ah, I see. Well, I am a lawyer, I move in legal circles.
People talk about different cases and one remembers
the more striking ones. Especially if the nephew of a
friend is involved. There's nothing remarkable in that,
surely?

JOSEF K

You move . . . in those circles?

HULD

Of course.

K'S UNCLE

Really! You're talking like a child.

JOSEF K
(*to Huld*)

And you say they are discussing my case in these circles?

HULD

It has certainly been referred to. You see, my moving in
these circles is of great advantage to my clients in many

ways. My illness restricts me of course – but I do receive visits from good friends of mine from the Court who keep me wonderfully well informed. There's a great friend of mine here in this room at this very moment, as a matter of fact.

He points to a dark corner. K turns. A Man is sitting in the shadows. He stands, walks slowly into the light.

This is my friend Albert K. This is his nephew Josef K and this is the Chief Clerk of the Court.

All murmur 'How do you do?'

I must say that it seems to me that we might take advantage of the Chief Clerk's presence to ask his advice in the matter of your case.

K'S UNCLE
A heaven-sent opportunity! Heaven sent.

CHIEF CLERK
If I can be of any assistance . . . I shall be only too . . .

HULD
Splendid. Let us draw up chairs –

A sound of smashing china from somewhere in the apartment.

They all turn.

JOSEF K
I'll see what's going on.

He goes out.

INT. HULD'S HOUSE: DARK CORRIDOR. NIGHT.

K peering. A hand slides into his. Leni whispers.

LENI
It's all right. I just threw a plate against the wall to bring you out.

Oh.

LENI

Come here.

She leads him to a room, opens the door.

In here.

They go in.

INT. HULD'S STUDY. NIGHT.

Leni takes him to sit on a large chest.

LENI

I thought you would come to me without me having to
get you out. You couldn't keep your eyes off me in the
bedroom, could you? And yet you kept me waiting.

JOSEF K

I had to listen to the old men rambling on, I couldn't
just run off without an excuse.

LENI

The fact is you didn't like me and you probably still
don't like me even now. Do you want to know what my
name is?

JOSEF K

What is it?

LENI

It's Leni.

She takes his hand.

Call me Leni.

K stares at her blankly.

Can't you think of anything else except your trial?

JOSEF K

I'm not sure I think about it enough.

LENI

I've heard you're too inflexible.

JOSEF K

Who said that?

LENI

Don't be so inflexible. There's no way you can defend yourself against this court, you have to admit your guilt, that's all. Make a full confession as soon as you can. That's the only way you can escape from them. And I'm going to help you. But you have to say my name first.

JOSEF K

Leni.

K pulls her on to his lap.

LENI

Ooh that's nice.

She clasps her arms around his neck.

JOSEF K

And if I don't confess my guilt, then you won't be able to help me?

LENI

No, then I won't be able to help you. But you don't want my help at all, do you? You're obstinate and you won't listen to reason. Aren't you? You're obstinate, aren't you?

She touches his face.

Look. I've got a physical defect.

She spreads two fingers.

Feel it.

He touches a web of skin between her fingers.

JOSEF K

Extraordinary.

He pulls the fingers apart and together a number of times.

What a pretty little paw.

He kisses her fingers.

LENI

You've kissed me!

She kisses his neck, slips his lap, he tries to catch her, falls with her to the floor.

Now you belong to me!

EXT. HULD'S HOUSE. NIGHT.

A stationary cab. Rain.

The house door opens. Leni and K.

LENI

Come whenever you want.

She blows a kiss and closes the door.

Uncle jumps out of the cab, rushes at K, shoves him against the wall.

K'S UNCLE

How could you do it? Do you realize the damage you've
done to your case? You sneak off with that dirty little
whore, who is obviously his mistress, you stay away for
hours, and we're all left sitting there – your uncle, your
lawyer and the Clerk of the Court – a man who has
complete authority over your case as it stands at present.
They're polite, they're diplomatic, they don't mention it,
they spare my feelings, but finally they fall silent and we
all sit there looking at each other. Finally the Clerk of the

Court gets up, he says good night and he goes. My friend is dumbstruck, he can't say a word, you've probably helped give him a complete breakdown and hastened the death of the man on whom you are totally dependent. And as for me – I'm soaked right through, soaked, wet through, soaked to my skin. How could you do it?

K is silent.

INT. BANK: K'S OFFICE. MORNING.

K swivelling slowly in his chair.

He slowly moves objects from one place to another on his desk.

His arm stretches out on the desk.

He sits quite still, head down.

INT. HULD'S STUDY. DUSK.

K sitting. Huld seated at a very large desk.

HULD

The proceedings are not public, you see. You must remember that. As a result of this, the Court records, above all the record of the charge, are not accessible to the accused or his defence. The consequent problem is that one does not know, or knows very imprecisely, what it is the initial plea has to contest. This does place the defence at a disadvantage, I freely admit. But it is quite deliberate. Defence counsels are not provided for under the law, they profess only on sufferance. The law intends, as far as is possible, to eliminate defence counsel altogether, so that the whole onus is placed on the accused man himself. But it would be quite wrong to infer from this that the defendant does not need a lawyer before this court. On the contrary, in no other court is a lawyer so necessary. And may I say in all humility that you are fortunate in your choice of lawyer. I have excellent contacts and I have already had a number of discussions – with – I must concede – limited success. Some officials have expressed favourable opinions, others much less favourable. The Chief Clerk of the Court, of course, to whom you behaved so unwisely in this very room, refuses, for the time being, to be at all moved by your plight. But on the whole I would say the outlook is moderately cheering. Nothing is totally lost. And if we can win over the Clerk of the Court to our side we can await subsequent developments without any qualms.

JOSEF K

I propose that I write a short account of my life – a survey of my life from every conceivable angle, recalling the minutest actions and events. An onerous task, I agree, but I believe it should be done and that the advantage of such a defence are indisputable. I intend to hand this defence in to the Court myself.

HULD

What you say is madness.

Leni comes into the room with tea for Dr Huld. She gives it to him. She stands behind K's chair. Huld drinks the tea. Leni strokes K's hair. They watch Huld drink.

Absolute madness.

INT. HULD'S: THE DARK HALL. DUSK.

Leni and K embracing. Leni whispers.

LENI

There's a painter called Titorelli. He paints for the Court. He paints the judges. Go to see him.

She gives him a piece of paper.

INT. BANK: K'S OFFICE. MORNING.

K swivelling slowly in his chair.

He slowly moves objects from one place to another on his desk.

His arm stretches out on the desk.

He sits quite still, head down.

A knock at the door. The Assistant enters. K stares at him.

> K'S ASSISTANT
> I'm sorry Herr K, I know you were not to be disturbed
> but the three gentlemen are still waiting to see you. I
> have told them that you are engaged on especially
> important work, but it is now two hours and they are
> quite distressed –

> JOSEF K
> I'm going out. My overcoat please.

He goes to the door.

INT. BANK: ANTE-ROOM AND K'S OFFICE. DAY.

*The three Businessmen. They stand as K comes out. The Assistant
brings his overcoat.*

> FIRST BUSINESSMAN
> Herr K, we are really very anxious to speak to you –

> JOSEF K
> You must excuse me, gentlemen, I'm afraid that after all
> I have no time to see you today. I have urgent business
> to attend to. I really must leave at once. Could you
> possibly come back tomorrow? Or perhaps we could talk
> on the telephone.

The Deputy Manager comes into the room.

DEPUTY MANAGER

So you're going out now, Herr K?

JOSEF K

Yes. I have business. Urgent business.

DEPUTY MANAGER

But these gentlemen have been waiting to see you for some considerable time.

JOSEF K

It's all agreed.

SECOND BUSINESSMAN

But I really must protest –

THIRD BUSINESSMAN

We wouldn't have waited all this time if –

DEPUTY MANAGER

Gentlemen, there's one very simple solution. If you're prepared to make do with me, I should be very glad to take over the negotiations in place of the Senior Clerk. Of course your business must be discussed straight away. Please come into my office.

The men go out with the Deputy Manager.

K leaves the room, stands still for a moment in the corridor, turns, goes back into his office.

The Deputy Manager is bending over K's filing cabinet. He looks up.

So you haven't gone yet? I'm looking for the Donner agreement. Do you know where it is?

K moves forward.

It's all right, I've got it.

The Deputy Manager goes back to his own office.

EXT. SLUM DISTRICT. DAY.

K walks down a street.

EXT. SLUM DISTRICT: TITORELLI'S HOUSE. DAY.

K stands outside a house, checking the address. There is a hole in the brickwork. A yellow steaming fluid is pouring out of this. Rats by a drain. At the bottom of the steps a small child lies howling.

On the other side of the front door a tinsmith's workshop. Three assistants hitting an object with their hammers. A big sheet of tin plate hanging on a wall reflecting light.

K goes into the house.

INT. TITORELLI'S STAIRWAY. DAY.

Young girls come running out of a flat, laughing, rushing up the stairs. K follows them. One Girl, slightly hunchbacked, about thirteen years old, slips on the stairs and then looks up at K as he approaches. She wears a very short skirt.

JOSEF K
Is there a painted called Titorelli living here?

She stands, slides up to him, pokes him in the stomach with her elbow.

Do you know the painter Titorelli?

The Girl stands even closer to him.

GIRL
What do you want him for?

JOSEF K
I want him to paint my portrait.

The girl giggles.

Paint your portrait?

She hits him gently, runs up the stairs. He follows.

She disappears round the next bend in the stairs. K turns the bend. All the girls are waiting for him, standing on either side of the stairs, smoothing their skirts. He passes between them.

They close in behind him. The Hunchback points him to a very narrow wooden staircase. At the top of it is a door made of boards. The name Titorelli is painted on it in red.

The door is flung open. A man in a nightshirt stands at it.

TITORELLI
(*to K*)
Come in, come in.

The girls rush up the stairs and try to push their way in.

Titorelli throws them out. The Hunchback slips into his room.

INT. TITORELLI'S ROOM. DAY.

K goes in. Titorelli whirls the Hunchback around and dumps her outside the door. He shuts the door.

TITORELLI
I am the painter Titorelli.

JOSEF K
You seem to be very popular.

TITORELLI
Oh, those girls! They're a damn nuisance. They get everywhere. Last night I found one of them under my bed.

The girls start to scratch on the walls. They can be glimpsed through the cracks in the wood.

VOICE

Titorelli, can we come in now?

TITORELLI

No!

VOICE

What about me? Just me?

TITORELLI

I said no!

K looks at an easel covered by a shirt, sleeves dangling.

JOSEF K

A girl called Leni gave me your name.

TITORELLI

I know Leni.

JOSEF K

She says you are trusted by the Court.

TITORELLI

I am certainly trusted by the Court. She's quite right. I take it you are an accused man?

JOSEF K

Yes. I am.

TITORELLI

And you would like some help from me?

JOSEF K

If that's possible.

TITORELLI

Let me ask you one question. Are you innocent?

JOSEF K

Yes. I am completely innocent.

I see. Well, if you're innocent, the whole thing is very simple.

Is it?

Yes, yes of course. But you are definitely innocent?

Definitely.

Well, that's the main thing.

Girls scratching on the wall.

But I understand that once the Court has made an indictment, it is firmly convinced that the accused is guilty and it can be budged from that conviction only with great difficulty.

With great difficulty? It can't be budged at all. The Court can never be budged.

Titorelli, is he going to go soon?

Shut up!

Are you going to paint him? Don't paint him! He's so ugly.

If you don't keep quiet, I'll throw you all down the stairs.

He whispers in K's ear.

Those girls belong to the Court too.

JOSEF K
Oh, do they?

TITORELLI
You don't seem to know much about the Court, do
you? But since you're innocent, you won't need to. I
can get you off by myself.

JOSEF K
How? You said yourself the Court can never be budged.

TITORELLI
Not head on, no. But it's different behind the scenes, in
the corridors, in this room, for example. You see, I
know them all, well, not all, but quite a few. I inherited
this post. My father was the Court painter before me.
It's a position handed on from father to son, you see.
And every judge wants to be painted just as the grand
old judges were in the old days, and there's no one else
who can do that except me. Do your understand?

JOSEF K
So your position is unassailable?

TITORELLI
Unassailable. Now, our aim is to get you acquitted,
right? So I have to ask you first what kind of acquittal
you want. There are three possibilities. Actual acquittal,
ostensible acquittal and indefinite postponement. Actual
acquittal is, naturally, the best, but I haven't the
slightest influence on that kind of verdict. Nobody has.
And to be quite frank, I have to tell you I've never come
across a single case of actual acquittal in my whole life.

JOSEF K
What about in years gone by?

TITORELLI

Oh, there are stories of such acquittal – but they're very hard to prove. The Court's final verdicts are never published, you see, they're not even available to the judges, so only legends about old legal cases have come down to us. The majority of these legends are in fact describing cases of actual acquittal – you can believe them if you like, but you can't prove them. Some of them are in fact very beautiful, very tender, inspiring.

JOSEF K

But you can't cite these legends as evidence before the Court, I take it?

Titorelli laughs.

TITORELLI

No. You can't.

JOSEF K

Then let's stop talking about 'actual acquittal'. Tell me about the two other courses.

TITORELLI

Ostensible acquittal and indefinite postponement. Why don't you take your jacket off? You look hot.

JOSEF K

Yes, it's unbearable. Can't you open a window?

TITORELLI

It won't open. But lots of air comes through the cracks.

JOSEF K

I'll take off my jacket.

Girls' voices.

GIRLS

He's taken off his jacket!

TITORELLI

Shut up! Right, let's take ostensible acquittal first. What happens is this – I write out a statement of your innocence. The text for this has been handed down by my father, by the way, and is unimpeachable. With this statement I go the rounds of the judges. I might begin with the judge I'm painting at the moment, for example. I explain that you're innocent and I offer to guarantee your innocence myself.

JOSEF K

And will he believe you?

TITORELLI

Not every judge will believe me, but once I get a sufficient number of judges to countersign the statement, I take it to the judge who is actually conducting your trial. This judge has the guarantee of a number of his colleagues, so he can order the acquittal with an easy mind and you walk out of the court a free man.

JOSEF K

A free man.

TITORELLI

Yes. But only ostensibly free. You see, my judges are the lowest grade of judges, they don't have the right to give a final, an actual acquittal. Only the very highest court, which is absolutely inaccessible to you, to me, and to all of us, can do that. You see, the difference between actual and ostensible acquittal can be demonstrated in a purely external way.
With actual acquittal all the documents are set aside. They vanish. The trial is deleted, as it were. With ostensible acquittal, the case records remain in circulation and one day some judge or other comes across them, looks through them, realizes the charge is still valid and orders an immediate arrest.

JOSEF K

And the trial begins again.

TITORELLI

The trial begins again. But of course there's always the
chance of obtaining another ostensible acquittal.

JOSEF K

But the second acquittal isn't final?

TITORELLI

No, no. It's ostensible. It can be followed by a third
arrest, a third acquittal, a fourth arrest, a fourth
acquittal and so on, *ad infinitum.*

He studies K.

So how do you like the sound of ostensible acquittal?

JOSEF K

Tell me about the other one.

TITORELLI

Indefinite postponement.
          (*He thinks.*)
That consists in preventing the trial from advancing
beyond its earliest stages. To achieve this, the defendant
and his helper must keep in constant contact with the
Court. You must'nt lose sight of your case for a
moment, you have to keep the case revolving in the
same small circle, you must submit yourself for regular
interrogation, visit all the judges who can influence your
own, keep the case from progressing, you see, by acting
with unswerving persistence and vigilance – but of
course there's no rest, there's no sleep, it can go on for
ever, you can never, as they say, drop your guard –

K stands.

GIRLS

He's up!

TITORELLI

Are you going? Is it the air? I'm so sorry. There's lots
more I wanted to say to you. I had to be quite brief. But
I hope I've made myself understood?

JOSEF K

Oh yes.

TITORELLI

Both methods have this in common – they prevent the
accused man from being sentenced.

JOSEF K

But they don't ensure any real acquittal.

TITORELLI

You've grasped the crux of the matter.

JOSEF K

You've been kind.

He goes towards the door.

TITORELLI

You don't want to be pestered by those girls, do you?
Use this door.

He climbs over the bed and unlocks another door.

Don't be afraid to climb over the bed, everybody does
it.

*K climbs on to the bed and suddenly sees through the open door.
He stares.*

JOSEF K

What's this?

TITORELLI
This? It's the Court offices. Why are you so surprised?

INT. COURT OFFICE. DAY.

K's P.O.V.

Benches in the Court offices corridor. A man sitting, his head in his hands. Another man standing in the half darkness.

INT. TITORELLI'S ROOM. DAY.

K climbs across the bed.

INT. COURT OFFICES. DAY.

K staggering, a handkerchief pressed to his mouth.

The girls rush to meet Titorelli. They seize his hands, hold on to him. Titorelli laughs.

TITORELLI
Can't come any further, I'm afraid! Cheerio! And don't be too long thinking it over.

K staggers down the corridor.

EXT. STREET NEAR HULD'S HOUSE. NIGHT.

L walking purposefully towards Dr Huld's house.

EXT. DR HULD'S FRONT DOOR. NIGHT.

K rings the bell. Silence. He rings it again. Two eyes at the peephole. The eyes withdraw. K bangs on the door. Silence.

The door suddenly opens. K falls in. He glimpses Leni in a chemise running down the passage. By the wall stands a skinny little man in shirt sleeves.

JOSEF K

Do you work here?

BLOCK

I'm a client. I'm here on legal business.

INT. HULD'S CORRIDOR. NIGHT.

K passes Block and turns to study him.

JOSEF K

Oh yes? She's your mistress, isn't she?

BLOCK

Good God no!

JOSEF K

What's your name?

BLOCK

Block. I'm a businessman.

JOSEF K

Where's Leni? Where's she hiding?

BLOCK

She's probably gone to the kitchen to make soup for the lawyer.

JOSEF K

Where's the kitchen! Take me there.

INT. HULD'S. THE KITCHEN. NIGHT.

Leni making soup. She wears an apron. K and Block come in.

LENI

Good evening, Josef.

JOSEF K

Good evening.

He goes to her.

Who is this man?

LENI
Oh, he's just Block.

JOSEF K
You were in your chemise. Is he your lover? Answer me.

LENI
Come into the other room and I'll explain everything.

JOSEF K
No. Explain here.

She tries to kiss him. He stops her.

Is he your lover?

LENI
Josef, you're not going to be jealous of Block?
(*To Block.*)
Rudi, I'm under suspicion. Say something.

BLOCK
(*to Josef*)
It beats me how you can be jealous of me.

JOSEF K
Yes, it beats me too.

Leni laughs.

LENI
Do you want to see the lawyer? Shall I announce you
first or take him his soup first?

JOSEF K
Announce me first.

Leni goes out. He calls her back.

Take him his soup first.

Leni goes to the stove.

LENI

Then I'll take him his soup. The only trouble is, he may fall asleep. He never takes long to fall asleep after his soup.

JOSEF K

What I have to say to him will keep him awake.

LENI

The minute he's had his soup I'll tell him you're here, so I can have you back with me as soon as possible.

JOSEF K

Oh, go and give him his soup. Get on with it.

LENI

Do be nicer. Please.

She goes out with the soup. K and Block are silent. K walks up and down the kitchen. Block watches him.

BLOCK

I've seen you before. I saw you in the Court offices some time ago.

JOSEF K

Oh. Did you?

BLOCK

I was sitting in the passage when you went through.

JOSEF K

Yes. I was there – some time ago.

BLOCK

I'm there practically every day.

JOSEF K

Tell me. Do you remember that everyone stood up
when I came in? Why did they do that? Did they think I
was a judge?

BLOCK

No no, not at all. We were standing up for the Usher.
We knew you were an accused man.

JOSEF K

Oh. But then, perhaps my behaviour struck you as
arrogant?

BLOCK

On the contrary.

JOSEF K

What do you mean?

BLOCK

The Court is full of superstitions. One of these
superstitions going the rounds is that you can tell from
the defendant's face – particularly from the outline of
his lips – what the outcome of his case is going to be.
Well, those people there on that day maintained that –
judging by your lips – you were certain to be convicted,
and pretty soon at that. So we didn't think you were
arrogant, we thought you were deluded. And so we felt
pity for you.

JOSEF K

My lips! I can't see anything special about my lips. Can
you?

BLOCK

Absolutely nothing at all.

JOSEF K

Superstitious rubbish.

Leni comes back into the kitchen. She looks at them and laughs.

LENI

Aren't you sitting close together, you two? Like old pals.

She takes the candle from Block, wipes his hand with her apron and kneels down to scrape grease off his trousers.

JOSEF K

What are you doing?

LENI

Cleaning him up. The lawyer is waiting for you. Why don't you go in? We've got to clean Block up for his bedtime.

JOSEF K

Bedtime? What bedtime?

LENI

Block's bedtime. He often sleeps here, don't you?

JOSEF K

He *sleeps* here?

LENI

Not everyone's like you, Josef, allowed in to see the lawyer any time they like. Look! It's eleven o'clock and the lawyer is happy to see you. Block's not so lucky. Are you? You know, sometimes I announce him and he doesn't get in to see the lawyer until three days later. And if he isn't on the spot when he's called for he has to be announced all over again. That's why I've let him sleep here, because it's even happened that the lawyer has rung for him in the middle of the night.

K looks at Block.

BLOCK

As time goes by, one becomes very dependent on one's lawyer.

JOSEF K

How much time has gone by, in your case?

BLOCK

Five years. It's been going on for over five years.

LENI

He loves sleeping here. Don't you? Would you like to
see his bedroom?

*She opens a door off the kitchen. K looks in. The room is
windowless, tiny, filled by a narrow bed. A niche in the wall holds
a candle, an inkwell and a pen. Piles of papers sit on the bed.*

JOSEF K
(*to Block*)

So you sleep in the maid's room?

BLOCK

That's right.

JOSEF K
(*to Leni*)

Oh, get him to bed!

LENI

I hope you're not going to be in such a bad temper with
the lawyer.

JOSEF K

Bad temper? Not at all. I'm simply going to tell him that
I'm dismissing him.

BLOCK

He's dismissing him!

Block rushes round and round the kitchen.

He's dismissing the lawyer! Oh my God! He's
dismissing the lawyer!

Leni runs at K. Block and Leni collide. She strikes him.

417

INT. HULD'S: THE CORRIDOR. NIGHT.

K runs up the corridor towards the bedroom. Leni chases him.

K opens the bedroom door. Leni puts her foot in the door, tries to pull him back. K twists her wrist violently. She cries out. He pushes her away, goes into the bedroom, shuts and locks the door.

INT. HULD'S BEDROOM. NIGHT.

Dr Huld is sitting up in bed.

>   HULD
> I've been waiting for you.

>   JOSEF K
> I'm going in a moment.

>   HULD
> I shan't let you in another time as late as this.

>   JOSEF K
> That suits me.

Pause.

>   HULD
> Sit down.

>   JOSEF K
> If you wish me to.

He sits.

>   HULD
> Did I see you lock the door?

>   JOSEF K
> Yes. That was because of Leni.

>   HULD
> Is she pestering you?
>   (*He laughs.*)

It's such a strange quirk she has. She just finds accused
men wildly attractive. She can't help running after them.
She falls in love with them all and indeed they all seem
to fall in love with her. Even that miserable worm Block
she finds attractive – just because he's an accused man.

Pause.

What do you think about that?

JOSEF K

Nothing.

Pause.

HULD

Did you come here tonight to see me for any particular
reason?

JOSEF K

Yes. I came to tell you that I'm taking my defence out of
your hands, as from today.

Huld stares at him.

HULD

Do I understand you correctly?

JOSEF K

I trust you do. I've been thinking about this for a long
time. My decision is final.

Huld pushes the quilt back and sits on the edge of the bed.

You'll get a chill.

Huld wraps the quilt around him.

HULD

Your uncle is a friend of mine and I've also become
fond of you in the course of time. I admit it quite
openly. I don't need to be ashamed of it.

419

JOSEF K

Let me make myself clear. I believe it is necessary to take much more drastic measures in this case than have been taken up to now.

HULD

You are impatient.

JOSEF K

No, it's not a matter of impatience. The case is closing in on me more and more. I am being slowly poisoned.

HULD

You know, I once saw beautifully expressed in a book the difference which obtains between legal representation in ordinary actions and legal representation in cases like this. This is what it said: in the first, the lawyer leads his client by a thread until the verdict is reached; in the second, he straightaway lifts his client on to his shoulder and carries him, without putting him down, as far as the verdict and beyond. And that is the truth. To be defence counsel in a case of this nature is a great and noble task, a task which I have never for a moment regretted, except perhaps now, when I find my work so completely misunderstood.

Silence.

Let me say this. I get the impression that what has misled you into misjudging my legal assistance is that you have been treated too well. I'd like to show you how other accused men are treated – perhaps you'll manage to learn something from it. I'm going to send for Block now, so kindly unlock the door.

K remains still for a moment. He then goes to the door, unlocks it and sits again.

Huld rings a bell. Leni comes in immediately.

Bring Block here.

Leni calls down the corridor.

LENI
Block! The lawyer wants you!

Huld gets back on to the bed and turns to the wall.

Leni slides behind K's chair and caresses him.

Block appears in the doorway. He enters cautiously.

Huld speaks from beneath the quilt.

HULD
Is Block there?

BLOCK
At your service.

HULD
What do you want? You've come at an inopportune
moment.

BLOCK
Wasn't I called for?

HULD
Yes, you were called for. But you've come at an
inopportune moment.

Pause.

You always do.

BLOCK
Do you want me to go away?

HULD
You may stay, as you're here.

Pause.

Yesterday I was with the Third Judge. He's a friend of mine. I gradually got the conversation on to you. Do you want to know what he said?

BLOCK
Oh, please.

Block bows as if about to go down on his knees.

Oh, please.

JOSEF K
(to Block)
What in God's name are you doing?

Leni puts her hand over K's mouth. He seizes both her hands and holds them tight.

Block kneels by the bed.

BLOCK
I'm kneeling, Dr Huld.

He strokes the quilt. Leni frees herself from K. She sits on the edge of the bed and looks down at Block. He looks up at her imploringly, glancing at Dr Huld. She mimes kissing Dr Huld's hand.

Block takes Dr Huld's hand and kisses it, twice. Huld does not move.

Leni bends over Huld and strokes his hair.

HULD
How has he been behaving himself today?

LENI
He's been quiet and industrious.

HULD
What's he been doing?

LENI

Well, so that he wouldn't disturb my work, I locked him
in his room. I peeped through the gap in the door every
so often. He was always kneeling on the bed reading the
papers you gave him. He was reading all day. He was
doing his best. I know he was. It wasn't until eight
o'clock that I let him out and gave him something to
eat.

HULD

You're praising him – which makes it even more
difficult for me to say what I have to say.

Pause.

What the Judge said was not favourable.

LENI

Not favourable?

HULD

Not favourable.

LENI

But how can that be?

HULD

He didn't even like it when I started to talk about Block.
'Don't talk to me about Block,' he said. 'But he's my
client,' I said. 'You're wasting your time,' the Judge
said. I said, 'Of course personally he's quite awful, his
manners are horrible and he's dirty, but as far as
organizing a legal case is concerned, he's
irreproachable.' I was exaggerating on purpose. But to
no avail. I am now forced to repeat what the Judge then
said.

Huld looks at Block for the first time.

'Block is cunning,' he said. 'He knows how to drag his

case out. But his ignorance is much greater than his cunning. What would he say, do you think, if he found out that his trial has not even begun yet, that the signal to begin it has not even been given?'

Block's face aghast.

K looks on, impassive.

INT. K'S SITTING ROOM. NIGHT.

K sitting still. A knock on the door.

> FRAU GRUBACH
> (*out of shot*)
> Herr K, there is a telephone call for you.

K slowly looks up. He stands and goes to the door.

INT. GRUBACH'S HALL. NIGHT.

K goes to the telephone.

> JOSEF K
> Josef K.

> MANAGER'S VOICE
> Herr K. This is Herr Deimen.
> (*Pause.*)
> From the bank.

> JOSEF K
> Oh, good evening, Herr Deimen.

> MANAGER
> You know of course the Italian firm Sitari?

> JOSEF K
> I do, yes.

> MANAGER
> Their chairman is arriving here tonight on business. But

he's very eager to see some of our art museums and monuments – that sort of thing – in the morning. I'd be so grateful to you if you would act as his guide. I mean, you know about art and you speak Italian. Could you possibly spare a couple of hours?

                    JOSEF K
Of course, Herr Diemen.

                    MANAGER
Wonderful. He wants an early start. Eight o'clock suit you?

                    JOSEF K
Certainly.

                    MANAGER
Thank you so much. I'll see you in the reception room.

K replaces the receiver and stands.

Frau Grubach is looking at him through a chink in the kitchen door.

INT. K'S BEDROOM. NIGHT.

K lying in his bed in moonlight. His eyes are wide open.

INT. BANK: RECEPTION ROOM. MORNING.

K enters the room. The Manager and the Italian are sitting in armchairs. They stand. The Manager introduces K to the Italian.

                    MANAGER
Signor Rossi has just been telling me that he doesn't actually have as much time as he'd hoped. He'll have to restrict his sightseeing. I've suggested you simply show him round the Cathedral. Do you think that's a good idea?

JOSEF K

Yes indeed.

The Manager looks at his watch.

MANAGER

He has an appointment now – so he would like to meet
you at the Cathedral at ten o'clock. Is that convenient?

JOSEF K

Of course.

ROSSI
(*to Josef K*)

I am very grateful to you. I look forward immensely to
seeing you at the Cathedral at ten o'clock.

They all shake hands. Rossi goes.

MANAGER

I'm also very grateful to you. But simply confining
things to the Cathedral won't be so demanding, will it?
He's a very important client, as you know.

INT. BANK: ANTE-ROOM. DAY.

K walking through the room. The telephone rings. He picks it up.

JOSEF K

Josef K.

LENI'S VOICE

It's Leni. How are you?

JOSEF K

Oh . . . I have to meet an Italian at the Cathedral . . .
later this morning.

LENI

The Cathedral?

426

JOSEF K

Yes, the Cathedral.

LENI

But why the Cathedral?

Silence.

They're hounding you.

K puts the phone down. He stands still. He murmurs.

JOSEF K

Yes, they're hounding me.

EXT. CATHEDRAL. DAY.

It is raining. The clock is striking ten.

K walking across the square towards the main entrance.

He looks about him. Rossi nowhere to be seen.

K walks to a side entrance. No sign of Rossi.

K walking round the Cathedral. Various doors are closed.

K walks back to the main entrance. The clock says ten-twenty. K looks about. There is no sign of Rossi. K enters the Cathedral.

INT. CATHEDRAL. DAY.

K goes to the bookstall. He looks through various guidebooks. An Attendant is counting change.

JOSEF K

Which would you say is the most reliable guide to the Cathedral?

ATTENDANT

This one.

427

JOSEF K

Thank you. How much is this?

ATTENDANT

One krone.

K gives her a note.

JOSEF K

Thank you.

He walks into the Cathedral and sits down in a pew.

He opens the guidebook and glances through it. He blinks, looks up.

In the distance, on the high altar, a great triangle of candle flames is sparkling. K puts the book down and stands up.

He walks towards the pulpit. A fat candle is burning on a pillar. Suddenly he turns. A man is watching him in the distance. He appears to be a Verger. He points vaguely to something behind K, nodding his head.

What do you want?

He moves towards the Verger. The Verger waves him away and limps off.

K follows the Verger and then stops. When K stops, the Verge stops. The Verger turns and points, as before.

K shrugs and walks back towards his pew.

He is suddenly aware of a small side-pulpit, with a lamp on. A Priest is standing at the foot of it. His hand is on the rail. He is staring at K. He nods at him. K crosses himself and bows. The Priest climbs up to the pulpit.

K looks at his watch in the dim light. Eleven a.m. The Priest tests the lamp on the pulpit. He screws it tighter.

K starts to walk back towards the entrance. He passes empty

pews. There is no one at all in the Cathedral. He finds his pew.
He picks up the guidebook and moves to the door.

PRIEST'S VOICE

Josef K!

K stops. He stares at the ground.

He looks up at the door in front of him.

Silence.

He turns his head slightly and looks back at the Priest. The Priest
is standing quite calmly, in the pulpit.

K turns round. The Priest beckons to him.

K suddenly runs towards the pulpit. He stops before he reaches it.

The Priest points to a spot just below the pulpit. K walks to it.

PRIEST

You are Josef K?

JOSEF K

Yes.

PRIEST

You are an accused man.

JOSEF K

Yes. So I've been informed.

PRIEST

Then you're the man I'm looking for. I am the Prison
Chaplain.

JOSEF K

Oh, are you?

PRIEST

I had you summoned here – to have a talk with you.

JOSEF K

No, no. That's not accurate. I came here to show an
Italian round the Cathedral.

PRIEST

Keep to the point. What's that you have in your hand?
Is it a prayer book?

JOSEF K

No. It's a guidebook to this Cathedral.

PRIEST

Put it down.

*K throws it away violently. It skids, twists and comes apart on the
Cathedral floor.*

Do you know that your case is going badly?

JOSEF K

I have that impression.

PRIEST

How do you think it will end?

JOSEF K

I don't know. Do you?

PRIEST

No, but I fear it will end badly. Your case may not get
beyond a lower court. You are considered to be guilty.

JOSEF K

But I am not. And anyway, how can any man be called
guilty? We're all human beings, aren't we? One human
being is just like another.

PRIEST

That's true, but that's how all guilty men speak.

JOSEF K

So you're prejudiced against me too?

PRIEST

No, I'm not prejudiced against you.

JOSEF K

Thank you. But people are prejudiced against me. My position is becoming more and more difficult.

PRIEST

You don't seem to understand the essential facts. The verdict does not come all at once. The proceedings gradually merge into the verdict.

Pause.

JOSEF K

So that's how it is.

Pause.

PRIEST

What do you plan to do next?

JOSEF K

Get more help.

PRIEST

You ask for too much help from other people. Especially women. Don't you see that's not the kind of help you need?

JOSEF K

Oh, I don't know. Women have great power. And this court is obsessed by women. Show an examining magistrate an attractive woman in the distance and he'll knock over his table and the defendant in order to get his hands on her.

The Priest leans over the balustrade and stares down at him.

In the background the Verger is putting out candles.

Are you angry with me? Perhaps you don't realize the kind of court you're serving?

Pause.

I'm only telling you what I've observed.

Pause.

I didn't mean to offend you.

The Priest raises his voice.

PRIEST
Can't you see what is going to happen to you? Can't you see what is staring you in the face?

Silence.

JOSEF K
Won't you come down here? You haven't got to preach a sermon. Can you come down?

PRIEST
Yes, I can come down now. I had to speak to you first from a distance – because – you see – I am quite easily influenced and tend to forget my duty.

He detaches the lamp from the hook on the pulpit, climbs down and gives the lamp to K.

JOSEF K
Can you spare me a little more time?

PRIEST
As much as you need.

JOSEF K
You're being very kind to me. I appreciate it. You're an exception among those who belong to the Court. I trust you more than any of them. I feel I can speak freely to you.

INT. CATHEDRAL. DARK AISLE. NIGHT.

They walk up and down the dark aisle, side by side.

PRIEST

Don't delude yourself.

JOSEF K

How am I deluding myself?

PRIEST

You're deluding yourself about the Court. In the
writings which preface the Law it says about this
delusion: Before the Law stands a door-keeper. A man
from the country comes up to this door-keeper and begs
for admission to the Law. But the door-keeper tells him
that he cannot grant him admission now. The man
ponders this and then asks if he will be allowed to enter
later. 'Possibly,' the door-keeper says, 'but not now.'
Since the door leading to the Law is standing open as
always and the door-keeper steps aside, the man looks
through the door. Seeing this, the door-keeper laughs
and says: 'If it attracts you so much, go on and try to get
in without my permission. But you must realize that I
am powerful. And I'm only the lowest door-keeper. At
every hall there is another door-keeper, each one more
powerful than the last. Even I cannot bear to look at the
third one.'
The man from the country had not expected difficulties
like this, for, he thinks, the Law is surely supposed to be
accessible to everyone always, but when he looks more
closely at the door-keeper in his fur coat, with his great
sharp nose and his long, thin black Tartar beard, he
decides it is better to wait until he receives permission to
enter. The door-keeper gives him a stool and allows him
to sit down to one side of the door. There he sits, day
after day, and year after year.
During all these long years, the man watches the door-

433

keeper almost continuously. He forgets the other door-keepers, this first one seems to be the only obstacle between him and admission to the Law. In the first years he curses his ill-luck aloud, but later when he gets old, he only grumbles to himself. He becomes childish and, since he has been scrutinizing the door-keeper so closely for years that he can identify even the fleas in the door-keeper's fur collar, he begs these fleas to help him to change the door-keeper's mind. In the end his eyes grow dim and he cannot tell whether it is really getting darker around him or whether it is just his eyes deceiving him.

But now he glimpses in the darkness a radiance glowing inextinguishably from the door of the Law. He is not going to live much longer now. Before he dies all his experiences during the whole period of waiting merge in his head into one single question, which he has not yet asked the door-keeper. As he can no longer raise his stiffening body, he beckons the man over. The door-keeper has to bend down low to him, for the difference in size between them has changed very much to the man's disadvantage.

'What is it you want to know now then?' asks the door-keeper. 'You're insatiable.' 'All men are intent on the Law,' says the man, 'but why is it that in all these many years no one other than myself has asked to enter through this door?' The door-keeper realizes that the man is nearing his end and that his hearing is fading, and in order to make himself heard he bellows at him: 'No one else could gain admission through this door, because this door was intended only for you. I shall now go and shut it.'

The walk on.

JOSEF K
The door-keeper deceived the man.

PRIEST

Don't be too hasty.

JOSEF K

It's obvious. The door-keeper didn't tell the man the
truth until it was too late.

PRIEST

He wasn't asked the question until then. And remember
he was only a door-keeper.

JOSEF K

But he had power! And he used it to destroy the man.
He's a criminal. He should have been dismissed.

PRIEST

But you've missed the point. The scripture is
unalterable.

K stops and stares at him.

The Priest walks on. K follows.

They walks on in silence.

JOSEF K

Aren't we near the main entrance?

PRIEST

No. We're a long way away. Why? Do you want to go
now?

JOSEF K

Yes of course I want to go. I have to go. I'm a senior
clerk at a bank. They're expecting me. I only came here
to show a business associate from abroad around the
Cathedral.

The Priest holds out his hand.

PRIEST

Well then, go.

JOSEF K

I don't think I can find my way alone in the dark.

PRIEST

Just keep to the wall on your left, keep right along that
wall and you'll find a door.

The Priest withdraws.

JOSEF K

Wait! Please! Wait!

The Priest turns.

PRIEST

I'm waiting.

Pause.

JOSEF K

Don't you want to hear anything more from me?

PRIEST

No.

JOSEF K

But you were being so kind to me, explaining things to
me, now you're letting me go as if you cared nothing
about me.

PRIEST

But it was you who said you had to go.

JOSEF K

Yes, you must understand that.

PRIEST

But you must understand what I am also.

JOSEF K

You're the Prison Chaplain.

PRIEST

Precisely. That means I belong to the Court. So why should I want anything from you? The Court doesn't want anything from you. It receives you when you come and it dismisses you when you go.

INT. K'S SITTING ROOM. NINE O'CLOCK. NIGHT.

K sitting still.

A ring at the front door. The door opens, closes.

Footsteps.

A knock on the door. The door opens. Two Men come in. They are portly, formally but shabbily dressed.

K stands up.

JOSEF K

You've come for me.

The Men nod.

K goes to the window and looks out.

WINDOW OPPOSITE. K'S P.O.V. NIGHT.

In a lighted window across the street babies are playing in playpens, stretching their hands out between the bars.

INT. K'S SITTING ROOM AND BEDROOM. NIGHT.

K turns and looks at the two Men, who stand patiently, holding their hats.

K mutters to himself.

JOSEF K

So they send old actors for me. They're trying to get rid of me on the cheap.
(*To the Men.*)

What theatre are you playing at?

FIRST MAN

Theatre?

They look at each other.

JOSEF K

Oh well, let's get on with it.

INT. GRUBACH'S HALL. NIGHT.

K goes out of the room. The two Men follow. He gets his hat from the hall. They go out.

EXT. GRUBACH'S HOUSE. NIGHT.

They come out of the house. The Men link arms with K.

They walk, passing from the light of street lamp into shadow, into light and into shadow.

K looks from left to right at their heavy double chins.

EXT. A DESERTED SQUARE. NIGHT.

The square is decorated with flower beds. The three come into the square. K suddenly stops.

JOSEF K

Why the hell did they have to send you, of all people?

The Men are passive. They stand holding on to K.

Well, that's it. I won't go any further.

They try to hoist K from the spot. He resists, simply by rooting himself to the ground.

You're going to have a hard job of it, you know.

Suddenly he sees Fräulein Bürstner at the corner of the square, climbing up a small flight of steps. She is caught in the moonlight.

K stops resisting. The Men looks at him, relax. He begins to walk in the direction of Fräulein Bürstner, the Men with him.

Fräulein Bürstner disappears. K speaks, half to the Men, half to himself.

JOSEF K

Yes, all I can do now, you see, yes that's absolutely right, all I can do now is to keep my mind calm and discriminating. I'm not going to leave this life like a raging idiot. Why should I? How can I put it? I don't want people to say of me that at the beginning of my case I wanted it to finish and at the end of it I wanted it to start all over again. Do I? Do you follow? I don't want that to be said. And frankly, I'm very grateful that you two half-dumb imbeciles have been sent to escort me. I'm grateful that it's been left to me to tell myself all that needs to be said.

EXT. BRIDGE. NIGHT.

They walk on to a bridge in the moonlight.

A Policeman appears. He looks at them. The two Men stop. The Policeman walks slowly towards them. The Policeman is about to speak when K abruptly propels them on over the bridge.

K looks back. The Policeman is looking after them. They turn a corner.

EXT. DESERTED STREET. NIGHT.

K runs. The Men are forced to run with him.

EXT. FIELDS AND QUARRY. NIGHT.

They walk through fields and arrive at a small quarry. The Men stop. They let go of K.

K stands still.

The Men wipe their brows.

Moonlight. The First Man goes to K, takes off his coat, waistcoat and shirt. He folds the clothes. K stands shivering.

The Second Man is looking about the quarry. He turns and waves.

The First Man leads K to a spot near the wall.

They lie him down.

They try to fit him comfortably between boulders.

The First Man takes out a butcher's knife, hold it, examines the edges.

The First Man hands the knife across K's chest to the Second Man, who hands it back.

K watches the knife.

The First Man hands the knife across K's chest to the Second Man, who hands it back.

K looks beyond them to the top storey of a house.

A window opens. A light flashes on. A figure leans a long way out, stretching out its arms.

K raises his hand towards the figure, spreading his fingers.

The First Man grasps K's throat. The Second Man drives the knife into the heart.

K looks up at the dim faces above him, as they look down at him, their cheeks touching.

JOSEF K

Like a dog!

The Dreaming Child

Adapted from the short story
by Karen Blixen

BRISTOL. 1861.

Moonlight. A garden gate. In background a drive leading to a large mansion.

Charley and Emily (18) at the gate. He is in dress uniform, with medals.

He clasps her, whispering. She pushes him away. He seizes her, kisses her. His hands hold and feel her body. She surrenders, resists, surrenders, resists.

MORNING. A GREEN HILL. BRILLIANT SUNLIGHT.

Emily on her horse galloping along the brow of a hill.

CHARLEY
(*VO whispering, urgent*)
Let me come to your room. Let me stay.

A GRAND BALL. 1861.

Emily walking down the stairs. Tom Carter walks towards her. Tom bows, kisses her hand. She moves on his arm through the ballroom. Various people greet the couple.

HOUSE IN SLUM. NIGHT. 1861

Midwife with Woman in labour. The Woman screams.

MIDWIFE
Breathe easy. Breathe easy.
(*to Mrs Jones*)
Hold her still.

MORNING. A GREEN HILL. BRILLIANT SUNLIGHT.

Emily on her horse galloping along the hill.

> CHARLEY
> (*VO whispering, urgent*)
> I sail tomorrow. Let me stay with you. Please.

THE GARDEN GATE. MOONLIGHT.

> CHARLEY
> Please.

He kisses her passionately.

THE GRAND BALL.

Emily walking down the stairs. Tom Carter walks towards her. He bows and kisses her hand.

SLUM HOUSE. NIGHT.

The Woman panting.

> MIDWIFE
> That's right. That's right.

EXT. THE MANSION. EARLIER IN THE NIGHT.

Moonlight. Charley and Emily walking in the garden. She breaks off a white rose from a bush and gives it to him. He looks at her gravely. They stand, looking into each other's eyes. He puts the rose to his lips.

THE MANSION. DAY. SUMMER. 1868.

Emily (25) in hammock asleep.

> CHARLEY
> (*VO whispering, urgent*)
> I beg you. I want you. I must have you.

THE BALL.

Tom and Emily dancing the mazurka. Charley by the wall watching.

He is suddenly surrounded by girls. They giggle.

> **GIRL**
> Charley, you're not dancing. Why aren't you dancing?

He grins.

THE WOMAN IN LABOUR.

The Midwife. Mrs Jones. The Woman lying still, eyes closed.

CHARLEY AND EMILY EMBRACING PASSIONATELY.

> **CHARLEY**
> It's natural. It's not wrong. You know that. In your heart.

She breaks away.

THE MANSION. DAY. SUMMER. 1868.

Emily (25) in hammock asleep.

> **CHARLEY**
> (*VO whispering*)
> I adore you.

THE DRIVE. MOONLIGHT.

Emily breaking away from Charley. She opens the gate, goes through it, shuts it and walks swiftly up the drive. He calls after her.

> **CHARLEY**
> (*hushed*)
> Emily!

She stops, turns. They stand looking at each other. She walks slowly towards him. She touches him gently.

EMILY
Charley, please. Please.

He seizes her. She turns away, violently. He holds her from behind, through the gate, kissing the back of her neck, pressing into her, his hands on her breasts. She struggles. He takes her hand and puts it on his groin.

She gasps. He turns her to him and kisses her. She responds to his kiss. Her hand stays where he has placed it.

CHARLEY
Yes. Yes.

She wrenches her hand away. He seizes her hand again and forces it towards him.

For God's sake!

THE MANSION. DAY. SUMMER. 1868.

Emily (25) in hammock asleep.

CHARLEY
(*VO whispering*)
For God's sake!

SLUM HOUSE.

The Midwife wrapping the new-born baby in a towel.

MIDWIFE
It's a lad.

EMILY AND PEGGY (BOTH 18) UNDRESSING IN A BEDROOM.

PEGGY
I danced with Charley White tonight. He's a flirt. He flirts with every girl in sight. He's a Don Juan.

Emily smiles into the mirror.

EMILY

I don't think so.

Peggy looks at her.

SLUM HOUSE.

The mother lies still. Her eyes are fluttering. She puts her hand into a purse and slowly brings out money. She puts the money into Mrs Jones's hand.

MOTHER
(faintly)

Keep him. Look after him. Keep him.

Mrs Jones stares at the money.

GARDEN. 1868.

Emily in hammock asleep.

CHARLEY
(VO whispering)

For God's sake!

THE GARDEN GATE. MOONLIGHT.

Emily running towards the house. Charley standing still, looking after her.

SLUM HOUSE.

The Mother's limp hand drops and is still. The baby crying.

MIDWIFE

She's gone.

EMILY IN HAMMOCK.

She sits up abruptly, brushes hair from her face, stares.

> MIDWIFE
> (*VO*)
>
> Who was she then?

> MRS JONES
> (*VO*)
>
> I don't know who she was.

SLUM HOUSE.

> MRS JONES
>
> I don't know who she was.

THE MANSION DAY. 1862.

Tom Carter's carriage draws up to the steps of the house. He jumps out of the carriage. Two Footmen and a Butler come to the door. He goes up the steps.

> BUTLER
>
> Good morning, Mr Carter.

> TOM
>
> Good morning.

> BUTLER
>
> Nice day for the racing, Mr Carter.

> TOM
>
> It is indeed.

INT. MANSION HALL.

Tom gives his hat to a Footman and goes up the stairs.

INT. MORNING ROOM.

Emily sitting. Tom comes into the room. He bends, kisses her hand.

> EMILY
>
> Such a lovely morning.

> TOM
>
> It is, yes. I'm afraid I'm a little late. The first race is at ten.

He takes her hand. She stands.

THE HOUSE. FRONT STEPS.

Tom and Emily walking down the steps to the carriage. The camera is on Emily's back as Tom turns to her.

> TOM
> (*casually*)
>
> Sad news. Charley White is dead. You remember Charley? Died of a fever. Off the China coast.

THE CARRIAGE.

Tom helps Emily into the carriage. As they sit, the camera rests on Emily's face.

> BUTLER
> (*VO*)
>
> Your Arab running today, Mr Carter?

> TOM
> (*VO*)
>
> Oh, she's running. Certainly.

> BUTLER
> (*VO*)
>
> Should be good going for her.

> TOM
> (*VO*)
>
> She likes it a bit harder than this.

> BUTLER
> (*VO*)
>
> Well, good racing, Mr Carter.

> TOM
> (*VO*)
>
> Thank you.

The carriage drives off.

INT. CHURCH WEDDING.

Tom and Emily standing at the altar. Organ playing. Emily's face is serene beneath her bridal veil.

EXT. CHURCH.

The doors open. Men come out carrying a coffin.

CONFETTI BEING THROWN. LAUGHTER.

COFFIN BEING LOWERED.

TWO WEEPING GIRLS.

> GIRL
>
> Oh Charley.

GIRLS CLUSTERED ROUND EMILY, TAKING TURNS TO KISS HER ON THE CHEEK.

SPADES THROWING EARTH ON TO THE COFFIN.

THE DREAMING CHILD

TOM AND EMILY BY THE SIDE OF THE GRAVE.

Emily's face is impassive.

GRAVEDIGGERS LEANING ON THEIR SPADES LOOKING INTO THE GRAVE.

HIGH SHOT FROM WINDOW IN THE HOUSE.

The Garden gate. Moonlight.

Charley standing alone.

Emily running towards the house.

THE GATE. CHARLEY'S P.O.V.

Emily entering the house by a back door. She shuts it.

Charley looks up at the house. A figure in the moonlight in the high window. A curtain falls.

SLUM STREET. 1868.

Children playing 'tig'. Dogs fighting. A carpenter sawing wood. A woman's voice screaming obscenities.

Jack (7) standing alone.

STAIRS.

Jack groping his way up dark stairs.

A broken window. Whistling wind.

THE LOFT.

Huge wet cold sheets, hung up to dry, swaying in the wind.

Jack carefully threads his way through them. One sheet catches him. He is trapped in it, fights his way out.

EMILY IN HAMMOCK.

Sound of a cloth flapping. She opens her eyes and looks across the lawn to the house.

HIGH WINDOW IN HOUSE.

A maid shaking a tablecloth out of the window. She looks across the lawn, stops shaking and pulls in the cloth.

JACK ASLEEP IN HIS BED. NIGHT.

A RAT IN THE ROOM.

JACK WAKES WITH A SCREAM.

SLUM STREET. DAY

Children playing 'tig'. Jack standing, watching.

> GIRL
> *(to Jack)*
> What are you thinking, then?

> JACK
> Thinking?

> GIRL
> You're always standing about thinking. Come on. We want to know what you're thinking.

> JACK
> I don't think I was thinking. I was just standing.

INT. HOUSE. SMOKING ROOM. NIGHT. 1868.

Tom, Rupert (Peggy's husband) and the Vicar with cigars. They have drunk one decanter of port and are well into the next.

In background through an arch is the Billiard Room. Emily is preparing to hit a ball. She is watched by Peggy and the Vicar's wife.

RUPERT

Saw it in the Chronicle this morning, I promise you. Votes for –

TOM

Sshh!

He looks toward the women in the Billiard Room.

The click of the ball.

Rupert lowers his voice.

RUPERT

Votes for women! Seriously. Down there in black and white. They're meeting on Thursday to work out their battle strategy!

He guffaws and drinks.

BILLIARD ROOM.

Emily hits the ball.

PEGGY

What a steady hand, Emily.

VICAR'S WIFE

And what a good eye.

EMILY
(*smiling*)

Thank you. I've always had a good eye, ever since I was a girl.

Voice from smoking room.

RUPERT

I mean – the idea that women –

TOM

Sshh!

SMOKING ROOM.

TOM

What would be the position of the Church, Vicar? Do
you think?

The Vicar drinks.

VICAR

The position of the Church? Well, my own view, quite
frankly and honestly, is . . . my own . . . purely personal
. . . view . . . is that the Lord would not in fact be in
favour. I strongly doubt myself that the Lord would be
in favour.

RUPERT

Quite so.

VICAR

After all, it could be argued and indeed has been argued
. . . that political power in women . . . a power . . .
mark you . . . unnatural, ungodly and corrupt . . . went
a long way to engender that most appalling of all
catastrophes . . . the French Revolution.

RUPERT

Exactly. Unsafe, old boy. Not a good bet. Bad form.

BILLIARD ROOM.

*Emily, billiard cue in her hand, about to hit the ball. Rupert's
voice is heard.*

RUPERT
(*VO*)

A dead duck, if you want my opinion. Totally out of
order. Absolute rubbish.

Emily hits the ball, expressionless.

KITCHEN.

Jack sitting in corner of the room. He suddenly laughs.

Mrs Jones and Miss Scott come in the door.

> MRS JONES
>
> Look at him. He's sitting there laughing to himself.
> What are you laughing at? He's a half-wit. He's cracked.
> Get up. Where's your manners? Say hello to Miss Scott.

Jack gets up. Miss Scott smiles at him.

*Mrs Jones picks up a basin of clean laundry and puts it on the
table. Miss Scott sits at the table, opens her sewing basket.*

> Here you are. There's plenty for you to sew in here.
> Torn sheets, torn underwear. I don't know what they've
> been up to. These toffs, they're not like us, you know.

She goes to the sink.

> (*To Jack.*)
> Eh! Come on you. Why haven't you done the washing
> up? Bloody waste of time, you are.

She hits him and pushes him to the sink.

JACK AT SINK WITH PLATES.

Mrs Jones and Miss Scott in background.

> MRS JONES
> (*muttering*)
> Working my fingers to the bone day and night. Don't
> get no more than tuppence for it. All on my own. Treat
> you like dirt.

SLUM STREET.

Jack is alone, bouncing a ball against the wall. A group of children come down the street, quite tidily dressed, carrying Bibles.

They see Jack. One of the boys whispers to the others.

They go to Jack and surround him.

> BOY I

Eh, Jack, where did you leave your brains?

> BOY 2

He hasn't got any.

> BOY I

What's this book?

> BOY 3

He can't read.

> BOY 2

He left his brains in the bog.

> BOY I

This is a Bible. It's all about God.

> GIRL

And Jesus.

> BOY 3

Jesus wouldn't have anything to do with him.

> BOY 2

Nor wouldn't God.

> GIRL

Yes, he would. God loves everyone.

> BOY 3
> (*to Jack*)

Get down on your knees then.

He pushes Jack.

> Get down on your knees and pray to God. Pray to God!
> Pray to God!

ALL THE BOYS
(jostling Jack)
Pray to God! Pray to God! Pray to God!

Jack hits Boy 3 in the face. The Boys retreat. Boy 3 starts to cry, holding his face.

BOY I
(to Jack)
Leave my brother alone. Bastard! We've all got brothers and sisters here. You got nothing.

Jack turns to the wall and continues to bounce his ball against it.

EXT. DARK STREET. NIGHT.

Tom Carter walking towards a small house. He knocks at the door. It opens. He goes in.

INT. SMALL HOUSE.

Maid and Tom standing in the hall.

MAID
She won't be a minute, sir. You wait in there.

SMALL ROOM.

Tom standing in the room.

Whore's voice offscreen.

WHORE
Tell him he can come in. Go on. But tell him how much first.

The Maid comes into the room.

457

> MAID

You can go in. But it'll be half a crown.

> TOM

I think I'll come back.

> MAID

Why? Can't you afford half a crown?

> TOM

I'll come back another time.

> MAID

She's very nice, you know. Very lovely and womanly.

Whore's voice offscreen.

> WHORE

Where is he? What's he doing? Is he shy?

> MAID
> (*smiling*)

Are you shy, darling? You won't be shy when she's finished with you.

Tom leaves the room and goes towards the front door. The Whore comes out of her room.

> WHORE

Where is he?

> MAID
> (*laughing*)

He's a shy little boy, Doll.

Tom slams the front door.

SLUM HOUSE. EVENING. CANDLELIGHT.

Miss Scott at the table sewing. Mrs Jones at the sink. Jack sitting in the shadows, dimly seen.

MISS SCOTT

I used to sew in all the big houses. And then they told
me I was too old. Because my eyes were beginning to
go. They told me I was too slow. But they were such
beautiful houses.

Mrs Jones goes out of the room with a bowl of washing.

JACK

What is a beautiful house?

Miss Scott turns to look at him.

MISS SCOTT

A beautiful house has lots of rooms in it. And big
windows. And marble halls. And satin and velvet. And
at night there are lovely candelabra with hundreds and
hundreds of glimmering candles. And the ladies walk
down the staircases in beautiful dresses.

JACK

What is a candelabra?

MISS SCOTT

Well, it's . . . it's a thing which holds all the candles in
it . . . hanging down from the ceiling. And they light up
the ladies, as they walk down the staircases in their
beautiful dresses.

They sit for a moment in silence.

And the children are so lucky.

JACK

Why?

MISS SCOTT

Because they have lots of dolls to play with and parrots
in cages and their mothers kiss them and call them
pretty pet names.

Pause.

JACK

Did my mother kiss me?

MISS SCOTT

Of course she did. Of course she did.

JACK

But why aren't there houses like that for everyone?

MISS SCOTT

There should be. There will be, one day. One day the tables will be turned.

JACK

The tables?

MISS SCOTT

One day the tables will be turned.

Mrs Jones comes back and goes to the sink.

Silence.

THE CARTERS' BEDROOM. NIGHT.

Emily lying in the bed, still. Tom comes into the room in his nightshirt.

He stands for a moment, uneasily. He looks at himself in a mirror.

THE CARTERS' BEDROOM. NIGHT.

Tom and Emily in bed making love.

She winces, turns her head away.

EMILY'S DRESSING ROOM.

Emily sitting on a chair in her nightdress. Her hands are clenched between her thighs.

Tom comes in. She sits easier. He stands looking at her.

TOM

Have I hurt you?

EMILY

No, no.

TOM

I never want to do that. Never.

EMILY

No. I know. I know that.

A CANAL.

Miss Scott and Jack walking along the side of a dark canal.

MISS SCOTT

I'm going to tell you something, Jack. The first moment I set eyes on you I said to myself 'That boy doesn't belong in this place. Look at his eyes. They're not like the other lads' eyes. That boy doesn't belong in this place.'

She ruffles his hair.

Your time will come, Jack. I swear to you.

In the street above the canal, a carriage goes by. Tom and Emily are in it.

A SLUM STREET.

The carriage stops outside a hovel. Another carriage stands along the street.

Tom helps Emily down from the carriage.

TOM

I shall wait for you.

Emily walks towards a hovel.

The door of another hovel opens. A Lady comes out of it hurriedly and walks towards her carriage. A Woman bursts out of the hovel carrying a slop bucket.

She throws the contents after the Lady.

WOMAN
Piss off, you crummy faggot! Stick your charity up your bum!

She slams the door.

The Lady passes Tom.

LADY
Animals.

Tom looks uneasily at the hovel Emily is approaching and follows her.

INSIDE THE HOVEL.

A Man at a table. A Woman in bed. Some children on the floor. Tom and Emily stand. She is holding a notebook in her hand.

THE MAN
We got nothing, Missus. She's ill. I'm lame. Two children dead. Nothing.

EMILY
I am to ask if this is a Christian family.

THE MAN
Oh yes, we're all Christians here, always have been.

EMILY
You attend chapel?

THE MAN
She goes to Sunday school every Sunday, don't you?

Oy! I'm talking to you!

A little girl looks up from the floor.

You go to Sunday School every Sunday, don't you?

The girl stares at Emily.

We're all Christians in this house.

Emily makes a note in her notebook.

The Woman in the bed turns over. She wheezes as she turns. She emits a small whimper.

EMILY

Here is a certificate for medicine for your wife's chest.

THE MAN

And what about a few bob, Missus?

EMILY

I shall be discussing your case with my colleagues.

Emily's eyes go to a bottle of beer on the windowsill.

THE MAN

Oh lovely, Missus, lovely.

Emily and Tom go in the direction of the door.

We got nothing. Two children dead. Nothing. She goes to Sunday school, every Sunday.

THE STREET. CARRIAGE TRAVELLING.

EMILY

He's a drunkard.

Tom smiles and takes her hand.

TOM

You are very strict.

EMILY

I am rational.

EMILY'S BOUDOIR. MORNING.

Emily sitting. Cook and Butler standing.

COOK

A bisque of oysters, Ma'am.

EMILY

Very nice. Yes?

COOK

We have some lovely whitebait, Ma'am. And I thought
fillets of salmon.

EMILY

Yes. Yes. Good. That will do very well.

COOK

And for the entrée, Ma'am, I suggest cutlets of pigeon.

EMILY

Be sure they're not overdone.

COOK

Oh, yes, Ma'am.

BUTLER

Certainly not, Ma'am.

EMILY

Overdone pigeon is uneatable. Last Thursday was most
unfortunate. What next?

COOK

Saddle of mutton, Ma'am. Roast quails with watercress.

BUTLER

You've forgotten the chicken, Cook.

COOK

Oh, yes. Poulard à la crème, Ma'am. With peas à la
Française.

EMILY

Let us omit the chicken this evening.

BUTLER

The chicken is omitted, Ma'am.

EMILY

And what do you have for dessert?

BUTLER

Cook is thinking of her very special vanilla mousse,
Ma'am.

EMILY

We shall look forward to that, Cook.

COOK

Thank you, Ma'am.

THE SLUMS. A PRIVY.

*Jack sitting in the privy. Screams, shouts, etc. from outside. A rat
races along the ground. Jack gasps. The door bursts open. A huge
Drunk Man lurches in.*

DRUNK

Get out of that you little bugger or I'll drown your face
in it!

EMILY'S BEDROOM.

Emily dressing, helped by two maids. One of them, Bess, is 16.

The bed is unkempt. Pillows and sheets rumpled and disordered.

EMILY

And how is your mother keeping, Bess?

BESS

Poorly, Ma'am. Poorly.

EMILY

Oh, is she still poorly?

BESS

There'll be no recovery there, Ma'am.

EMILY

Have faith. Have faith.

BESS

Yes, Ma'am.

EMILY

And your sister?

BESS

She's having a little baby, Ma'am.

EMILY

Oh, is she? How nice.

BESS

We're all so happy, Ma'am.

EMILY

Yes, yes. That's enough, the dress is perfect. Leave it.
Make the bed.

DINING-ROOM.

*At the table Tom, Emily, Uncle Edward and Sir George and
Lady Downing.*

EMILY

Tom is naive. He is an innocent. He believes everything
these people tell him.

TOM

Sometimes they're telling the truth.

466

LADY DOWNING

They simply want money. They'll say anything to get money. And do anything too.

SIR GEORGE

Anything.

TOM

They are desperate.

UNCLE EDWARD

They are doomed. Doomed to eternal degradation.

LADY DOWNING

Not eternal, surely?

SIR GEORGE

Surely not eternal?

UNCLE EDWARD

Earthly degradation feels like eternity.

TOM

You can be poor and dignified.

EMILY

And poor and drunk.

LADY DOWNING

And poor and filthy.

SIRE GEORGE

Revoltingly filthy.

UNCLE EDWARD

The poor *are* filthy but that's because they have no water to wash in.

LADY DOWNING

If we gave them water would they know what to do with it?

Sir George roars with laughter.

SIR GEORGE
That's a good one.

EMILY
We are talking about charity. Are we not? If you are
responsible for charitable funds, you have to be
detached, hard-headed, rigorous, while of course
remaining sympathetic to the plight of the poor.

UNCLE EDWARD
You're my favourite niece. I find the contrast between
the suppleness of your body and the rigidity of your
mind piquant.

TOM
Rigid? Emil's mind is in no sense rigid. It is
independent, rational and fearless.

EMILY
Thank you.

TOM
And it is allied to a most tender sensibility.

UNCLE EDWARD
I think the man is in love.

BEDROOM.

TOM
You are perfect. Quite perfect. You are a queen.

*Emily smiles stiffly. He caresses her neck and twists a curl. She
puts her hand up and straightens her hair.*

SLUM HOUSE.

Miss Scott sewing at the table.

Suddenly, from outside, sounds of running feet, cries, shouts.

The door bursts open. Jack runs in. His knee is bloody.

MISS SCOTT
What have they done? What have you done?

Jack limps up the stairs.

JACK'S BEDROOM.

Jack sitting on his bed holding his leg. Miss Scott comes in with a bowl of water and a cloth.

MISS SCOTT
Here, I'll wash it.

She begins to wash his knee. He winces.

There, there. It'll be all right.

JACK
You said . . . I lived somewhere else once.

MISS SCOTT
I did. I know that it's true.

JACK
Were there . . . lots of trees . . . where I lived?

MISS SCOTT
Oh yes. Great and beautiful trees. Elm trees, poplars, oak trees, willows, stretching as far as the eye can see. And they are still there, those trees, waiting for you to come back.

JACK
But if I lived there – how did I come to be here?

She holds him to her.

MISS SCOTT
I think that one day . . . one day, a long time ago . . .

469

you were suddenly lost and nobody could find you.
Nobody knew where you were. It has happened to so
many children. And then one day they are found.

                    JACK

Are they?

CLOSE-UP. EMILY. CARTERS' BEDROOM. NIGHT.

                    TOM
                   (*VO*)
You are perfect. Quite perfect. You are a queen.

Emily smiles. Tom's hand caresses her neck.

BACKYARD. SLUM.

Jack and other children.

                    JACK
I've got a mother and father. They've got lots of horses
in their stables. I know all the names of all the horses.

                    BOY I
Bollocks!

                    BOY 2
What are they?

Jack stares at them.

                    BOY 2
What are their names? What are the names of all the
horses?

                    BOY 3
He doesn't know their names!

                    BOY I
They haven't got any names.

BOY 2

And they haven't got any manes and they haven't got any tails!

Jack stares at them.

SLUM STREET.

A very small funeral procession going down the street. Mrs Jones a couple of neighbours, etc.

JACK'S BEDROOM.

Jack sitting alone, still.

SLUM HOUSE. KITCHEN.

MRS JONES

Here you are. Miss Scott has left you three things. Isn't that nice? She's left you this little thimble, this pair of scissors and this little black chair. She's left it all to you. Wasn't that nice of her?

JACK

Won't she ever come back?

MRS JONES

No, she won't come back. When people die they're dead. And as for you, you're going to start working. You understand me, lad? You're going to start working instead of dreaming. You're going to collect the laundry from the houses and take it back when it's done. You're going to earn your keep. You're big enough.

A LAKE. DAY.

Tom and Emily walking by the lake.

TOM

What do you think is wrong?

EMILY

I can't say.

They walk on.

TOM

It's six years.

They walk on.

Perhaps there's nothing wrong. Perhaps it's just fate.

EMILY

Perhaps I'm barren. Perhaps I cannot bear children.

They walk on.

TOM

Would you consult a doctor?

EMILY

I have done so.

TOM

You have done so?

EMILY

Yes.

He stares at her.

TOM

You did not inform me.

EMILY

No.

TOM

You went alone?

EMILY

No, no. With my maid.

Pause.

TOM

Which doctor?

EMILY

Dr Symmonds.

They walk on.

TOM

What did he say?

EMILY

He said it is impossible to establish conclusively whether a woman is barren or not.

They walk on.

Perhaps you are sterile?

He stops. She stops. He stares at her.

TOM

That is out of the question.

Silence.

EMILY

It seems to me there is no way of knowing anything about any of these matters.

A ROOM IN A HOUSE.

Tom dressing. The whore in a corset brushing her hair.

WHORE

Ah, you're a ram sir. A right ram.

TOM

Am I?

WHORE

A right ram.

She laughs.

TOM

Am I truly?

WHORE

Oh, you are truly. Truly.

TOM

And is that . . . what women want?

WHORE

Well they don't want little lambs darling, do they? They don't want little baa lambs? Anyway your wife is a woman. Isn't she? Why don't you ask her? Go home and ask her what women want.

Tom hits her, knocking her across the room.

TOM

How dare you!

DRAWING-ROOM. HOUSE.

Tom and Emily sitting on a sofa drinking tea. He puts his cup down and takes her hand.

TOM

Let me ask you . . . would you consider . . . adopting a child?

EMILY

Adopting?

TOM

I am considering the future. I am thinking of the future of the firm. It is important – for the firm – that I have a son. The family thinks this.

Silence.

EMILY

But he would not be a real son.

TOM

He would become one.

He picks up his cup and sips tea.

Give it thought.

INT. HOUSE. STAIRS.

The Head Gardener followed by two Under Gardeners climbing the stairs with great trays of flowers.

THE MORNING ROOM.

Emily sitting reading. A knock at the door. She looks up. The Butler comes in.

BUTLER

The Gardeners are here Ma'am.

He ushers the Gardeners and the Housekeeper into the room.

GARDENERS

Morning, Ma'am.

EMILY

Yes, Fibbs. What do you have?

FIBBS

I think I have a good catch here, Ma'am. I think they'll look nice in all the rooms.

Emily examines the flowers.

EMILY

Oh, the roses have opened at last. Thank goodness.
(*suddenly*)
No white. I told you no white roses to be cut.

FIBBS

My apologies, Ma'am, I forgot.

EMILY

Don't forget.
(*to the Housekeeper*)
Yellow roses in the West Room, pink in the South.

FIBBS

How do you like these Delphiniums, Ma'am?

EMILY

Very handsome. Delphiniums in the North Room. Lily of the Valley in the Blue Room. Lilac in the Chintz Room. As usual.

SLUM STREET. DAY.

The street is very narrow and very crowded.

Tom is in his carriage. The Coachman is forcing his way through the crowd.

•

TOM'S DRESSING ROOM. HOUSE. 1862.

He is opening an envelope. He takes a letter out and reads it.

A girl's voice reads the letter. She has a country accent.

GIRL
(*VO*)

There's something I think you should know. When you were at sea, all those years ago, just before you come home to be married, your wife had a romance with Charley White. I saw them together with my own eyes, by the garden gate, in obscene embrace.

He tears the letter up and throws it into a basket.

SLUM STREET.

The carriage moving slowly through the crowd. Jack, wheeling a wheelbarrow full of laundry, crosses in front of the carriage. He stops and stares at the horse. The horse rears violently and comes down hitting the wheelbarrow. Jack falls, the wheelbarrow topples, the laundry spilling into the gutter.

A crowd gathers round.

> TOM
> *(to Coachman)*

Is the boy all right?

The Coachman looks down.

> COACHMAN

Seems all right, sir.

> TOM

Bring him to me.

The Coachman gets down, picks the boy up from the gutter, carries him to the carriage and seats him next to Tom.

Are you hurt, lad?

Jack shakes his head.

Why didn't you move? You just stood there.

> JACK

I thought the horse was such a fine horse. He is, isn't he?

> TOM

He is that.

> JACK

What's his name?

> TOM

His name's Bruno. Now where do you live?

JACK

In Pewter Street.

TOM
(*to Coachman*)

Take us to Pewter Street.

The carriage drives on.

TOM

How old are you?

JACK

I'm seven, sir.

They ride on.

TOM

And what do you like best in the world?

JACK

I like thinking.

Tom looks at him.

TOM

Thinking? What do you think about?

JACK

I think about places I might have been to before.

TOM

Before? Before what?

JACK

Before I was here.

TOM

But you're only seven years old. You can't have been to many places?

JACK

But I haven't always lived here, you see.

TOM

Really? Where else have you lived?

Jack does not answer. The carriage drives on.

Where else have you lived?

Pause.

JACK

I don't remember.

MRS JONES' HOUSE.

Mrs Jones. Tom. Jack.

TOM

My horse knocked him over. My fault. Here's some money for the laundry.

She takes the money.

MRS JONES

Are you sure the lad didn't bring it about himself?

TOM

No, no absolutely not.

He looks at Jack and then at Mrs Jones.

Is he your son?

MRS JONES

My son?
                    (*She laughs.*)
No, he's not my son. He's nobody's son.

She cuffs Jack.

Come on, get on with it. Put those sheets in the sink.

Jack goes to the sink. Tom speaks to Mrs Jones in a low voice.

TOM

Then who were his parents?

MRS JONES

Don't ask me, sir. Only met his mother the once. She
died in this room.

THE HOUSE. PARK.

Emily and Peggy walking.

PEGGY

You're so exasperating! What is it you keep saying that
you'll tell me? But that you still haven't told me? I shall
faint if you don't tell me.

EMILY

Oh, I wouldn't bother to faint. I shall tell you.

PEGGY

Yes, please, please tell me.

EMILY

We're adopting a child. A boy.

Peggy stops walking.

PEGGY

But why?

EMILY

Tom wants an heir. He needs an heir.

PEGGY

But . . . ?

Pause.

EMILY

I can't have children.

Pause.

PEGGY

Why not?

EMILY

I don't know. Nobody knows.

Pause.

PEGGY

Emily . . . married life . . . can be difficult. It can take
time to . . . in our case it was nearly two years before
Robert was born.

They walk on.

Anyway, I have been told that the only women who are
truly infertile are those disgraceful women who . . .
betray their husbands. That is an established fact. Those
women can never have children.

EMILY

You believe that is true?

PEGGY

I do. Certainly.

EMILY

Well, be that as it may . . . Tom and I have been
married for six years.

PEGGY

Who is he . . . this child?

Emily laughs.

EMILY

I don't know. We haven't met yet. The truth is – I can't
tell anyone else this, anyone in the world – but the truth
is I'm indifferent. Tom wants it but I am indifferent.
Can I be blunt? Can I tell you the truth?

PEGGY

Yes.

EMILY

I'm glad I never had a child. I'm obviously not a mother. I was not born to be a mother.

PEGGY

How can you – ?

EMILY

No, no. It's true. So you see, it's all for the best. We won't have to . . . think about it ever again . . . having a child, I mean.

(*She smiles.*)

And I shall keep my figure.

She looks at Peggy.

Not that you haven't, Peggy. You have, of course.

They walk on.

Yes, I am sure it's for the best.

THE HOUSE. LIBRARY.

Tom at his desk. Emily comes in.

EMILY

May I have a word?

TOM

My dear. Of course.

She sits.

EMILY

I've been thinking about your idea. Of adopting a child.

TOM

Oh yes? Yes, I've been waiting to hear . . . what you thought.

EMILY

It is something . . . that you really feel we should do?

TOM

Yes. It is.

EMILY

Then I won't oppose it.

He stands, goes to her, sits by her.

TOM

But what do you actually feel . . . about it, yourself?

EMILY

I'm not enthusiastic. But I won't oppose it. I can see it makes sense.

TOM

The family needs a son.

EMILY

The family needs a son. And if we do do it, I of course will support you with all my heart.

TOM

I am grateful to you.

He takes her hand.

I must tell you . . . I think I've found the boy.

She looks at him.

THE GARDEN GATE. MOONLIGHT.

Charley and Emily kissing violently. She breaks away.

SEPIA. SLOW MOTION.

Charley and Emily inside her bedroom door. A long, lingering, sensual kiss.

SLUM HOUSE.

A Doctor examining Jack. Tom and Mrs Jones in the room.

DOCTOR
Breathe in. Breathe out. In. Out. Open your mouth. Say 'Aaah'. All right, put your shirt on.

He turns to Tom.

Perfectly fit.

Tom gives the Doctor money.

Thank you very much. Good afternoon.

TOM
Now, Mrs Jones . . .

MRS JONES
I'm going to have to tell you, Mr Carter, that I've laid out a lot of money on that child over all these years.

TOM
Yes, yes. Of course. I appreciate that.

He takes notes from his wallet and gives them to her.

Mrs Jones examines the notes.

I hope this is acceptable.

MRS JONES
Oh thank you very much sir. That's very nice of you, sir. And – can I say – that if you ever want any washing done yourself you know where to find me. And you can see that my laundry is the highest class.

TOM
I can indeed, Mrs Jones.

LAWYER'S OFFICE. DAY.

The Lawyer is looking at his notes. Tom and Emily are sitting.

> LAWYER

Mother dead?

> TOM

Yes.

> LAWYER

Father absent?

> TOM

Not seen these seven years.

> LAWYER

Birth certificate?

> TOM

No.

> LAWYER

The father did initially provide money for the keep of
the child?

> TOM

So I understand.

> LAWYER

And then disappeared. You deduce from that he had no
further interest in the child?

> TOM

We do.

> LAWYER

That seems to me a reasonable deduction.

He turns a page.

You propose a trial period of six months?

TOM

We do.

LAWYER

If he proves satisfactory you will give him a name?

TOM

Yes.

LAWYER

And if he proves unsatisfactory you will pass him on?

Pause.

EMILY

Yes.

LAWYER

Well, I can see no legal objection to this procedure and to your assuming the guardianship of this child.

TOM

Thank you.

EXT. STREET. LAWYER'S OFFICE.

Emily and Tom walking towards their carriage.

EMILY

I want to go and collect the boy by myself, Tom. Do you mind?

TOM

No, no. Of course. Excellent.

EMILY

After all I shall have to get to know him
                    (*she laughs*)
if I'm to be his mother. Won't I?

TOM

You will indeed.

THE DREAMING CHILD

SLUM HOUSE. THE LOFT.

Mrs Jones is hanging the sheets. Jack is holding the tub.

MRS JONES
You know what's going to happen the day after
tomorrow, don't you?

JACK
No.

MRS JONES
Get away. Haven't you guessed?

JACK
No.

MRS JONES
Mr and Mrs Carter are going to take you to live with
them.

He stares at her.

They're going to take you to live with them in their big
house.

JACK
Are they my mother and father?

She cackles.

MRS JONES
That's right! They're your old mama and papa! They
wondered where you'd got to and then they found you
in the middle of all the dirty washing.

JACK
But how did they know it was me?

MRS JONES
By the smell, you fool.

THE NURSERY.

Emily placing a gollywog on the bed. The Nurse setting up a doll's house. Bess and another Maid bring in a rocking horse.

BESS

Where shall we put this Ma'am?

EMILY

Yes, yes, the rocking horse.
                    (*She looks about the room.*)
By the window. That's the place for it. And put that hobby horse against the wall in the corner.

BESS

It's a beautiful rocking horse, Ma'am.

EMILY

Yes, it is.

BESS

It took Bert ages to make it. He hoped you'd like it, Ma'am.

EMILY

I do like it. Tell him I like it very much.

Another Maid appears at the door carrying a number of dolls in her arms. The Nurse goes to her and takes some of the dolls.

NURSE

Shall I put these on his bed, Ma'am?

EMILY

No, that's too much. Much too much. Take them away. We really don't want to spoil him, do we?

SLUM HOUSE. KITCHEN.

Mrs Jones is washing Jack and combing his hair.

THE DREAMING CHILD

MRS JONES

You'll have to give yourself a good wash every day in
that house, you will. That's what they do, that lot. They
give themselves a good going over every day. So you'd
better remember that. You're a lucky lad and don't
forget it.

She studies him.

There you are. Look how nice you look. With your hair
all nice and wet.

SLUM HOUSE. STREET.

Emily's carriage draws up. The Coachman helps her out.

Children rush to hold the horse. Some of them surround Emily.

CHILDREN

Give us a penny, Missus. Give us a penny.

The Coachman pushes a number of the children away.

COACHMAN

Go on! Hop it!
(to a boy)
Which is Mrs Jones's house?

BOY

That one there.

COACHMAN

That one there, Ma'am.

*She walks through the children. They watch her approach the
house.*

KITCHEN.

*Jack standing on his chair looking out of the window. He sees
Emily walking towards the house.*

He is in silhouette.

She walks to the door and out of sight.

KITCHEN.

Emily comes in. He turns. They look at each other.

Mrs Jones waves at him to get down from the chair. He remains there. She bobs to Emily.

Silence.

MRS JONES
This is him, Missus.

Silence.

JACK
I'm so glad you've found me, mother.

Emily looks at Mrs Jones sharply. Mrs Jones stares at her. Emily slowly looks back to Jack.

I've waited for you for such a long time.

Emily remains still, frowning.

Now I'm coming home . . . to be with you . . . at last.

He steps down from the chair and stands looking at her.

EMILY
It is . . . very nice to meet you. I hope you will be happy with us.

JACK
I'm already very happy. I can feel it here.

He touches his chest.

Here.

He goes to her, puts his hand up to her hair and strokes it.

I knew you at once. You are my mother. I would know you anywhere.

She stares at him.

And now you kiss me.

She hesitates, then bends and kisses him on the cheek.

He smiles.

EMILY

Well . . . you must say goodbye to Mrs Jones.

JACK
(to Mrs Jones)

Goodbye.

EMILY

I should think you might thank Mrs Jones for all she has done for you.

JACK

Oh, yes that is quite right. Thank you, Mrs Jones, for looking after me so well. If you hadn't looked after me I think I'd have been dead and I'd never have found my mother. So it's good not to be dead.

MRS JONES

Well, you be a good boy. And don't give no one no cheek. Respect your betters.

STREET.

Emily and Jack come out of the house. The group of children stare at them in astonishment.

DOORWAYS IN THE STREET.

Women come into the doorways to watch Emily leading Jack to the carriage, whispering to each other.

STREET.

JACK

It's Bruno.

(to the horse)

Hello Bruno.

Jack turns to the children.

Ta ta.

VARIOUS CHILDREN

Ta ta, Jack.

*Emily and Jack get into the carriage. The carriage drives away.
The children stand looking after it.*

THE CARRIAGE. TRAVELLING.

Emily remains still, looking straight ahead.

THE CARRIAGE CROSSING CLIFTON BRIDGE.

THE GORGE. JACK'S P.O.V.

*Through the bridge railings the river seen flowing through the
gorge. Boats on the water.*

JACK SLIPS HIS HAND INTO EMILY'S HAND.

THE MANSION. DRIVE.

The carriage going down the drive towards the house.

SEPIA. SLOW MOTION. NIGHT.

Emily leading Charley through the hall to the foot of the stairs.

She turns to him and kisses him.

THE MANSION. DRIVE.

The carriage going down the drive towards the house. It stops.
Jack jumps down and stares up at the house.

He runs in.

THE HALL.

The staff lined up.

Jack runs in, stops dead. He looks at them. Emily enters.

> EMILY
> (*to the staff*)
> Here is Jack. As you all know, he's come to live with us.
> Now, Jack, this is Mr Rogers, this is Mrs Hurt.

He goes to them.

> JACK
> Hello. I don't think we've met.

> EMILY
> And here is Winnie, Maude, Alice, Margaret, Mary,
> Mary 2, Phoebe, Rose, Dolly, Sophie, Rachel, Bess,
> Clementine, Bridget, Barbara, Lily, Daffie, John,
> William, James, Kenneth, Dick (*etc., etc.*).

The men bow. The women bob. Jack bows to some of them. Bess
catches his eyes and giggles.

He runs into the drawing-room. Emily walks after him.

DRAWING-ROOM.

> JACK
> Is the parrot dead?

> EMILY
> No, she's not dead. She lives in another room.

                    JACK
Didn't she like this room?

                    EMILY
She never lived in this room.

                    JACK
Oh. Are you quite sure?

A little dog runs into the room, barking.

                    EMILY
Come here, come here.

She picks the dog up.

                    JACK
It's all right, mother. He knows me.

*He picks up a poker from the fireplace and holds it up. The dog
stands on his hind legs and puts his paws on the poker.*

You see? He knows me well. But I've forgotten his
name.

                    EMILY
Nap.

                    JACK
Yes. Nap.

HALL. STAIRCASE.

Jack running upstairs.

Emily and the Nurse walk up after him.

NURSERY.

Emily and Nurse reach the door of the nursery and go in.

Jack is standing in the middle of the room.

NURSE

Isn't he clever, ma'am? He knew where his room was.

JACK

Of course I knew!

He looks slowly around the room, at each object.

What . . . are all these things?

EMILY

They're toys.

NURSE

They're all your toys, Jack. Haven't you had any toys before?

The Nurse picks up a Jack-in-the-Box. The Jack jumps up. Jack starts.

This is called a Jack-in-the-Box.

EMILY

Your name is Jack. You could be a Jack-in-the-Box yourself, couldn't you?

He takes her hand and clasps it.

JACK

I don't know.

Tom comes into the room.

TOM

Hello! You've arrived!

Jack stares at him.

JACK

So you are my father. I thought so.

He runs into Tom's arms.

TOM

That's right. I'm your father!

Tom picks Jack up and throws him up and catches him.

And my goodness you're heavy.

Jack laughs and then touches Tom's chest.

JACK

You're not wearing your medal.

TOM

Who told you about my medal?

JACK

Nobody.

TOM

Yes, they did. Someone's been gossiping. All right. I'll
go and find it in a second and put it on. Would you like
that?

JACK

Oh, yes.

Emily leaves the room.

EMILY'S BEDROOM.

Emily sitting, her hands clasped, still.

THE MANSION. NIGHT.

*Moonlight. Charley and Emily walking in the garden. She breaks
off a white rose from a bush and gives it to him. He looks at her
gravely. They stand, looking into each other's eyes. He puts the
rose to his lips.*

NURSERY. EVENING.

Jack in bed. The Nurse.

JACK

I knew it all along, you know. I knew I would come
home in the end.

NURSE

You'll have to close your eyes and sleep.

JACK

I didn't know where to find them, you see. But it was all
right because they found me.

NURSE

Now if you want me just ring this bell and I'll come. I'm
just up the stairs.

She goes out.

He looks slowly around the room.

THE DOLLS.

THE HOBBY HORSE.

THE ROCKING HORSE.

THE JACK-IN-THE-BOX.

THE HALL. NIGHT.

A grandfather clock ticking.

NURSERY.

The rocking horse. Chimes from the clock.

JACK ASLEEP.

Chimes.

A RAT AT NIGHT.

JACK WAKES WITH A SCREAM.

TOM ASLEEP IN BED. EMILY'S EYES ARE OPEN.

JACK LYING IN BED. HIS EYES OPEN.

The Nurse comes in.

> NURSE
>
> There, there. Was it a bad dream? There, there.

> JACK
>
> Can the curtains be open?

> NURSE
>
> Surely, why not?

She opens the curtains.

> Is that better?

> JACK
>
> Oh, yes. I like the light, even at night.

EMILY LYING IN BED. HER EYES OPEN.

HOUSE. KITCHEN.

Jack at the sink washing up plates. Maids drying plates. The Cook comes in.

> COOK
>
> What's he doing? Who said he could do that?

> MAID
>
> He just came in and started washing up. We didn't know what to do.

> COOK
>
> Hey lad that's not your job. You're not supposed to do that.

JACK

But I know how to do it. I know how to make all the plates clean. And I've only ever broken one plate.

COOK

It's not your job.

NURSERY.

Jack on rocking horse slowly rocking. Emily comes in.

EMILY

Now Jack I've been talking to Cook. Washing up plates is something other people do. The maids do it. It's their work. It's not right for you to do it.

JACK

I mustn't do it?

EMILY

That is correct. You must not do it.

She leaves the room. He rocks on the horse.

SEPIA. SLOW MOTION.

Charley and Emily in her bedroom. He is kissing her breasts.

SERVANT'S HALL.

The Servants at a table with their tea.

BESS

Lovely jam, Cook.

COOK

They don't like it much upstairs.

BUTLER

They do like it, Cook.

COOK

They don't like it. That's the truth of it. She left it all over her plate this morning.

A bell rings. They look up.

BUTLER

That's the drawing-room. Right, Bridget. Up you go.

Bridget gets up from the table.

BESS

Well, I think it's the best jam I've ever tasted.

DRAWING-ROOM.

The bell-pull swinging. Bridget comes into the room and looks about. There is no-one in sight. She leaves the room.

Jack crouching behind an armchair, grinning.

He stands and watches Bridget walk across the hall. She goes through the green baize door. The green baize door swings shut.

He stares at the door.

SERVANTS' HALL.

Bridget comes into the room.

BRIDGET

There was no-one there.

BUTLER

What do you mean there was no-one there?

FOOTMAN

It must have been a ghost. We've got tons of ghosts in this house.

The bell rings. They look up.

BUTLER

Dining-room. Go on Bess.

FOOTMAN

Give my love to the ghost.

DINING-ROOM.

Jack crouched behind a chair.

Bess comes into the room. She looks about. The bell-pull is swinging gently.

She suddenly sees Jack's foot poking out from behind a chair.

She goes round the table and stands looking down at him.

He looks up and giggles.

BESS

You're a naughty lad. But I won't tell anyone it was you. We'll just keep it a secret, between ourselves.

ORCHARD. DAY.

Tom and Emily walking in the orchard. They see a number of servants collected under an apple tree.

Jack is sitting on an upper branch of the apple tree. He is throwing apples down. The servants are applauding.

SERVANTS

Eh, look at him. Good boy! Look at that! Light as a feather.

EMILY

Should he be doing that? Isn't it dangerous?

TOM

No, no. Of course not. There's no harm in it. Look at him. See how agile he is.

EMILY

Yes, he is agile. Light and agile.

TOM

They all love him. All the servants love him.

CONFERENCE ROOM. FAMILY SHIPPING OFFICE.

Mr Rudd, Emily's father. Emily and Tom.

EMILY

Yes, I think he possesses native intelligence. I
recommend we engage a tutor.

MR RUDD

The trial period is six months?

TOM

Yes.

MR RUDD

Tell me . . . has he religious sensibilities?

TOM

That is not yet known.

MR RUDD

I meant – is there a background of religion?

Pause.

EMILY

No, there is not.

Pause.

MR RUDD

So he's a savage?

EMILY

Not at all.

MR RUDD

Let me remind you of certain basic facts. The illegitimacy of a child is the result of the immorality of its mother. And the immorality of the poor is passed on from generation to generation.

Silence.

Will you bring him to church?

TOM

He'll make nothing of it.

MR RUDD

He'll make nothing of God?

Pause.

EMILY

He knows nothing of God.

ME RUDD

He's a creature of God.

EMILY

He does not know that.

Pause.

MR RUDD

That is blasphemous.

EMILY

Ignorance is not blasphemy.

MR RUDD

Ignorance in itself is not blasphemy. Ignorance of God is.

TOM

He is seven years old.

Pause.

MR RUDD

You must establish the level of his *actual* intelligence –
quite apart from his *native* intelligence. A native
intelligence is in itself useless, without merit. You're
looking at a future for him where he will be asked to
exercise the most serious responsibilities. Will he be able
to undertake such responsibilities? Will he have the
courage, the will, the determination, the faith? Or will he
be temperamentally and intellectually incapable? I suggest
you embark on a proper and exhaustive investigation.

EMILY

Oh, father! He's our son! Don't talk of him as if he's
a . . . !

MR RUDD

Your son? He's not your son.

Silence.

EMILY

No, he's not our son. But neither is he . . . a thing.

Pause.

TOM

Let us engage a tutor.

THE HALL. DAY.

*Jack standing on the top of a ladder cleaning candles in a
chandelier.*

*The Housekeeper, the Butler, Bess and other Maids are watching
him. A Footman holds the ladder.*

BUTLER

We could have done with you here years ago, son!
 (*to the others*)
He's going to make our lives a lot easier, this lad.

FOOTMAN
I never had no head for ladders myself.

BUTLER
Apple trees, chandeliers, he can do the lot.

HOUSEKEEPER
Come on then, Jack. Down you come.

JACK ON TOP OF THE LADDER.

He looks down. He starts to climb down.

THE HALL.

Jack descending. He jumps the last few steps on to the floor. Bess cuddles him.

BESS
Would you like a plum?

She takes a plum from her apron.

Look what I've got. A lovely plum. Just for you.

Jack takes the plum.

JACK
I like plums.

BUTLER
She doesn't give everybody her plums, you know.

FOOTMAN
I've always been after her plums myself. No luck so far.

Sound of a carriage arriving. Bridget turns from the front door.

BRIDGET
They're back!

The servants go gravely about their business, taking the ladder with them. Jack eats his plum.

SHIPYARD. DOCK. DAY.

A large hoarding: CARTER AND RUDD, SHIPPERS.

*Tom, Emily and Jack walking along the dock towards Mr Carter.
(Tom's father) who is talking to his foreman.*

MR CARTER

Ah, you've brought the little lad along, have you?
> (*He kisses Emily.*)

How pretty you look, my dear. You have a bloom on
your cheeks. And how's the little lad? Now, tell me little
lad – do you like big boats?

JACK

Yes, I do.

MR CARTER

You see that one? The biggest one? Do you know where
it's going?

JACK

No.

MR CARTER

It's going to Africa.

JACK

Where is Africa?

MR CARTER

It's on the other side of the world. It's all the way round
on the other side of the world.

TOM

You'll go there one day, Jack.

MR CARTER

You will. You'll go in a big boat.

JACK

I don't think I'll ever go to Africa.

MR CARTER

Of course you'll go to Africa. Your name is Carter isn't it?

Tom and Emily glance at each other.

All men by the name of Carter sail to Africa. And they sail to China too. And Jamaica. And do you know why? Do you know why all men by the name of Carter sail to any port in the world? I'll tell you. Because these are Carter boats. Do you know what I mean by that?
(*To Tom.*)
Does he know what I mean?

TOM

He will.

MR CARTER

Come on then. Come and have a look at your boat.

They walk up the stepladder on to the deck of the boat.

INT. SHIPPING OFFICE.

Mr Rudd at the window watching the group walk up the stepladder on to the boat. He focuses on Jack.

DECK OF BOAT.

Sailors are cleaning the sails. The group stop to watch.

MR CARTER

Do you know what they're doing, son? They're cleaning the sails so they'll go faster through all the big waves. They're making sure the boat is all shipshape and Bristol-fashion.

There is a sudden gust of wind. A sail fills and blows out the other side. Jack gasps and clutches Tom's hand.

ANOTHER PART OF THE DECK.

Mr Rudd watching, sees Jack shrink back and clutch Tom's hand. He frowns and shakes his head.

THE GROUP ON THE DECK.

MR CARTER
What's the matter? Are you nervous, lad? Nothing to be nervous about.

EMILY
He's not at all nervous. He was just taken by surprise.

MR CARTER
(*to Jack*)
Like to come down and have a look at the hold, see all the things we're taking to Africa?

JACK
Oh yes, sir.

Mr Carter turns and calls.

MR CARTER
Hello there, Bo'sun! Take us down to the hold.

THE HOLD.

Bo'sun, holding a lantern, leading the group.

MR CARTER
You see lad we take all these trousers and all these shirts and all these saucepans all the way to Africa. All the way to Africa. And the African people love our saucepans, don't they Bo'sun?

BO'SUN
They do, Mr Carter.

MR CARTER

And tell the lad what we bring back from Africa.

BO'SUN

Well, we bring back palm oil for soap, gum and beeswax and of course we bring back elephants' teeth.

MR CARTER

But no elephants.

QUARTER-DECK.

Jack stands by the wheel, his hands on it.

TOM

How would you like to take this ship out to sea yourself, Jack? It's a great thing to do at night. You navigate by the stars, you see. They show you the way to go.

Jack turns to Emily.

JACK

Do the stars know the way to Africa?

EMILY

Oh, yes. Oh, yes.

THE HOUSE. EMILY'S BOUDOIR.

Fish in a small aquarium. Jack and Emily are feeding them.

JACK

They're such big fish. I like them very much because of the way they swim round and round and up and down. But I think they're dangerous.

EMILY

Dangerous? Why?

JACK

Yes, they're dangerous. We must watch out for the dog.

We must stop the dog jumping into the bowl. They might bite him.

EMILY

No, no. The fish and the dog are very old friends. And these fish don't bite.

JACK

Don't they?

EMILY

No.

JACK

Then I'm wrong?

EMILY

You are wrong. Yes.

JACK

I'm glad I'm wrong because I like these fish very much and I wanted to say one other thing.

EMILY

What?

JACK

Can you leave these curtains open at night?

EMILY

Yes. If you want. But why?

JACK

So that they can look out at the moon.

Emily looks out of the window.

FLASH.

Charley at the gate in the moonlight looking up.

THE DREAMING CHILD

THE DRIVE OF THE HOUSE. AFTERNOON.

Jack running with the dog.

JACK
Come on, Nap! Come on, Nap!

Jack jumps on the garden gate and begins to swing backwards and forwards on it.

Emily is walking across the lawn. She stops.

EMILY
Get down from there! Stop it! Stop doing that! Get away from that gate!

He jumps down from the gate.

She walks towards him swiftly and hits him. He falls, scraping his knee. He cries out, holds his knee. She stands still. The dog barks.

Jack gets to his feet and runs into her arms. She holds him.

You might have fallen off the gate, you see. You might have fallen off and hurt yourself. I didn't want you to hurt yourself.

THE COACHMAN.

He stands at the side of the house, observing this scene.

THE NURSERY. NIGHT.

Jack wakes out of a dream, sweating.

GREEN BAIZE DOOR.

The green baize door leads to the Servants' Quarters.

Jack in his nightclothes walks towards it in the moonlight. He slowly pushes it open and looks inside.

THE SERVANTS' STAIRS.

JACK AT THE DOOR.

He lets the door close behind him and begins slowly to ascend the stairs. The stairs are dark. He falters, shivers, goes on.

He reaches the top of the stairs and walks on to a narrow landing.

THE LANDING.

Bess is standing with a candle looking at him. She whispers.

> BESS
>
> What are you doing up here?

> JACK
>
> I came to find you.

He goes to her. She cuddles him.

> BESS
>
> You shouldn't come up here, really. It's not allowed.

Jack stares at her.

> JACK
>
> What's up here, then?

> BESS
>
> This is where the servants live. This is where we sleep. Do you want to have a quick look at where I sleep?

> JACK
>
> Yes.

> BESS
>
> Take my hand then and keep quiet.

She leads him along the landing to a door and opens it.

BESS'S ROOM.

Bess and Jack go in.

> **BESS**
>
> This is my room. Do you like it? Look. It's got a nice window. I was sharing it with two other girls but they both took ill and went to the infirmary so I've got it all to myself now.

She takes him to her bed.

> This is my bed. Look. Do you like my doll? My mum made it all by herself. She gave it to me. She's dead now. She died only the other day, my mum.
> > (*She kisses the doll.*)
> I love my doll.

Footsteps on the landing.

> Sshh!

She puts her arm round him. They both crouch down.

SERVANTS' FLOOR. CORRIDOR.

The Housekeeper, holding a candle, staring at the door of Bess's room, which is ajar.

THE HOUSE. HALL. MORNING.

Morning prayers. The family and all the staff.

Tom leading the gathering in the Lord's Prayer. After the general 'Amen' there is a moment's silence.

Jack suddenly speaks.

> **JACK**
>
> But where is God?

Everyone is still. Jack turns to Tom.

I would like to see God. And speak to him. Just as I
speak to you. Can I do that?

*Frozen silence. Suddenly Bess giggles. Jack looks across at her
and laughs briefly. Emily turns to look at Bess. Bess, aware of
Emily's look, stops giggling.*

TOM

No. You cannot.

SCHOOLROOM.

Tutor and Jack.

TUTOR

Now, boy, tell me. Can you read?

JACK

No, sir.

TUTOR

Can you write?

JACK

No, sir.

TUTOR

What do I mean by the word 'write'?

JACK

Writing is making signs.

TUTOR

Signs?

JACK

Yes. Like a man in a lighthouse. When he flashes his
light he is sending signs. Writing is sending signs.

TUTOR

Who told you that?

514

JACK

Nobody. I just thought that when I was thinking.

HOUSE. LANDING. DAY.

Jack bouncing a ball on the stairs. He hears footsteps. The Housekeeper is leading Bess towards Emily's boudoir. She knocks on the door and enters with Bess.

Jack bounces the ball down the stairs, catching it off the wall. He stops still at the bottom of the stairs. He hears sobs from above. He bounces the ball back up the stairs, suddenly stops. Boudoir door opens. The Housekeeper comes out with Bess. The Housekeeper turns back into the room.

HOUSEKEEPER

Thank you, Ma'am. Good afternoon, Ma'am.

She closes the door.

Bess, sobbing, is led away. Jack stands looking up.

GREEN BAIZE DOOR.

It swings. comes to a close.

BESS'S BEDROOM.

Jack standing at Bess's made-up bed. The room is empty.

THE TACK ROOM. DAY.

Jack helping the Coachman fix the harness on to the horse. Jack moves close to the horse's head.

COACHMAN

Don't go so close. He can bite.

JACK

He won't bite me.

COACHMAN

Well, I reckon he probably won't, he likes you, all right.
But he's been a bit jumpy ever since –

He stops.

JACK

Ever since what?

COACHMAN

He was a tearaway once, this horse. A tearaway. Nobody
could ride him. Nobody. Except Madam. Madam was
the only one who could sit on him. He loved her. I
could never handle him – and I can handle most – but
she would just talk to him, that's all, just whisper to him
and he was like a baby. But then one day –

JACK

One day what?

COACHMAN

One day she turned her back on him. Treated him like a
stranger. Had him gelded. Put him in harness. Broke his
heart.

JACK

Why did she do that?

COACHMAN

Well, he was a tearaway. He was too strong for her. In
the end.
         (*He puts his face close to Jack.*)
I shouldn't have told you. Now you won't tell Madam I
told you. Will you?

JACK

No, I won't.
         (*He strokes the horse.*)
So he's not a tearaway any more?

516

COACHMAN

Oh, no. He'll never be a tearaway again in this life.
>   (*He strokes the horse.*)

Never in this life. Oh, I forgot something.
>   (*He picks up a doll from a shelf and gives it to Jack.*)

Here you are. Bess's doll. She said I was to give it to
you. As a farewell present.

FAIRGROUND. A HEATH.

*Crowds of people moving in all directions. Music. Coconut shies.
Side-shows. 'The Strongest Man in the World', 'Bearded
Woman', etc.*

*Emily and Jack standing at a coconut shy. He throws his ball at
a coconut and hits it.*

MAN

Good shot, sir! Bullseye!

EMILY

That was a very good shot. What a good eye.

JACK

You try, Mother. Please.

EMILY

No. I can't do it. I don't know how to do it.

JACK

Just throw it.

EMILY

Shall I? Shall I? What, like this?

She throws it and hits the coconut. Jack applauds.

JACK

Good shot!

MAN

Excellent, Madam. Bullseye! Now you're both entitled
to prizes. One for the lady and one for her little boy.

EMILY

Aren't we lucky? I would like that little pepper pot. Jack,
what would you like?

JACK
(*pointing*)

I'd like that.

MAN

What? This?

JACK

Yes please.

MAN

It's a salt cellar.

JACK

Yes please.

MAN

Here you are then.

The Man gives the salt cellar to Jack. Jack gives it to Emily.

JACK

It will be nice company for your pepper pot, Mama.

FAIRGROUND. LATER.

Emily and Jack walking in the crowd.

JACK

Did you lose me in a crowd when I was small? In a
crowd at a fair like this?

EMILY

Did I lose you?

JACK

You must have lost me because you found me. So I
must have been lost.

EMILY
(*lightly*)

Yes. Then that is what must have happened. I must
have lost you in a crowd at a fair. And then I found you.

She ruffles his hair.

CAMERA OBSCURA.

*The camera pulls back into the interior of Clifton Observatory.
Tom is operating the camera obscura.*

*The fairground is projected on to the drum of the camera obscura.
The image of Emily and Jack becomes smaller as they walk out of
the fairground.*

PEGGY'S HOUSE. GARDEN.

*Peggy and Emily sitting on a bench. In background two small
Children with a Nurse.*

PEGGY

He seems to be a good-natured child.

EMILY

Oh, yes. He is.

PEGGY

Everyone loves him.

Pause.

Don't they?

EMILY

They seem to.

Pause.

PEGGY

And you?

Pause.

EMILY

I cannot . . . love him.

PEGGY

Oh?

EMILY

It is not in my heart. Perhaps I have no love in my heart.

Pause.

PEGGY

That cannot be true.

EMILY

It could be true. I think I have a desert where my heart should be. An empty space.

PEGGY

That is not possible.

EMILY

How do you know?

PEGGY

I know. I know you have a real heart.

EMILY

Everything is real. A warm heart is real. A cold heart is also real.

PEGGY

You do not love the child because you did not bear him.

EMILY

Do you love your own children simply because you bore them? Or because of their natures? Or because of your nature?

They look at each other. Emily turns away and gazes across the garden.

SEPIA. SLOW MOTION.

Charley making love to Emily on her bed.

PEGGY'S GARDEN.

Emily gazing across the garden. She suddenly becomes aware that Peggy is crying quietly.

EMILY

What is it?

PEGGY

Nothing. Nothing.

EMILY

Tell me.

PEGGY

No. It's nothing.

They sit still.

Are you saying you have never loved?

Emily gives her a handkerchief.

EMILY

Wipe your tears away, my dear.

They look into each others eyes. Emily smiles slightly.

Wipe your tears away.

FIVES COURT. DAY.

Tom and Jack playing fives. Jack is very quick on his feet. He hits the ball firmly.

TOM

Excellent! Well hit! Well struck! You're a natural!

Jack grins.

SCHOOLROOM. DAY.

The Tutor and Jack. The Tutor is standing by a globe of the world. Tom is seated by the window.

TUTOR

Where is India?

Jack is silent.

TUTOR

Where is India?

JACK

Round the corner.

TUTOR

Round what corner?

JACK

Round the corner of that globe.

TUTOR

Are you being impertinent?

Pause.

JACK

But India is just round the corner of that globe.

TUTOR

There are no corners on a globe, you idiot!

Pause.

JACK

No. That is correct.

TUTOR

What did you say?

JACK

That is correct.

TUTOR

Are you telling me that what I tell you is correct?

JACK

Yes, sir. What you said was correct. A globe does not have corners. A globe is round. I see that. There are no round corners. A corner stops and then turns sharply to the right or to the left.

Pause.

You see, sometimes I say things that I don't understand. I hear myself say something I don't understand. But I am only seven.

TUTOR

Is India next to China?

Pause.

Is India next to China?

JACK

No, sir. It's just round the corner from China.

OFFICE AT SHIPYARD.

Mr Rudd. Emily. Tom.

MR RUDD

So you are in favour?

TOM

He's a good lad. A strong lad. He has a mind. He's still a child of course. But he has a mind.
(*to Emily*)

Would you not say?

EMILY

Oh, certainly. Certainly.

Pause.

MR RUDD

So you both feel confident that you would like to put your seal on this?

Pause.

TOM

Yes, sir.

MR RUDD

I have heard that the boy is sometimes quite high-spirited . . . somewhat . . . unpredictable . . .

TOM

He has plenty of spirit, certainly. That's a benefit. Is it not?

EMILY

To be high-spirited is hardly a sin.

MR RUDD

Think carefully. You are taking upon yourselves a son for life.

(*to Tom*)

A son who will inherit your estate and run your worldly affairs after your death.

Pause.

Emily?

EMILY

I support it.

MR RUDD

You have never brought him to me –

EMILY

You have never asked for him to be brought to you. You have shown no interest in him whatsoever –

MR RUDD

Since your mother is dead, I did not feel –

EMILY

My mother would have received him.

MR RUDD

Will you allow me to receive him now?

Emily looks at Tom.

TOM

No, sir. I'm afraid not. We have consulted you, of course – but the decision is ours. There seems to your daughter and to me little point in your receiving him now. Emily and I will confirm shortly that we will formally adopt him. I have the right to do this and I shall do it.

He looks at Emily.

We shall do it.

Tom and Emily stand.

Thank you for your courteous interest.

Mr Rudd stands.

MR RUDD

I bow to your conviction.

EMILY

Thank you.

MR RUDD

When will you tell the boy that you are formally
adopting him?

TOM

Never.

EMILY

He has never been told that he has been on six months
trial. There is no need to tell him. Ever.

THE DOWNS. DAY.

Tom, Emily, Jack and the dog on the Downs.

Tom is running with Jack on his shoulders, followed by the dog.

*Tom is neighing like a horse. He stops. Jack jumps off and runs
back to Emily.*

JACK

He's very tired, I think. I'm quite heavy on his
shoulders. Do you think I should let him run with me
again?

EMILY

Oh yes. Let him run with you just one time more.

Jack runs to Tom.

JACK

Do you want to run with me again or are you too tired?

TOM

Tired? Horses are never tired. Up you come.

Jack climbs on to his shoulders and they run.

Emily stands watching.

SERVANTS' HALL. AFTERNOON.

*A Footman is playing the fiddle. Some of the Maids are dancing.
Jack is sitting with the Cook, eating a fruit pie.*

The Butler is singing.

BUTLER

Oh I never thought she would be
    false or ever prove untrue,
As we sailed away from Bristol
    Quay on board the Kangaroo

Everybody joins the chorus including Jack between gulps of pie.

So farewell to dreams of married life
    to soapsuds and the blue
Farewell to all the laundry girls
    and the washing powder too
I'll seek some far and distant clime,
    no longer can I stay
And on some Chinese Hottentot
    I will throw this life away

NURSERY. EVENING.

*Jack climbing into bed. The Nursemaid tucking him in. Emily
comes in.*

NURSEMAID

Evening Ma'am.

EMILY

Evening Rose.

Emily sits on the bed.

Did you like Cook's party? Did you eat her jam?

JACK

I ate her pie and I sang a song with everybody.

EMILY

You can sing another song tomorrow, at the children's party. You're going to meet other children. Are you looking forward to that?

JACK

I don't know yet. I've never been to a children's party. What will I have to do?

She takes his hand, looks into his eyes.

EMILY

You'll just . . . have a nice time.

She kisses his cheek, blows out his candle and goes to close the curtains.

JACK

No, please.

EMILY

Yes, yes. Of course. You want to see the moon.

She leaves the curtains and goes out.

Moonlight in the room.

NURSERY. DAY.

Nurse with Jack. She is dressing him.

NURSE

There. Don't you look handsome? I bet you'll be the handsomest boy there. Won't you? I bet you're excited. Are you excited? I bet you're looking forward to the party? You'll have a lovely time. And you'll meet some lovely boys and girls. Now you look at yourself in the glass.

Jack stands looking at himself in the glass.

PEGGY'S HOUSE. DAY.

The children's party.

In background the Mothers, Nursemaids. Chatter.

In foreground a Punch and Judy show. The Children watching.
Most of the Children laughing. Jack frowning. Judy hits Punch
violently. The Children laugh and applaud.

Jack stands and moves away. A Girl (10) joins him.

> GIRL
>
> Who did you like best? Punch or Judy?

> JACK
>
> I didn't like Punch or Judy.

> GIRL
>
> Oh. Your name's Jack isn't it?

> JACK
>
> How did you know that?

> GIRL
>
> I just knew. Where were you born?

> JACK
>
> I was born here.

> GIRL
>
> Where?

> JACK
>
> In Bristol.

> GIRL
>
> But who was your mother?

> JACK
>
> My mother is here.

GIRL

Where?

JACK

In this room. She is standing over there. In her pink
dress.

The Girl turns to look across the room at Emily and then turns back.

GIRL

Don't be silly.

JACK

I'm not silly.

GIRL

Well, you are silly. What you said was silly.

JACK

Why?

GIRL

That lady is not your mother.

JACK

Yes, she is.

GIRL

No, she is not. She found you in a slum. My mother
told me. You're just being 'tried out' – to see if you can
be a son. But you're not a real son. And that lady is not
your real mother.

EXT. FIELD. DAY.

*Tom at the gate on his horse. He is bending to close the gate. The
horse is frisky. Tom takes him on and turns back to the gate.*

*Jack is with Bruno and the Coachman. Jack undoes the saddle
and bridle and gives them to the Coachman. The Coachman's
face is blank.*

Tom closes the gate and looks across the field.

Jack slaps the horse.

Tom watches the horse gallop free across the field.

THE FISH IN THE AQUARIUM.

Jack watching them, still.

GREEN BAIZE DOOR.

The door swings and comes to a stop.

SERVANTS' STAIRS.

Jack climbing the stairs.

BESS'S EMPTY ROOM. DAY.

Jack standing at the window looking out.

FRONT STAIRS. LANDING.

Emily on landing.

EMILY

Jack! Where are you?

BESS'S ROOM.

A faint echo 'Where are you?'

Jack does not move.

THE LAWN OUTSIDE THE HOUSE.

Snow.

High up, the figure of Jack looking out of a window.

TOM ON THE LAWN LOOKING UP.

THE HALL.

Emily with the Doctor.

> **DOCTOR**
> Yes, yes. A little fever. Nothing to worry about. Keep
> him in bed. No excitement.

NURSERY.

> **EMILY**
> Now just sip this.

He sips.

> **JACK**
> Do you know, in my house the stairs were so dark and
> so full of holes that you had to grope your way up it on
> your hands and knees or you would fall through the
> holes and land on your head. And there was a window
> broken by the wind and on the landing there was a great
> mountain of snow, taller than me.

> **EMILY**
> But you're in this house now. There are no broken
> windows in this house.

> **JACK**
> Oh, yes, this is a beautiful house. But I have another
> house. A dark house. A house of dirt and rats.

> **EMILY**
> You must be quiet.

> **JACK**
> In the street where my dark house was there was an old
> lodging house. The people who had got plenty of money
> slept in beds but the others had to stand up to sleep,

with a rope under their arms. One night the house caught fire and burned down. The people who were in bed were all burnt to death because they couldn't get their trousers on quick enough. But those who were standing up to sleep were the lucky ones because they could get out quick.

EMILY

Ssshh. Ssshh.

JACK

And in my house the sheets on the line tried to suffocate you and smother you. They were half wet and alive. They were animal sheets. They wanted to eat you up. They wanted to suck out your life from you.

EMILY

Ssshh. You are never going back to that house.

JACK

Never?

EMILY

Never. Never.

DRAWING-ROOM. PARROT IN CAGE.

In background, open door leading to hall. The Doctor can be seen talking to Tom and Emily in the hall.

The Parrot speaks.

The camera tracks past the Parrot into the hall.

EMILY

Is he dying?

DOCTOR

He is growing weaker. It is difficult –

EMILY

But is he dying?

DOCTOR

Madam . . .

EMILY

Why is he dying? He's not ill.

DOCTOR

Madam you must –

EMILY

I am aware that children die. Poor children die. They die of diseases. They die because they are poor. But Jack has no disease and he is no longer poor. So why is he dying?

DOCTOR

I cannot say. There is no clear –

EMILY

I simply don't understand why he is dying! I mean – what is he dying *of*?

NURSERY.

Parrot in the room.

PARROT

Dying *of* . . .

Jack looks up. Opens his eyes.

JACK

Dying?

TOM

We were talking to Peg Leg the parrot, old chap.

JACK

Is Peg Leg dying?

534

TOM

No, no. He won't die for another hundred years.

JACK

Do you remember Miss Scott, Mama?

EMILY

No, Jack. I didn't know her.

JACK

Oh, you did, really. If you could remember properly.
She was so poor she came to live in our slum because
she had no money. But she remembered you, Mama.
She sewed your wedding dress. It was white satin. But
when she died she left me a pair of beautiful scissors but
I left them at my other house. Can I have them? They
are mine. I want to cut a white rose from the bush.

SLUM HOUSE.

Mrs Jones and Emily.

MRS JONES

No. I don't recall no scissors. And I don't remember no
Miss Scott. Never heard of her. Nobody left him no
scissors. It's all in the boy's dreams, Missus. He was
always a dreamer. Used to sit in that corner and dream
to himself. He just dreamed up those scissors.

ARCADE. BRISTOL.

*Emily's carriage draws up at the arcade. She walks through the
arcade to a haberdashery store.*

INT. HABERDASHERY STORE.

Emily with Saleslady. She is looking at a pair of scissors.

EMILY

Yes. Thank you. These will do. What do they cost?

SALESLADY

Nine-pence, Ma'am.

EMILY

Here you are.

Emily becomes aware of something taking place at the other end of the store. She puts the scissors into her handbag and walks across the store to an open door.

A number of women are standing in the doorway looking into the room. The room is crowded. All women.

A Woman at the far end of the room is speaking.

During the course of her speech a number of women turn and leave abruptly. At one point Emily recognises Bess, the young Maid. Bess looks at her briefly and then away.

SUFFRAGETTE

Remember! Women who owned property possessed a vote until 1832. That right was taken away from us. We are – all of us – regarded as good only for domestic duties. We are excluded from any other role in the world in which we live. We are regarded as inferior, without conscience, without intelligence – as frivolous – as morally suspect. We must no longer submit to these definitions of our sex. We demand the vote – for all women. We demand recognition of our dignity, our intelligence, our honesty. We will no longer live in submission.

EMILY'S FACE.

EXT. HOUSE. RAIN.

Mr Rudd walking up the steps.

A Maid opens the door. She curtseys.

Emily comes across the hall.

EMILY

Father.

DRAWING-ROOM.

Doctor. Tom. Emily. Mr Carter. Mr Rudd.

DOCTOR

I don't know that he is dying. But if he is we don't know why.

Pause.

All I can say is . . . it's not a thing I would ordinarily say . . . it's his flame . . . I speak as a man, not as a doctor . . . it's his flame . . . which is going out. It's as if . . . the eight years of his life have been enough for him. It's as if . . . he doesn't want any more of his life.

EMILY

How can you say that? How dare you? Who is this man? Leave this house.

The Doctor leaves the room and the house.

Tom looks at her.

She walks up the stairs.

The three men stand in silence. Mr Rudd turns to Tom.

MR RUDD

I'd like to see the boy.

Tom looks at him.

Where is his room?

Tom pauses and then goes to the bell-pull and pulls it.

> MR CARTER
> (*muttering to himself*)
> I don't understand it. I just don't understand it.

The Housekeeper comes into the room.

> TOM
> Show Mr Rudd to the boy's room.

NURSERY. CORRIDOR.

Housekeeper leading Mr Rudd to the nursery.

> MR RUDD
> Thank you.

He goes in.

NURSERY.

The Nurse jumps up.

> NURSE
> Oh, sir . . .

> MR RUDD
> Would you leave us for a moment please?

She goes out. Mr Rudd stands looking down at Jack. Jack opens his eyes.

> Not feeling well?

> JACK
> Oh, quite well, sir.

> MR RUDD
> Bit of a headache I expect.

> JACK
> A little one, yes sir. Not a very big one.

Pause.

MR RUDD

Still, you're lying in a very nice room.

JACK

Oh yes. I love my room.

MR RUDD

You came to see one of my ships once upon a time. But
we didn't say hello.

Jack smiles.

JACK

Hello.

Pause.

MR RUDD

You'll be feeling better by tomorrow. We could have a
game of dominoes. Do you know how to play
dominoes?

JACK

No, sir.

MR RUDD

I can teach you how to play. When you're feeling better.
It's a very interesting game. People play it in China and
Africa and sometimes . . . when the sea is very calm . . .
people play it in the middle of the ocean.

He leaves the room.

EMILY'S BEDROOM.

She is sitting still, her hands over her face.

THE NURSERY.

Emily and Jack.

JACK

Yes. And when you were standing with my father at the gate in the moonlight you plucked a white rose from the bush and you gave it to him.

She stares at him.

NURSERY. LATE AT NIGHT.

Emily. Tom. Mr Rudd. Mr Carter. Nurse. Jack's fever is high. He is delirious.

JACK

Do you know . . . I sometimes wonder where I am. I sometimes wonder who I was.

EMILY

Ssshh. Ssshh.

JACK

Who was I?

THE SERVANTS' HALL.

The Servants sitting about the room, silent.

DRAWING-ROOM.

Emily and Tom sitting at the window.

His head is in his hands. He is sobbing. She is gazing out of the window.

HOUSE. THE HALL.

The Servants going up and down the stairs and across the hall about their work. They are in mourning.

MORNING ROOM. DAY.

Emily and Housekeeper and Butler.

EMILY

Mr Rudd in the West Room. Mr Carter in the North Room. The Misses Ames in the Damask Room. Miss Gibbs in the Chintz Room. Mrs Thistlewaite in the South Room. Lilies in all rooms.

Silence.

The Housekeeper and Butler wait. She looks at them.

Mr Rudd in the West Room.

The Housekeeper and Butler stand uncertainly.

Lilies in all rooms.

FAMILY VAULT.

The family. The small coffin.

MR RUDD

Although young Jack was not strictly a member of the family, I recommended that he be buried in the family vault. My son-in-law and my daughter were on the point of adopting him. Formally. Therefore I think this burial is appropriate.

TOM

Thank you, sir. We had indeed grown very close to the boy, very attached to the boy. His death is a matter of great sadness to us. It seems to us also that this burial is appropriate.

Tom picks up the prayer book and reads.

'Man that is born of a woman hath but a short time to live and is full of misery. He cometh up and is cut down, like a flower.
    In the midst of life we are in death.'

EMILY'S FACE.

THE COFFIN GOING INTO THE VAULT.

The iron gates close.

A HIGH WINDOW. DAY.

Emily standing still by the window looking out.

A HIGH WINDOW. NIGHT.

Emily standing still by the window looking out.

MORNING ROOM. DAY.

Emily sitting still. Tom comes into the room.

TOM

Emily?

She does not look at him.

EXT. HOUSE. MOONLIGHT.

Emily looking down from a high window.

INT. HALL. STAIRS.

Emily on the stairs in her nightdress pouring water into a flower pot. The water spills down the side of the pot on to the carpet.

Housekeeper comes up the stairs, goes to her, takes her arm and helps her up the stairs.

Tom is standing on the first landing looking on.

CORRIDOR. HOUSE. DAY.

Emily and the Housekeeper come round the corner into the corridor. Emily stops dead.

CLOSE-UP. HER EYES.

EMILY'S POV.

Charley standing still at the end of the corridor.

The shot is held. He does not move.

CLOSE-UP. HER EYES.

THE CORNER OF THE CORRIDOR.

Emily and Housekeeper. Tom looking on. The Housekeeper guides Emily along the corridor.

SLUM STREET. MORNING.

Emily gets out of her carriage and walks towards Mrs Jones's house.

MRS JONES'S KITCHEN. MORNING.

> EMILY
>
> The last time I came to see you, Mrs Jones, you said that Miss Scott did not leave Jack a silver pair of scissors. You also said you did not remember a Miss Scott.

> MRS JONES
>
> I said that, yes I did say that. But I was wrong. I do remember a Miss Scott. There was a Miss Scott. My memory is bad, Missus.

> EMILY
>
> And there was also a little black chair with roses painted on it.

> MRS JONES.
>
> A little black chair?

EMILY

With roses painted on it.

MRS JONES

Oh, the little black chair. Oh, yes. Well I don't know what happened to that.

Emily looks at the kitchen shelf. She goes to it and picks up a silver thimble.

EMILY

Whose thimble is this?

Mrs Jones is silent.

Is this your thimble?

MRS JONES

No, Ma'am. It belongs to the boy. She left it to the boy.

EMILY

So you didn't sell the thimble? Why not?

MRS JONES

Well, it belongs to the boy.

EMILY

I shall take it.

MRS JONES

Yes, yes. How is the boy, Ma'am?

EMILY

I wish you well.

She goes. Mrs Jones starts to fold sheets feverishly. She mutters to herself.

MRS JONES

These ladies . . . these people . . . all these fine ladies . . . they come down here . . . poke their nose . . . come down here . . .

544

SLUM HOUSE. NIGHT.

The Mother lying on the table. She puts money into Mrs Jones's hand.

>   MOTHER
>   (*faintly*)
> Keep him. Look after him. Keep him.

Mrs Jones stares at the money.

EMILY'S BEDROOM.

Emily lying in her bed. Eyes open. The thimble on a little table beside the bed.

PEGGY'S HOUSE.

Peggy and Tom.

>   TOM
> She has stopped speaking. Ever since the boy died.
> Hardly a word. She seems to be somewhere else. She
> lies in her room. Please. You are her dearest friend.
> Talk to her.

EMILY'S BEDROOM.

Emily and Peggy.

>   PEGGY
> I'm concerned for you. Why do you say so little? What
> are you thinking? Why do you keep to your room? Your
> devoted husband worries for you. Why don't you speak
> to your husband?

Emily remains silent.

> Why don't you speak to your husband? What has he
> done?

EMILY

He has done nothing.

PEGGY

He believes he has done something. He believes he has done something to offend you.

EMILY

He has done nothing.

PEGGY AND TOM.

Tom walking about the room.

TOM

Is it grief? Is she grief-stricken? It was sad, yes, the death of the boy, very sad. But surely – rationally – not a matter for such grief? How can one feel such grief for someone who . . . five and a half months ago . . . was a total stranger? How can one feel such grief about the death of a total stranger? Do you understand what I'm saying? He was not a blood relation!

PEGGY

He was a child of rare spirit.

TOM

But not a blood relation. I do not understand what is happening to my wife. I can make no sense of it.

HOUSE. BOUDOIR.

Emily and Peggy.

EMILY

I am very sorry he is so distressed. I did not . . . intend that.

Pause.

But yes. It is true. Somewhere . . . inside me . . . is a

knot . . . which I have never been able to untie. It is tied
so tight. I cannot untie it.

HOUSE. LIBRARY.

Tom at his desk. He is sitting still, neither reading nor writing.

There is a knock on the door. Emily comes in. He stands.

EMILY
It is such a beautiful morning. Do you have time to take
a walk?

A WOOD. MORNING.

*Tom and Emily walking through the wood. The wood is black in
the shade, brilliant green in the sun. They walk through shade
into sun into shade.*

They come out into a field. Wild flowers.

A cuckoo. They listen.

*Emily bends, picks up a bird's egg broken in two. She tries to put
it together.*

TOM
What are you doing?

EMILY
It's broken. I'm trying to put it together but I can't do
it.

They walk on.

TOM
I thought we might make a journey to France. Wouldn't
you like to see France again? It's really such a beautiful
country. Do you remember it? We were there so briefly.
I thought perhaps this time –

EMILY

There is something I want to tell you. Shall we sit?

They both sit on a tree stump.

Birdsong.

Cumulus clouds.

A breeze along the rye. Long billows.

They sit still.

That boy was my child.

TOM

Yes, of course, yes. He was our child.

EMILY

No. He was *my* child. My own child.

TOM

What are you talking about?

Pause.

EMILY

He was my son. I gave birth to him.

TOM

I don't think . . . you know what you're saying.

EMILY

Oh, I do know. I do know what I'm saying. He knew too. He knew. He was right. He was my son.

Pause.

TOM

But you cannot have children.

EMILY

But I did. I had him.

Pause.

TOM

Go on. I'm listening to you.

EMILY

Thank you.

TOM

I'm listening to you.

Pause.

EMILY

Charley White was my lover. When you were in China. Charley was my lover. And then he died. But when you were still in China my son was born.

She stands and begins to walk backwards and forwards.

Charley was going on such a long voyage. I couldn't bear it. I could not bear him going. He begged me to let him stay the night with me. Can you imagine? Can you imagine? He begged me to let him stay the night with me. We stood by the garden gate. He was so . . . powerful. His ardour . . . transfixed me. I was his white rose. I was adored. He adored me. That night I collapsed into his arms.

Silence.

The boy was our son.

Silence

Jack was our son but I never told him so. Oh I wish I had done so. I wish I had told him so.

Pause.

When Charley begged me at the gate I felt it to be . . . so dangerous, out of the question, appalling, impossible, insulting, disgusting, criminal, unthinkable. But why? Why did I think that? Why do you make us – encourage us – to think in that way? You must know that he begged me out of his love for me. He spoke out of his love, out of his great heart, out of his passion. He wanted to give me all the life of his soul and his blood. He offered it to me and I took it. I received it. I opened my life to his life. I gave myself to him.

Pause.

But then later I was frightened. When the baby was born I gave him away. And I didn't see him again until I found him.

She sits down.

And if I were back at that moment again, if I were standing with Charley at that gate, in that moonlight, again, I would do as I did then. I would walk back with him, through the garden, as I did then. And I would let him stay the night with me, and let him love me, before, in the morning, he was to go so far away for so long, so far away for ever.

They sit still.

Because there is a grace in the world, you see. And I have found it.

Birdsong.

Do you understand?

He looks at her.

TOM

Yes.

Birdsong.

I understand.

The camera slowly tracks back across the field.

Breeze along the rye. Long billows.

Emily and Tom remain sitting on the tree stump, in the receding distance.